The International Library of Ethics, Law and Technology

Volume 18

More information about this series at http://www.springer.com/series/7761

Massimo Durante

Ethics, Law and the Politics of Information

A Guide to the Philosophy of Luciano Floridi

Springer

Massimo Durante
Department of Law
University of Turin
Turin, Italy

ISSN 1875-0044 ISSN 1875-0036 (electronic)
The International Library of Ethics, Law and Technology
ISBN 978-94-024-1148-5 ISBN 978-94-024-1150-8 (eBook)
DOI 10.1007/978-94-024-1150-8

Library of Congress Control Number: 2017947052

Printed on acid-free paper

This Springer imprint is published by Springer Nature
The registered company is Springer Science+Business Media B.V.
The registered company address is: Van Godewijckstraat 30, 3311 GX Dordrecht, The Netherlands

Preface

Ivan Locke, the eponymous hero in the film "Locke" (2013), is on an hour-and-a-half night drive towards his destiny, in the sole company of his inexorable sense of responsibility. As a construction foreman, Locke is well aware of the difficulties inherent to the building process: like forging one's own life or assuming responsibility for a life not yet born, it is a process fraught with formidable challenges and tragic moral choices. Living up to our moral obligations can be so taxing that we risk destroying everything: "Make one little mistake and the whole world comes crashing down", as Locke remarks. The only recourse we have in dealing with moral choice is to take what Goethe called the "right path". For Locke, this means journeying through the night, compelled by a sense of responsibility towards an urgent and inescapable moral call that cannot be postponed (as indeed most moral calls cannot). Locke spends the entire journey on his car phone with a series of invisible off-screen characters representing the real or phantasmal interlocutors of his moral life. While listening to these conversations, we come to realize that the process of creation – whether it be of a building or of a life – is not just about producing something ex novo but about becoming aware of our limits and assuming full responsibility for them. The film ends, significantly, at dawn, with some dramatic release of tension. However, it offers no definitive resolution, for as in real life, responsibility is an endless journey, and moral life is a dawn that gives rise to an infinite series of new days.

Like Locke's incessant telephone calls, a book is also an attempt at creating a meaningful conversation with unseen interlocutors. A book is a response to those who have inspired us and addresses itself to our imagined audience, the readers, in order to further that conversation. As soon as a book has been written, it is the author's turn to retreat from view, leaving space for the reader's response. This, then, is what writers and readers do: by imbuing words with meaning, they exchange information with the absent other. Writing and reading are thus also about overcoming solitude and creating connections, for they impart our lives with meaning, the only true tie that binds. In this sense, people are made up of information. Information allows us to experience meaning that goes beyond and transcends the individual, drawing us into an overarching whole. Information lies at the core of our humanity.

Humanity, however, is nothing more than the empty space across which we seek to communicate with one another, and every epoch has been concerned with a specific, idiosyncratic perception of what humanity means. Our epoch is informational. It brings to completion our self-understanding as informational systems that produce, process and exchange information with other informational systems in an environment that is constituted of information. Luciano Floridi was the first to recognize the full breadth and depth of this assertion. What makes Floridi's philosophy so remarkable is that he treats information not only as a means of deconstructing and understanding our reality but also, and above all, as a means of constructing and, it is hoped, of improving it.

This is the reason for my long-standing engagement with the philosophical meditation of Floridi. The present book aims to keep that conversation alive and to invite to it all of those willing to embrace these three notions: we construct our world and ourselves informationally; by constructing our world and ourselves, we thereby become aware of our limits; it is precisely these limits that make us become human beings.

***

The long-standing theoretical conversation I have been engaged in with Ugo Pagallo and Luciano Floridi has always been, and continues to be, an enriching and inspiring intellectual experience, and I wish to thank them both. This book would not have been possible without them. To Ugo, I am particularly grateful for the constant reminder of Hegel's claim that philosophy is its own time comprehended in thought and for impressing upon me that ours is the age of the technological. Luciano taught me the fundamental Kantian lesson that constructivism is the only way to hold together knowledge and responsibility without privileging either. Thank you for this. Great lessons are to philosophical enterprises what rafts are to castaways.

Over the course of many conversations with Luciano Floridi, I have come to a better understanding of several crucial philosophical topics that have brought about major improvements to this book. I am also indebted to Patrick Allo, Pompeu Casanovas, Ugo Pagallo, Giovanni Sartor, Mariarosaria Taddeo and Herman Tavani for their insightful remarks, shared ideas and bibliographical suggestions. Many of the considerations in this work are also the outcome of fruitful interactions with graduate and Ph.D. students at the Law Department of the University of Turin.

I would also like to thank the Springer editorial team and, notably, Christopher Wilby, Senior Publishing Assistant at Springer, for having encouraged me to commit myself to this project, for his input at several stages of the work and for his precious support throughout the entire process of producing the book. The anonymous reviewers appointed by Springer provided me with valuable suggestions and kept me on the right track. My thanks also to Laura McLean for her linguistic revision of the manuscript.

Finally, I would like to thank a bright young girl, full of life and joy, for having taught me a most important lesson. “I don’t like people who suddenly stop walking and then stand there looking at you, insisting that you need to stop, too”, she told me once. “I think people should keep walking together and looking straight ahead”. And she is quite right. The only way we can walk together is by moving forward as one and looking straight ahead, sharing this *something yet to come*, politics, love and democracy; it is not ours to know exactly what. This book is dedicated to her.

Turin, Italy
8 May 2017

Massimo Durante

Contents

Introduction

The Information Revolution

We live in information societies. The term "information society" was originally used to describe (mainly sociologically and economically) the impact of networked and digital information and communication technologies (ICTs) on our societies and the way society has been transformed by the growth and dissemination of information. However, the change driven by ICTs is much more profound. It is altering our representation and understanding of reality and of ourselves by putting to the test our most traditional and deep-seated categories and agencies. We are witnessing an information revolution, or informational turn, that Luciano Floridi (2010) has dubbed the "fourth revolution", to follow the Copernican, the Darwinian and the Freudian revolutions:

> After Nicolaus Copernicus (1473–1543), the heliocentric cosmology displaced the Earth and hence humanity from the centre of the universe. Charles Darwin (1809–1882) showed that all species of life have evolved over time from common ancestors through natural selection, thus displacing humanity from the centre of the biological kingdom. And following Sigmund Freud (1856–1939), we acknowledge nowadays that the mind is also unconscious and subject to the defence mechanism of repression. So we are not immobile, at the centre of the universe (Copernican revolution), we are not unnaturally separate and diverse from the rest of the animal kingdom (Darwinian revolution), and we are very far from being standalone minds entirely transparent to ourselves, as René Descartes (1596–1650), for example, assumed (Freudian revolution) (Floridi 2010, 8–9).

This process of reassessing human nature is indeed peculiar[1] and forces us to stop thinking of ourselves as "standalone entities, but rather [as] interconnected informational organisms or *inforgs*, sharing with biological agents and engineered artefacts a global environment ultimately made of information, the infosphere" (Floridi 2010, 9). We are thus part of a global environment made up of information, the infosphere, which is constituted, in turn, by "all informational processes,

[1] As Floridi points out (2010, 8–9): "Oversimplifying, science has two fundamental ways of changing our understanding. One may be called *extrovert*, or about the world, and the other *introvert*, or about ourselves. [...] Since the 1950s, computer science and ICTs have exercised both an extrovert and an introvert influence, changing not only our interaction with the world but also our self-understanding".

services, and entities, thus including informational agents as well as properties, interactions, and mutual relations" (Floridi 2010, 9; 2003). It may be useful to recall that such an informational universe is constituted by both analogue and digital data (Floridi 2010, 24). This informational representation transforms the world, not in what the world is (i.e. in noumenal sense), even if in a certain sense it does touch on the ultimate nature of reality,[2] but in how we know and experience the world (i.e. in phenomenal sense). This leads to an important philosophical consequence that is relevant, as we will see through throughout this volume, both from a theoretical standpoint and a practical standpoint:

> The criterion of existence – what it means for something to exist – is no longer being actually immutable (the Greeks thought that only that which does not change can be said to exist fully), or being potentially subject to perception (modern philosophy insisted on something being perceivable empirically through the five senses in order to qualify as existing), but being potentially subject to interaction, even if intangible. To be is to be interactable, even if the interaction is only indirect" (Floridi, 2010, 12).

Our networked and globalized world is thus subjected to the methods, practices and innovations of information technology, and reality is disaggregated into the elements and the data of interoperable software coding and reconstituted into novel social, economic, political, ethical and legal forms. Rendition of the world and of reality as information is creating new conditions of possibility for the emergence of new opportunities as well as of unpredicted policy vacuums and problems. To gain an understanding and be able to manage these opportunities, vacuums and problems requires scholars to elaborate an original and complex epistemological and ethical framework that can account not only for the consequences of the growth of information (the quantitative dimension) but also for the reontologization of reality brought about by that growth (the qualitative dimension). As remarked by Hegel, there is a point at which quantity becomes quality. Thus, this framework cannot just consist of regional epistemologies and standard, applied microethics. On the contrary, it is necessary to elaborate a more general epistemological analysis of information and to develop an innovative, applicable macroethics that are broader in their scope and capable of handling the profound transformations affecting the fabric of our own reality.

Scholars must firstly revise the long-standing and traditional epistemological tendency to consider reality in terms of stable and enduring structures ultimately based on or reducible to the objective existence of a material world. Secondly, it is crucial to understand that our reality is increasingly the outcome of information automated processes and software agents' behaviours that are capable of producing morally, politically and legally loaded consequences for humans, which cannot be

[2] Floridi (2010, 12): "What we are currently experiencing is therefore a *fourth revolution*, in the process of dislocation and reassessment of our fundamental nature and role in the universe. We are modifying our perspective on the ultimate nature of reality, that is, our metaphysics, from a materialist one, in which physical objects and processes play a key role, to an informational one. This shift means that objects are de-physicalized in the sense that they tend to be seen as support-independent (consider a file)".

understood and accounted for by means of established and traditional categories and forms of agencies, based on a rigid and impervious anthropocentric perspective. Thirdly, it is becoming increasingly difficult to determine the agent that is to be held morally, politically or legally responsible in a network of relations and interactions that requires a more comprehensive and systematic understanding of the whole environment in which agents behave and interact.

To help us address these issues, we turn to Luciano Floridi's work in the field of information theory. We believe that Floridi's philosophy and ethics of information is the finest conceptual prism through which to decode the informationally reontologized reality and to frame in theoretical and practical terms the problems that are brought about and fostered by the ongoing information revolution.[3] The main thrust of Floridi's work is both centripetal and centrifugal: centripetal, in that it concerns the centrality of information as the main mode of understanding and representing reality, and centrifugal in that it concerns decentralization of the anthropocentric perspective within that understanding and representation of reality. However, this should in no way lead us to conceive of and label Floridi's philosophy in terms of posthumanism. Posthumanism – and post-humanist thought – only just begins to broach the profound changes that philosophy must concern itself with in our technological age. While philosophy is still concerned with the human capacity to provide questions with relevant answers, there has been a dramatic shift in the theoretical strategy taken to accomplish this task. This strategy requires us to realize that we depend on technologies just as technologies depend on us. We cannot escape this complex circularity, which calls us to responsibility as constructionist human beings (*homo poieticus*) who build their world through constant interaction with technologies in terms of constraining affordances that, while not dictating agents' behaviour, do configure the environment in ways that shape agents' engagement. Any instance of the universe may be experienced as an informational object (constituted by a packet of information) by an epistemic agent at the proper level of information. Accordingly, agents need not be thought of anthropologically, but as information systems that create, store, disseminate and exchange information, by interacting with each other and participating in the construction of the infosphere. This requires philosophy to accomplish a double turn: to adopt a non-anthropocentric and constructionist approach to theoretical and practical issues. We believe that Luciano Floridi's theory of information paves the way to this pivotal philosophical turn. Our book aims to show what this philosophical turn requires conceptually. We therefore need to adopt a theoretical hypothesis to guide our analysis and investigation. This may easily be summed up by stating that Luciano Floridi is "the last humanist" and "the first constructionist".

[3] For an introduction to Floridi's philosophy and ethics of information, see the *Journal of Experimental and Theoretical Artificial Intelligence* (2015); Beavers and Jones (eds.) (2014); Demir (ed.) (2010 and 2012); Allo (ed.) (2011); *Etica & Politica/Ethics & Politics* (2011); *Metaphilosophy* (2010); *Knowledge, Technology and Policy* (2010); Ess (2009); and *Ethics and Information Technology* (2008).

Luciano Floridi: "The Last Humanist" and "The First Constructionist"

The claim that Floridi is the last humanist may be understood in two ways. It can be interpreted in the sense that Floridi is the last of the humanists, that is, he is a philosopher who has finally given up on an anthropocentric approach to theoretical and practical issues in our technologically mediated society. It can also be interpreted in the opposite sense, meaning that Floridi is the last possible humanist, that is, a philosopher who believes that the only way at present to support humanism in a technologically mediated society is to endorse a non-anthropocentric approach to theoretical and practical issues. In this work, we wish to show that both interpretations are true. A non-anthropocentric approach to theoretical and practical issues is required by the fact that technology is so profoundly embedded in our world that our lives, i.e. the way we relate to each other and the environment, are technologically mediated. Today, a uniquely anthropocentric perspective is not sufficient theoretically or practically to account for all of the different types of interactions we might experience.[4] Floridi's ontocentric approach, however, does not displace the role of human beings; on the contrary, it highlights and reinforces it, since it expands the class of both moral agents and patients. On the one hand, this means that there are more sources of morally relevant actions, while on the other, there are more patients to whom we owe moral respect. This may lead us in the long run to increase the sense of universality and hospitality on which we wish to construct our information societies. This leads us to another aspect of our hypothesis: the relevance of a constructionist perspective.

Philosophy has long been characterized by a deconstructionist perspective, which has mainly concerned itself with a strong *pars destruens* of the philosophical narrative. Philosophers set out to denounce humanism, how its promises were regularly unfulfilled and to what extent human culture, norms and values could not prevent even the most ominous and ruthless tragedies. Against this backdrop, technology has been repeatedly evoked in support of this negative view and to demonstrate the human tendency to progressively lose control of reality. A faithful and unadorned account of the human condition was, in this perspective, the best that philosophy could be expected to offer us. *Good news is no news*. However, times have (slightly) changed. Our generation is more concerned with a *pars construens* of the philosophical narration. We have no special reason to support optimism (which, in fact, we do not), given that we live, think and work in an age of crisis. Nonetheless, this has provided us opportunities for rethinking our mindset and renegotiating our relationship with traditional and deep-seated categories, values and agencies. Crisis is not somewhere out in the world; it is an integral feature of Western societies as we

[4] Floridi (2013, XV): "[Ethics] is still largely centred on a standalone, Cartesian-like, ratiocinating, human individual […] when the world has in fact moved towards hybrid, distributed, and multiagent systems (there is probably more 'moral agency' occurring at the level of governments, nongovernmental organizations, parties, groups, companies, and so forth, than in the life of millions of individuals)".

have constructed them. That is why we have to adopt a constructionist perspective with regard to theoretical and practical issues.

Luciano Floridi is not only the last humanist. He is also the first constructionist, because he believes that constructionism today is both theoretically and practically the first methodological commitment of the philosophical inquiry.[5] Theoretically, constructionism is concerned with the understanding of philosophy in terms of "conceptual design":

> By 'conceptual design' I mean to refer to a *constructionist* (not a *constructivist*) philosophy that can explain (better: account for) our semantic artefacts and design or re-purpose those needed by our new infosphere. [...] I much prefer speaking of *conceptual design*, especially in view of the fact that design is neither discovery nor invention, nor a matter of tinkering, fixing, or improving, but indeed the art of implementing requirements and exploiting constraining affordances intelligently and teleologically, in order to build artefacts in view of a specific goal. Philosophy as conceptual design is therefore a realistic philosophy, which treats semantic artefacts as mind- *and* reality-co-dependent, in the same way as a house is not a representation but the outcome of a specific architectural design both constrained and afforded by the building materials (Floridi 2013, 2).

This means that philosophy is mostly fashioned by the set of questions being posed and the answers being answered for a specific purpose.[6] Philosophy is not some sort of picture of the world or of the intrinsic nature of the system we are analysing. Rather, it provides a way to construct models of systems that delimit the range of the consistent answers that might be offered to the relevant questions. Floridi's epistemic constructionism is the theoretical foundation of and counterpart to the ethical conception of the *homo poieticus*, i.e. the demiurgic attitude of informational agents that are called upon to design technologies and to construct their world in a responsible manner. In practical terms, this means that we bear responsibilities for the way we design technologies and construct our world through interaction with others and the environment. It also means, however, that we are not just creators but also created entities that are part of a whole that is always cocreated. Constructionism is not meant to restore the sense of human narcissism that a radical non-anthropocentrism approach is meant to displace. Floridi's notion of ethical

[5] Floridi (2013, 2): "I take [philosophy] to be a foundationalist enterprise (something not very fashionable these days). Again, relying on the previous analogy and the conceptual undercurrents, I do not take philosophy to be in business of repairing but rather in that of building the raft while swimming, to paraphrase Neurath. The emphasis is on the radical and difficult nature of the philosophical task ahead of us, not on any anti-foundationalist suggestion. Understanding philosophy as conceptual design means giving up not on its foundationalist vocation, but rather on the possibility of outsourcing its task to any combination of logico-mathematical and empirical approaches. At the same time, understanding philosophy as conceptual design enables one to avoid epistemic relativism at the expense of representationalism".

[6] Floridi's philosophical inquiry moves from problems (i.e. a set of questions and answers) and develops through them. In this perspective, the constructionist view advocated in his philosophy may be put into relation with Deleuze's and Guattari's (1994) understanding of the philosophical task, as Floridi himself remarks (2013, 2, footnote 2).

constructionism is not so much concerned with the *egopoietic* construction of the self as it is with the *ecopoietic* construction of the environment in which we live:

> We shall be in serious trouble if we do not take seriously the fact that we are constructing the new physical and intellectual environments that will be inhabited by future generations. [...] The task is to formulate an ethical framework that can treat the infosphere as a new environment worth the moral attention and care of the human inforgs inhabiting it. Such an ethical framework must be able to address and solve the unprecedented challenges arising in the new environment. It must an *e-nvironmental ethics* for the whole infosphere. This sort of *synthetic* (both in the sense of holistic or inclusive, and in the sense of artificial) *environmentalism* will require a change in how we perceive ourselves and our roles with respect to reality, what we consider worth our respect and care, and how we might negotiate a new alliance between the natural and the artificial. It will require a serious reflection of the *human project* (Floridi, 2013, 18; the last emphasis is ours).

The Structure of the Book

This book is organized in two parts. The first is devoted to the presentation and analysis of the main theoretical tenets and issues of Luciano Floridi's theory of information. The goal is not to provide the reader with an exegesis of Floridi's thought but to attempt to trace the reasoning and strategies that have guided his philosophical construction and theoretical choices. We will highlight the most original acquisitions of Floridi's thought, that is to say, his contribution to the theory of information, from a philosophical and ethical standpoint, as well as to the philosophical tradition as such. While Floridi is steeped in and highly versed in the philosophical tradition, he makes a concerted effort not to remain tethered to this tradition, which he in fact successfully revamps in several crucial ways, as we shall discuss.

Part I specifically Chap. 1 is concerned with methodology. Floridi develops and makes use of the method of levels of abstraction, which is the philosophical basis of his constructionism. This method is widely applied by Floridi in his theory of information and is very often referred to in the present book because of its crucial importance. Its philosophical significance, which rests on a fruitful reading of Kant's transcendentalism coupled with the employment of specific notions (i.e. observables, variables and gradients of abstraction), derives from the fact that it enables Floridi's theory of information to escape from the Scylla and Charybdis of both subjectivism and objectivism. Since all entities are perceived, understood and experienced at a specific level of abstraction by an epistemic agent (there is no level of abstraction-free entity), all agents bear an inevitable epistemic responsibility for the adopted level of abstraction. Chapter 2 is concerned with the transformation of our world engendered by the information revolution stemming from the technological evolution of ICTs. This evolution shapes our world in a way that has been devised by Floridi in terms of an informational environment. This requires a change of paradigm in the study of technology and in the comprehension of our world, which requires us to rethink the notion of space, from Newton to Leibniz and Kant. This chapter thus focuses on the informational nature of the environment in which we live and act in. Accordingly, we explain the infosphere, the laws that are meant to govern it and the essential principle that underlies the ontology of the informational environment. Chapter 3 is concerned with the role of human beings in the transformed technological scenario of the informational environment. Human beings can no longer be understood as standalone entities, legislators of all things, according to a deep-seated anthropocentric perspective. Floridi suggests we adopt an ontocentric approach, based on the notion of informational object, in order to consider the role of agents and patients in a non-anthropocentric perspective and to extend the class of what counts as a moral subject. In this chapter, our aim is hence to elucidate how a non-anthropocentric approach does not necessarily turn into an anti-humanistic rhetoric that inflates postmodern philosophy; it instead strengthens the notion of human responsibility. This point is further remarked upon and analysed in Chap. 4, which is concerned with the morality of artificial agents. Investigation of the revised notions of agency and autonomy from the informational standpoint sheds further light on the moral experience of accountability and responsibility. As for the patients of the moral experience, the extension of the class of moral agents in the direction of non-human agents can help us to better grasp the role of humans in moral responsibility and to tackle more adequately new theoretical and practical problems arising from the current interaction with artificial autonomous agents. Finally, Chap. 5 deals with the informational construction of the self (personal identity). This subject concludes Part I of the book because the informational construction of the self is no longer understood in a traditional way as the fundamental starting point of philosophical reasoning, but rather as the dynamic result of interaction with other entities and with the environment. Furthermore, it is the notion of informational construction of the self (i.e. the idea that we are constructed by a consistent packet of information that may be experienced at different levels of abstraction) that enables us to recognize that our personal identity is not a fixed, built-in entity to which one can gain immediate access with no regard to context or purpose.

Part II is devoted to the presentation and analysis of the main consequences of Floridi's theory of information expounded in Part I, primarily from a normative perspective concerning the fields of politics and law. Our purpose is twofold. Firstly, we intend to measure the concrete relevance of Floridi's speculation in the area of practical reason with reference to law and politics. Secondly, we aim to better understand the normative dimension of information, i.e. in what sense and to what extent information can function as a rule of behaviour, by providing people with the background against which they build their beliefs about reality, make decisions and behave, by interacting in a multi-agent system, in which they increasingly rely on information and depend on information and communication technologies (ICTs). In the end, we believe that our reflection on Floridi's theory of information will enable us to sketch out the general framework of an informational approach to politics and to law, which are becoming so important to our globalized, networked societies of information.

Part II specifically Chap. 6 deals with the philosophical foundation of pluralism, one of the main consequences of Floridi's theory of information. Floridi's approach allows us to give an ontological foundation to pluralism understood in informational terms. An ontological foundation of pluralism, or, in other words, a pluralistic conception of being, is central from a theoretical and practical standpoint, because it provides us with a deeper understanding of Floridi's ontological approach to ethical issues (concerned with the requirements of hospitality, universalism and pluralism). Moreover, it provides a way out from the quicksand of a merely relativistic attitude to the crucial idea and fundamental value of (the respect of) differences in our pluralistic societies. Chapter 7 is thus concerned with the ontological interpretation of informational privacy. This chapter develops and applies the idea of the ontological construction of personal identity in the field of management and protection of our constitutive information. It explores the notion of privacy as constructed and understood in informational terms and consistent with the progressive digitization of our personal identity in the information society. The informational approach to privacy provides us with an understanding of how personal data may be accessed, inferred and aggregated and thereby manipulated and put at risk. It also discusses how the ontological friction assuring the protection of privacy needs to be balanced with the opportunities resulting from the creation and sharing of informational resources. The first two chapters of Part II, like the last chapter of Part I, are mainly concerned with the effects of the informational revolution at the individual level. The remaining chapters of Part II turn to the social aspects. Chapter 8 is concerned with the philosophical foundation of the information society. This chapter revisits the political and legal tradition of contractualism by reconsidering the structure of the conflict (from which political and legal modernity emanates) and the statute of their participants. Notably, this perspective is intended to defeat the "human narcissism" on which the traditional anthropocentric construction and understanding of the society are based. Such a perspective requires us to envisage a new social or natural contract for the globalized, networked information society, which acknowledges a third perspective, namely, that of the infosphere. This chapter establishes the philosophical premises of the last two chapters, which are concerned with politics and law. Chapter 9 describes an informational approach to politics. The information revolution has a strong impact on our conception of politics, since it affects two basic political ideas in the modernity: regulation (the relation between rulers and ruled) and space (a territory governed by a sovereign power). Politics is no longer understood, in descriptive terms, as a form of control over a territory and, in normative terms, as the art of taking collective decisions. In the information age, politics is understood as the efficient and effective management of and control over the life cycle of information, which surpasses the spatial boundaries of nation states. Against this backdrop, the subject of politics is no longer the dichotomy or dialectics between rulers and ruled, which characterizes the idea of government. It is instead the dichotomy or dialectics between what is governable and what is ungovernable that characterizes the notion of governance when understood as a measure of the degree of complexity of our information societies. Chapter 10 is concerned with an informational approach to law. The information revolution can affect the law in many ways: firstly, it multiplies the sources of norms (legal information); secondly, it entails competition between different normative systems; and thirdly, it changes the reality that law is expected to govern, since it reontologizes the reality.

Technological normativity is thus embedded in our societies and in our democracies alike. This not only implies that we move from state regulation to a multi-agent and multilevel form of technologically mediated regulation; there is a major turn at stake: our normative mindset towards the representation of reality. Our normative beliefs guiding our decisions and behaviours are no longer regulated and based on a traditional and deep-seated representation of reality; they depend on an informational representation that is increasingly made up of virtual realities, informational objects and streams of information. This changes the reality of what is subject to the law.

Luciano Floridi's theory of information revisits many aspects of the current paradigm of philosophy, opening up original and unexplored paths of research and reflection. His approach to philosophical and ethical issues sows the seeds for a different way of understanding and for dealing with old and new theoretical and practical problems concerned with the role of information and ICTs in information societies. Innovative and radical, Floridi's thought is often challenging and confrontational. Not everybody is expected to agree with it. Overall consensus is not required and often not even hoped for. We only wish that our book might offer some readers with valid reasons and arguments for supporting Floridi's approach and require others to strengthen their reasons and arguments for dissent.

References

Allo, P. (ed.). 2011. *Putting Information First: Luciano Floridi and the Philosophy of Information*, Hoboken: Wiley-Blackwell.

Beavers, A.-F., and D. Jones, (eds.) 2014. Philosophy in the Age of Information: A Symposium on Luciano Floridi's The Philosophy of Information. *Mind and Machines* 24 (1): 1–141.

Deleuze, G., and F. Guattari. 1994. *What Is Philosophy?* New York: Columbia University Press.

Demir, H. (ed.). 2010. Luciano Floridi's Philosophy of Technology: Critical Reflections. *Knowledge, Technology & Policy*, 23.

———. (ed.). 2012. *Luciano Floridi's Philosophy of Technology: Critical Reflections*. Dordrecht: Springer.

Ess, C. 2009. Floridi's Philosophy of Information and Information Ethics: Current Perspectives, Future Directions, Introduction to a Special issue on "Floridi's information and Computer Ethics". *The Information Society – The Philosophy of Information, its Nature, and Future Developments* 25 (3): 159–168.

Ethics and Information Technology. 2008. Special issue edited by C. Ess on "Luciano Floridi's Philosophy of Information and Information Ethics: Critical Reflections and the State of the Art", 10(2–3).

Etica & Politica/Ethics & Politics. 2011. Symposium on "Luciano Floridi's Philosophy of Information", XIII, 2.

Floridi, L. 2010. Information Ethics, Its Nature and Scope. In *Moral Philosophy and Information Technology*, ed. J. van den Hoven and J. Weckert, 40–65. Cambridge: Cambridge University Press.

———. 2013. *Information Ethics*. Oxford: Oxford University Press.

Journal of Experimental and Theoretical Artificial Intelligence. 2015. Special issue edited by Jones, D. and A. Beavers on Inforgs and the Infosphere: Themes from Luciano Floridi's Information Ethics and Philosophy of Artificial Intelligence, 27(1).

Knowledge, Technology and Policy. 2010. Special double issue edited by Demir, H., and M. Taddeo on Luciano Floridi's Philosophy of Technology: Critical Reflections. 23(1–2) and 24(3–4).

Metaphilosophy. 2010. Special issue edited by P. Allo on Luciano Floridi and the Philosophy of Information 41(3): 247–459.

Part I

Theoretical Tenets and Issues

Methodological Issues

1

Abstract

The information revolution engendered by the evolution of digital information and communication technologies (ICTs) is a central issue that needs to be investigated and examined against the backdrop of a mature and comprehensive theory of information that has clearly formulated methodological premises rooted in the philosophical tradition. Only then can we gain a deeper understanding of our relationship with technology today. Luciano Floridi's theory of information, which encompasses both a philosophy (The philosophy of information. Oxford University Press, Oxford, 2011a) and an ethics of information (Information ethics. Oxford University Press, Oxford, 2013; see also Floridi 2008a, b), satisfies this inescapable methodological requirement. The method that Floridi develops (the method of levels of abstraction) can be applied to the entire range of issues with which his theory of information is concerned. This method is indeed very fruitful, since it avoids the pitfalls of the Scylla of subjectivism and the Charybdis of objectivism. In the present chapter and throughout this whole book, we will illustrate and make use of Floridi's method while attempting, whenever possible, to lay bare the profound philosophical underpinnings of the subjects evoked in our analysis. In so doing, we hope that every thesis presented in this text is rooted in a thoughtful understanding of the history of philosophy.

1.1 Introduction

Many scholars recognize – and even take for granted – the manifold impact of ICTs on our society, including its moniker, the so-called information society. This impact, which is widely assumed to be social, economic, legal, moral, political and so forth, poses the question of normativity (Durante 2010): i.e., whether this impact shapes or determines what guides our behaviours and thereby our own society. However, only a few scholars recognize that this impact is also or mainly epistemic. Among

M. Durante, *Ethics, Law and the Politics of Information*, The International Library of Ethics, Law and Technology 18, DOI 10.1007/978-94-024-1150-8_1

them, Luciano Floridi stands out. Let us start by presenting some of Floridi's views on this crucial, preliminary point. First, he points out that this impact carries with it both risks and benefits (Floridi 2010, 6–7):

> ICTs have been changing the world profoundly and irreversibly for more than half a century now, with breath-taking scope and at a neck-breaking pace. On the one hand, they have brought concrete and imminent opportunities of enormous benefit to people's education, welfare, prosperity, and edification, as well as great economic and scientific advantages. [...] On the other hand, ICTs also carry significant risks and generate dilemmas and profound questions about the nature of reality and of our knowledge of it, the development of information-intensive sciences (e-science), the organization of a fair society (consider the digital divide), our responsibilities and obligations to present and future generations, our understanding of a globalized world, and the scope of our potential interactions with the environment.

Secondly, he suggests us that the impact of ICTs, which relates to the whole life-cycle of information, is epistemic about both the world and ourselves (Floridi 2010, 8):

> ICTs have made the creation, management, and utilization of information, communication, and computational resources vital issues, not only in our understanding of the world and of our interactions with it, but also in our self-assessment and identity.

Then, on this account, he reminds us that a theoretical lack of balance affects the information society and leads us to mistake ICTs for merely *enhancing* or *augmenting* technologies, since it prevents us from realizing how profound the transformation of our understanding of reality and of ourselves driven by the ongoing information revolution actually is. This lack of balance calls for a viable philosophy of information (Floridi 2010, 7–8):

> The information society is like a tree that has been growing its far-reaching branches much more widely, hastily, and chaotically than its conceptual, ethical, and cultural roots. [...] The risk is that, like a tree with weak roots, further and healthier growth at the top might be impaired by a fragile foundation at the bottom. As a consequence, today, any advanced information society faces the pressing task of equipping itself with a viable philosophy of information.

In recent decades, Floridi has promoted and developed such a theoretical approach, which is condensed in his book, *The Philosophy of Information* (Floridi 2011a). We will explore and take advantage of this theoretical approach in order to construct our own argument in part two of this book. What is at stake is whether this approach provides us with the philosophical language capable of dealing with the aforementioned lack of balance. The answer requires a three-step conceptual analysis: (1) how technology is to be devised, in order to prove that it structures our understanding of reality and of ourselves; (2) how epistemology is to be conceived, in order to show that there is one level of explanation of reality and of ourselves consistent with the technological rendition of reality and our technologically-driven self-assessment; (3) how information is to be considered, in order to demonstrate that the consistent level of explanation is informational. The analysis will also require us to envisage the conceptual ground on which this consistency may be based. Our hypothesis is that this conceptual ground is offered by Floridi's construction of the informational nature of levels of abstraction, as the *unity* of the irreducible plurality of observers and observations, and his semantic treatment of informational resources as *constraining affordances* by means of a *minimalist* and *constructionist* approach (Floridi 2011b, 294).

1.2 Technology as Constraining Affordances

Luciano Floridi's thinking encourages us to realize how radical and profound the epistemic impact of technology over the society and its inhabitants is, not least for the very reason that both of them are already part of the world that ICTs are *re-ontologizing* (a technical term used by Floridi that will be clarified later in this section):

> What is in question is a quieter, less sensational, and yet crucial and profound change in our conception of what it means to be an agent and what sort of environment these new agents inhabit. It is a change that is happening [...] through a radical transformation of our understanding of reality and of ourselves. [...] In this sense, ICTs are not merely re-engineering but actually re-ontologizing our world (Floridi 2010, 10–11).

This requires us to better understand how technology may be said to have an impact on society. At the same time, we need to avoid three common mistakes with regards to our understanding of technology: (1) instrumentalism; (2) techno-determinism; (3) empiricism. Let us briefly analyse these possible misunderstandings concerning the impact of technology on society.

1.2.1 The Limits of Instrumentalism

Technology is not purely instrumental. This is for two reasons. First, the relation between means and ends is not entirely dependent on the structure or form of the instrument to be adopted, but also and above all on the act through which this instrument is concretely oriented towards an end in a specific situation. This means that every instrument is designed for an end, but the use that is made of it towards a particular end can always differ from the use for which it was originally designed (which also includes also *re-purposing*). The history of technology offers plenty of examples of instruments that have been used for aims different from those for which they were created. On this basis, we cannot speak of the mere instrumentality of technology, for it is impossible to define in advance the overall class of ends for which an instrument might actually be employed. Second, every instrument is designed and constructed to meet a given class of needs. However, it is difficult, if not impossible, to identify from the start the role and weight a particular instrument will have, that is, whether or not this mean will be able to meet a wider class of needs than originally envisaged. From this standpoint, it is also impossible to refer to the mere instrumentality of technology, since one cannot identify in advance the whole class of needs a specific instrument will be able to meet. The notion of the non-instrumentalism of technology should lead to a more mature conception of technology, according to which, if technology cannot be merely understood as a set of means to dispose of, it can be understood as the environment in which we live. The case of computer-based technology is paradigmatic. Not only is the computer meant to meet a nearly unlimited class of needs in its malleability (Moor 1985), but it is also no longer viewed as a mere instrument. On the contrary, technologies today re-ontologize the environment in which we live, which steadily challenges the offline/online distinction (Floridi 2010, 11–12):

> While a dishwater interface is a panel through which the machine enters into the user's world, a digital interface is a gate through which a user can be present in cyberspace. […] It follows that we are witnessing an epochal, unprecedented migration of humanity from its ordinary habitat to the infosphere itself, not least because the latter is absorbing the former.

This is recognized as the ecological approach of Luciano Floridi's philosophy of information, which introduces the idea of 'infosphere'. In this perspective, it is worth noticing as well that most of the current figures of speech concerning ICTs and computer-based technologies (the Net, being online, digital natives, virtual reality, surfing the web, cloud-computing, intelligent ambient, second life and so forth) are spatial rather than instrumental metaphors (see Floridi Floridi 2010, 11). The idea that technology re-ontologizes the world is epistemic (as we will see below, it affects the way in which we experience the world at a determined level of abstraction) and not *deterministic*. This point deserves further clarification, as it is often a question of misunderstanding that underlies notions of strict social engineering or techno-determinism that underestimate the impact of *the moment of complexity* (Taylor 2001) characterizing our globalised world.

1.2.2 The Limits of Techno-determinism

Technology creates new possibilities that can be understood as *affordances* (Wellman et al. 2003; Benkler 2006; Kallinikos 2011). People are enabled by new technologies to do what they were not able to do before, although this does guarantee that they actually will do it. As suggested by Benkler (2006), technology makes it easier (or more difficult) to perform some actions and human interactions. *Ceteris paribus*, Benkler says, the easiest things to do are more likely to be done, whereas the most difficult ones are less likely to be done. However, the other variables never remain constant. This is why strict technological determinism (according to which, if we are provided with a technology *t*, we can expect the emergence of the social relation or structure *s*) is false (Benkler 2006). As pointed out, strict social engineering and techno-determinism fail to appreciate that complexity is an emergent property of our society.

In the complex, networked society of information, subjects are subjects of relations that, along with informational fluxes, are established through their networked connections and interactions. This concept is strongly emphasized by Floridi, who comes to consider that being interactive becomes the criterion itself for existence (Floridi 2010, 12):

> Finally, the criterion for existence – what it means for something to exist – is no longer being actually immutable (the Greeks thought that only that which does not change can be said to exist fully), or being potentially subject to perception (modern philosophy insisted on something being perceivable empirically through the five senses in order to qualify as existing), but being potentially subject to interaction, even if intangible. To be is to be interactable, even if the interaction is only indirect.

To be a subject is thus to be subject to interaction. This affects the information society, and qualifies its complexity. The complexity of society is therefore expressed by the fact that the outcomes of multiple interconnected subjects' interactions are not foreseeable in deterministic terms (Taylor 2001). This last consideration requires us to endorse a non-deterministic conception of the apparent impact that technology has on society. To endorse a non-deterministic conception from a socio-technological point of view, however, does not amount to downplaying the importance of such an impact.

On the contrary, technology is correctly viewed as a set of affordances (Wellman et al. 2003; Benkler 2006; Kallinikos 2011), but affordances that are also 'constraining', since they shape the environment in which we operate, namely, in which we are called upon to decide, act and interact. ICTs present both possibilities as well as constraints that shape our environment, but they do not bias our decisions and behaviours in any deterministic way. Our decisions and behaviours can properly be interpreted as responses – active and creative, and thus not-deterministically biased – to the constraining affordances that shape our environment: this approach, which is conceived in terms of *constraining affordances*, on the side of technology, and *active responses*, on the side of human agents, defeats both techno-determinism and cyber-optimism and raises the issue of human responsibility at the top of the agenda. Let us reiterate that the way in which ICTs shape the environment is epistemological rather than merely empirical: this is why empiricism is limited in explaining the complex impact of ICTs on society.

1.2.3 The Limits of Empiricism

Thirdly and lastly, the practical (social, legal, ethical, political, etc.) impact of ICTs must not be separated from their epistemological impact, i.e., the way an epistemic agent experiences reality as constructed by information objects (Floridi 2010). Too often, studies on digitalization have treated the impact brought about by the evolution of ICTs simply as a quantitative phenomenon or one of many organizational devices rather than conceptualizing the information revolution as a qualitative phenomenon that entails, epistemologically, a *re-ontologization* of the whole of reality that is then conceived as an *infosphere*. This aspect is highlighted in Floridi's philosophy of information (Floridi 2007, 61; see also Floridi 2003):

> In order to grasp the ICT scenarios that we might witness and experience in the near future, it is useful to introduce two key-concepts [...], those of "infosphere" and of "re-ontologization". *Infosphere* is a neologism I coined years ago [...]. It denotes the whole informational environment constituted by all informational entities, their properties, interactions, processes and mutual relations. It is an environment comparable to, but different from cyberspace (which is only one of its sub-regions), since it also includes off-line and analogue spaces of information. *Re-ontologizing* is another neologism that I have recently introduced in order to refer to a very radical form of re-engineering, one that not only designs, constructs or structures a system (e.g. a company, a machine or some artefact) anew, but that fundamentally transforms its intrinsic nature [...]. Using the two previous concepts, my basic claim can now be formulated thus: digital ICTs are re-ontologizing the very nature of (and hence what we mean by) the infosphere, and here lies the source of some of the most profound transformations and challenging problems that our information societies will experience in the close future, as far as technology is concerned.

Technology (notably ICT) is no longer merely concerned with instruments to be used but with a radical transformation that gives shape, chiefly epistemologically, to our environment and hence to our engagement in the world. The idea of technology as (designing) the environment we inhabit in terms of constraining affordances is deeply affected by a conception of informational space (i.e., the infosphere), which is thought of as starting from the properties of information (*rectius*: informational resources). Those properties are thus the constraining affordances that model the agent's epistemic experience of reality. Before we focus our attention upon this crucial point, we have to understand first what it means for epistemology to be conceived in terms of constraining affordances.

1.3 The Epistemological Principle of Complementarity

We have been speaking thus far of constraints and affordances from a technological perspective. Now, we shall expound on these concepts from an epistemological standpoint. To this aim, we will make use of Mauro Ceruti's (Ceruti 2009) epistemological investigations, which draw attention to the importance of the principle of complementarity as the guiding idea of epistemology.

To start with, we have to note that the process of *decentralization* brought about by the technological architecture of the Net and, more generally, by the complexity of networks and ICTs – and which has promoted wider access to information and participation in user-generated content (Benkler 2006) – has also been remarked upon and explained in epistemological terms. As Ceruti (2009, 5) puts it:

> Contemporary epistemological reflection instead refers the concept of decentralization to two equally fundamental facts: the *proliferation* of the real in objects, levels, spheres of reality, and the awareness that such proliferation is always translated in the language and in the communication of *an observer* [*our transl.*].

This process of decentralization has also been singled out by Luciano Floridi (2011a) and formulated in informational terms, with reference to a cluster of concepts (proliferation or flourishing of informational objects, the levels of abstraction, the semantic role of the informee, etc.). We will make further note of them later in this chapter. For the moment, suffice it to note that, according to Floridi, decentralization endorses a universalistic approach based on the notion of informational object: namely, any entity can be described and experienced by an epistemic agent as the sum of well-formed information. Let us move back to our main question.

The process of "decentralization of the image of the cosmos" comes together and is coupled with an analogous process of "decentralization of our ways of thinking that cosmos" (Ceruti 2009, 5). Such processes (the role of the observer and a new interpretation of the laws of nature) have brought about an epistemological switch from the "science of necessity" to the "science of game" (Ceruti 2009, 10):

> To talk of a game in order to describe the evolutionary and historical processes of social and natural systems is to hint at a deeper understanding of the mechanisms guiding the *history of nature*. [...] Evolutionary processes always depend upon insoluble interaction among general mechanisms that operate as constraints – "laws" – and the variety, the individuality, the spatial-temporal singularity of the events. Nature and history all the time play interesting games: i.e., games that do not necessarily have a winning strategy in mind from the start. The course of the game always occurs within and though the interaction between rules posed as constraints and as constituents of the game, chance, and the contingency of particular events and of particular choices, and the strategies of the players in utilizing the rules and chance so as to construct new scenarios and new possibilities (Ceruti 2009, 10) [*our transl.*].

Constraints limit the sphere of possibilities not in the sense of being a cause of a determined, necessary effect, but, rather, in the sense that, by delimiting the sphere of possibilities, they afford new opportunities. This point has been accurately articulated by Ilya Prigogine and Isabelle Stengers (Prigogine and Stengers 1981, 1076):

> A constraint [...] does not merely delimit the possibilities; it is also an opportunity. It is not simply imposed from the outside onto a pre-existing reality, but participates in the construction of an integrated structure and determines in the light of a particular occasion an entire spectrum of intelligible new consequences.

The idea of science as a "game" is thus based on abandoning the view of science as an asymptotic process of approximation towards a unique and fundamental place of observation and explanation. Rather, the game consists precisely in the reintroduction of the observer within the system of observation and explanation (Ceruti 2009, 39–40). The categorical universe of science ceases to appear as something unitary, homogeneous and fixed once and for all; on the contrary, it appears to be characterized by an irreducible plurality of observers' viewpoints (Ceruti 2009, 43). This leads to a key epistemological consequence:

> The irreducibility of the observers' points of view *hic et nunc*, their presence in every description, in every strategy, indeed, in every matter of heuristics, sparks off an image of the development and structure of knowledge according to which the *possible universes of*

> *discourse are never defined exhaustively, but are constructed and dependent on the network of concrete relations of antagonism, complementarity and cooperation between the multiple viewpoints at play* (Ceruti 2009, 43) [*our transl.*].

What does this imply? Such an epistemological approach not only endorses a necessary pluralism of observers' viewpoints, but asserts that the epistemic question is no longer that of reconciling different points of view; rather, the question is to understand how different points of view produce themselves reciprocally (Ceruti 2009, 44):

> The real reversal in perspective consists in the recognition of the irreducibility of the points of view or, what is more, in the recognition of their proliferation in different directions and at different levels. There is a plurality of points of view belonging to concrete subjects like those adopting different systems of categorical references to judge the same evidence. There is also a plurality of points of view within the same subject endorsing, with regard to some problems and ends, different systems of categorical references, logics and forms of thinking (Ceruti 2009, 96) [*our transl.*].

This understanding of knowledge is therefore no longer characterized by the need to establish a synthesis between these different viewpoints (which can overrule some points of view in favour of others). On the contrary, it is characterized by the image of antagonism, cooperation and complementarity between different systems of categorical references. In this perspective, the epistemic attention is focused instead on the conceptual matrices that make these systems or viewpoints antagonistic, concurrent or cooperative. According to this approach, the unity of knowledge is not expressed by synthesis but, rather, by complementarity (Ceruti 2009, 98) and epistemology can be said to be inspired by a principle of complementarity that is an "essential precondition for every epistemological inquiry" (Ceruti 2009, 97).

Different points of view as well as different forms of discourse should not be conceived as mutually alternative, but rather as antagonistic, concurrent or cooperative, according to the differences between conceptual matrices that make them differ from one another. Each one can participate in the construction of knowledge within the constraining affordances that characterize their respective conceptual matrix: this perspective requires us to move from a conception of epistemology based on *representation* to a conception of epistemology based on *construction* (Ceruti 2009, 103) which entails, as suggested by Floridi 2011b, a *maker's knowledge* approach.

The consequence is profound: the irreducible pluralism of viewpoints displayed by the principle of complementarity does not merely imply that antagonist or cooperative discourses concur in the construction of knowledge, according to the interplay between their conceptual matrices; it implies that the whole cognitive universe is constituted as a *polysystemic subject* (Ceruti 2009, 111) that turns out to be the sphere of antagonism and cooperation between systems that are characterized by different logics, hierarchies, subjects and viewpoints:

> This image of the subject as being composed by multiple systems constitutes a mode of thought which decisively orients many of the most interesting contemporary studies into the nature of the subject at whatever level they are placed (Ceruti 2009, 111) [*our transl.*].

Such an epistemological perspective is therefore crucial in order to account for what may be called the subject or the system of explanation. In fact, it is important to conceive the epistemic foundation of our understanding of the world on the basis of the requirements displayed by the principle of complementarity, according to which the subject or the system of explanation may be understood as a place for the unfolding of antagonism and cooperation between systems characterized by different logics, subjects and viewpoints. This not only requires that different levels of explanation (i.e. models that are formed on the basis of different conceptual matrices) can concur in (a) the construction of a heterogeneous basis of information, but also that (b) information is conceived as semantic structures that are necessary in the construction of differences between conceptual matrices. In other words, differences between levels of explanation are to be traced back to differences between conceptual matrices (i.e., sets of constraining affordances), since the epistemic framework of complementarity is based on the "recognition of the multiplicity of places of observations and explanations" (Ceruti 2009, 120).

The question, therefore, is to understand whether a theory of semantic information establishes the epistemic conditions for the recognition of a plurality of observers, observables and levels of observation, as semantic differences between conceptual matrices. In this respect, we should not forget a crucial point, which is often underestimated in the analysis of the philosophy of information, namely, that *all* levels of abstraction are, according to Floridi, *informational*. We will come back to this key point. For the moment, let us formulate our hypothesis in general terms.

Our hypothesis is that Floridi's philosophy of semantic information accomplishes this task; we also seek to argue that the reason for being able to do so lies in his methodological treatment of *epistemological levelism* (Floridi 2011a, 47), coupled with his notion of *informational resource* conceived in terms of constraining affordance. If so, the implication would be significant: we would now have a philosophical language that bridges the philosophies of technology and epistemology, both conceived in terms of sets of constraints and affordances, through the understanding of the properties of informational resources, which give shape (design) to the informational environment, where we make decisions, act and interact.

1.4 Epistemological Levelism: The Method of Levels of Abstraction

The main method of Luciano Floridi's philosophy of information is *the method of levels of abstraction* (Floridi 2011a, chap. 3; see also, 2008c), which entails the "recognition of the multiplicity of places of observations and explanations" (Ceruti 2009, 120). Floridi's understanding of levelism – the idea that reality can be studied at different levels – is not ontological but rather epistemological (Floridi 2011a, 47):

> I agree with Heil and Schaffer that *ontological levelism* is probably untenable. However, I shall argue that a version of *epistemological levelism* should be retained, as a fundamental and indispensable method of conceptual engineering (philosophical analysis and construction) in PI [philosophy of information], albeit in a suitably refined version.

This form of criticism – to opt out of ontological levelism and opt for epistemological levelism – resembles Kant's *transcendental* approach, as Floridi remarks (Floridi 2011a, 58; 2011b, 293), by stating where his assessment agrees with Kant's (Floridi 2011a, 59):

> The attempt to strive for something unconditioned is equivalent to the natural, yet profoundly mistaken, endeavour to analyse a system (the world in itself, for Kant, but it could also be a more limited domain) independently of any (specification of) the level of abstraction at which the analysis is being conducted, the questions are being posed and the answers are being offered, for a specific purpose.

Floridi endorses Kant's transcendental approach, "which considers the conditions of possibility of the analysis (experience) of a particular system", whilst he "does not inherit from Kant any mental or subject-based feature" (Floridi 2011a, 60). It should be noted that two aspects here might lead to confusion about Floridi's transcendental approach. First, Floridi's method of levels of abstraction does not disregard the role of "any mental or subject-based feature", as if it were endorsing some forms of descriptivism or "naïf naturalism" that are already displaced by Floridi's constructionism (Floridi 2011a, 75–77; 2011b, 285). Rather, mental or subject-based features may qualify as *gradients of abstraction* without being able to denote the nature of levels of abstraction, which is just informational, as we will see below. Secondly, what is crucial in Floridi's transcendental approach is the idea itself that analysis (*experience*) is something that stems from a set of *questions being posed and answers being offered for a specific purpose.* This problem-based approach should be conceived in terms of a "conceptual constructionism" (Floridi 2011a, 24), as in Deleuze and Guattari, *What is philosophy*, Deleuze and Guattari 1994. We should now take a step back and explain, in short, what a *level of abstraction* (LoA) is, according to Floridi's epistemological levelism.

In general terms, levels of abstraction are "interfaces that mediate the epistemic relation between the observed and the observer" (Floridi 2011a, 76). They are mediations that articulate and put into communication the different poles (e.g. the observer and the observed, or mind and world) of the irreducible difference that the conceptual core of epistemology seems to consist of. More analytically, levels of abstraction can be described as according to the following cluster of definitions:

> A *level of abstraction* (*LoA*) is a finite but non-empty set of observables. No order is assigned to the observables, which are expected to be the building blocks in a theory characterized by their very definition (Floridi 2011a, 52).
>
> An *observable* is an interpreted typed variable, that is, a typed variable together with a statement of what feature of the system under consideration it represents (Floridi 2011a, 48).
>
> A *typed variable* is a uniquely named conceptual entity (the *variable*) and a set, called its *type*, consisting of all the values that the entity may take (Floridi 2011a, 48).

Epistemological levelism, based on levels of abstraction, endorses pluralism without falling into *relativism* or *perspectivism*, since "the explicit reference to the LoA makes it clear that the model of a system is a function of the available observables, and that it is reasonable to rank different LoAs and to compare and assess the corresponding models" (Floridi 2011a, 75; 2011b, 292). In other words, the necessary choice between levels of abstraction is not only subjective, but is goal-oriented, that is, it depends on the goal of the *analysis*. This sheds light on why we have been emphasizing the idea of analysis: the 'right' level of abstraction is never independent from a set of questions and answers nested around the specific purpose for which it is adopted. Comparison and assessment of different level of abstraction and of their corresponding models are made possible by *gradients of abstractions* that may be defined as follows:

> A Gradient of Abstraction (GoA) is a formalism defined to facilitate discussion of discrete systems over a range of LoAs. Whilst a LoA formalizes the scope or granularity of a single model, a GoA provides a way of varying the LoA in order to make observations at different levels of abstraction (Floridi 2011a, 54).

Returning to what we have already noted regarding mental or subject-based features, this point can be briefly clarified here. The crucial epistemic dualism of mind and world can be tackled from two different perspectives: one which singles out either 'mind' or 'world' as the correct explanation for the process of knowing; and another which focuses attention on the idea that the conceptual core of epistemology resides in the irreducible 'difference' between instances (e.g., mind and world) to be articulated. According to the former, the epistemological discourse is a chain of discrete points located between the two poles of mind and world: i.e., from pure mentalism to strong naturalism. According to the latter, the question is at what level this seminal, irreducible difference is established. In Floridi's views, mentalism or naturalism can qualify as *disjoint gradients of abstraction* (Floridi 2011a, 56), and the fundamental conceptual core of epistemology resides in the informational nature of *all* levels of abstraction, as we will see shortly, since information, as well-formed, meaningful and veridical data, (which is in itself a distinction or a difference that makes a difference [MacKay 1969; Bateson 1973]), already includes, at its essential level, the notion of an irreducible difference, according to which it is possible to speak of an *informational ontological pluralism*, in order to describe Floridi's epistemological position (Durante 2010b).

Epistemological levelism also endorses realism without falling into *descriptivism*, since "for a typed variable to be an observable, it must be interpreted, a correspondence that has inevitably been left informal. This interpretation cannot be omitted: a LoA composed of typed variables called simply *x*, *y*, *z*, and so on and treated rather formally, would leave one with no hint of its domain of application" (Floridi 2011a, 75; 2011b, 282). In plain terms, an observable is an interpreted typed variable, which requires both *interpretation* of the typed variable and a previous *choice* about which observables and hence which types are appropriate to a phenomenon to be regarded. Do we need to have an account of such a phenomenon in advance? Does this expose us to circularity? "How, then, is that to be determined without circularity?" (Floridi 2011a, 76). Let us examine what enables levels of abstraction to model the world or its experience, generating and committing the agent to informational spaces, in a 'realistic' way:

> Here, I may stress that the behaviours at a moderated LoA must adequately reflect the phenomena sought by complying with their constraints and taking advantages of their affordances; if not, then either the definition of the behaviour is wrong or the choice of observables is inappropriate. When the definitions of observable must incorporate some 'data', the latter behave like constraining affordances and so limit the possible models" (Floridi 2011a, 76).

All levels of abstraction are thus informational: they allow an epistemic agent to experience the world in terms of informational objects. This does not mean that the informational level is just one among many other levels of abstraction. Rather, it is the informational construction of an object that allows an epistemic agent to *vary* the levels of abstraction at which she can experience the object. Data, which constitute information, require levels of abstraction to be processed, and levels of abstraction require data as constraining affordances to delimit the possible range of information constructs. This mutual relation is not that of infinite regress but, on the contrary, defines Floridi's constructionism (Floridi 2011b, 282–283) and allows us to comprehend why knowledge is not some sort of picture of the world, i.e., of the intrinsic nature of the system it analyses. Rather, it is a way to construct models of systems that delimit the range of coherent responses that can be given to the related questions (Floridi 2011b, 302). Let us now shift our attention to the concept of data as *constraining affordances*, underlying the constructionist approach of Floridi's semantic philosophy of information and providing us with a language that bridges together (the normativity of) technology and epistemology.

1.5 Informational Resources as Constraining Affordances

According to Luciano Floridi's philosophy of information, information is conceived, primarily, as semantic information. The approach, which is most commonly expounded in order to understand what is semantic information, is a *databased approach*, according to which information may be said to consist of data. More analytically, the general definition of (factual) semantic information conceived in terms of data is the following (Floridi 2010, 50):

> [DEF] *p* qualifies as factual semantic information if and only if *p* is (constituted by) *well-formed*, *meaningful*, and *veridical data*.

Syntax, meaning and veridicality are the properties of data that constitute semantic information. Even if our own attempt here is to explain normativity in the semantic terms of informational resources (*data* + *meaning*) conceived as *constraining affordances*, we have to acknowledge that the normativity of syntactical structures ("rules that govern the chosen system, code, or language", Floridi 2011a, 84) already affects the semantic definition of information. Exploring the intricacy of a broadly understood syntax ("what determines the form, construction, composition, or structuring of something", Floridi 2011a, 84) and semantics goes beyond the scope of the present text, so let us return to the basic implication of the general definition of semantic information.

Floridi himself suggests that a close relationship exists between information and knowledge. More precisely, one of the advantages of the general definition of information in terms of semantic information is the following (Floridi 2010, 51):

> The second advantage is that [DEF] forges a robust and intuitive link between factual semantic information and knowledge. [...] Knowledge and information are members of the same conceptual family. What the former enjoys and the latter lacks, over and above their family resemblance, is the web of mutual relations that allow one part of it to account for another. [...] Build or reconstruct that networks of relations, and information starts providing the overall view of the world that we associate with the best of our epistemic efforts. So once some information is available, knowledge can be built in terms of explanations or accounts that make sense of the available semantic information. [...] In this sense, *semantic information is the essential starting point of any scientific investigation* (emphasis ours).

Although a matter of heated debate, Floridi holds that information can upgrade to knowledge when information is conceived as a building block, which encapsulates truth, in a "web of mutual relations that allow one part of it to account for another". Knowledge upgrades information not because it accumulates the selected information (in this most common perspective, knowledge is what lessens the informativeness of information, its *newness*, and transforms it into some stable and durable view of the world) but, first and foremost, because it already conceives an *explanation* as a network of relations. We have seen that the epistemic plurality of explanations (i.e., the principle of complementarity discussed in Sect. 1.3) is rooted in the ontological plurality of informational resources (Durante 2010b), conceived as data + meaning, since datum itself is fundamentally defined as follows (Floridi 2011a, 85):

> Dd datum $=_{\text{def.}}$ x being distinct from y, where the x and the y are two uninterpreted variables and the domain is left open to further interpretation.

We can see both the distinctiveness and the intertwinement of (the two uninterpreted variables constituting) a datum (referred to by Floridi as "diaphoric definition of data", Floridi 2011a, 85), the original, crucial source of the informational relatedness (Durante 2010b) of the web of mutual relations. This also means that a datum is nothing *per se* or, to put it better, that nothing is a datum *per se*. "A datum is a relational entity" (Floridi 2011a, 87). It is not at all immediately visible what follows from the construction of data in terms of *relata*. For the data being related (i.e., not accessible *per se*), it means that data can never be accessed or elaborated independently of a *level of abstraction*. As Floridi puts it (Floridi 2011a, 85–86), the presence of data can be "empirically inferred from, and required by, experience" but it cannot be epistemically accessed as such. However, it is precisely the relatedness of data that plays a crucial role - and this is a key conceptual point of the analysis - when data are accessed and elaborated at any given level of abstraction, since the relational nature of data constitutes the *normativity* of the domain of variables left open for further interpretation.

Let us formulate this point by making use of Floridi's perspicuous terms, which will eventually draw us back to our first undertaking: proving that Floridi's philosophy of semantic information generates a conceptual language that bridges the philosophies of technology and epistemology through his informational conception of constraining affordances and his notion of constructionism as conceptual engineering (Floridi 2011b, 283). Indeed, Floridi himself remarks upon what we may call the *normative* dimension of data, namely that data can be an "external anchor" (Floridi 2011a, 85) for our information, since:

> Understood as relational entities, data are *constraining affordances*: they allow or invite certain constructs (they are *affordances* for the information agent that can take advantage of them) and resist and impede some others (they are *constraints* for the same agent), depending on the interaction with, and the nature of, the information agent that process them (Floridi 2011a, 87).

Data are constraining affordances as *relational entities*, since this relatedness is the reason why data cannot be accessed or elaborated independently of a level of abstraction. We can now grasp why semantic information is the fundamental starting point for any scientific investigation, since data, which constitute information, are essential in the construction of a web of mutual relations, *precisely because* they are not accessible per se. In other words, data understood as constraining affordances are "answers waiting for the relevant questions" (Floridi 2011a, 77; 2011b, 294).

Here lies the philosophical foundation of Floridi's constructionism, which is rooted in the *relational* nature of data conceived as constraining affordances. This also means that his constructionism is always entrenched in human responsibility (Floridi 2011b, 300) since data are not understood as *sources* of information but as *resources* for information. This distinction is an important one, since it forges a robust, although not always patent, link between constructionism and responsibility. Let us first quote Floridi (2011a, 77) to clarify this point:

> Note, however, that the fact that data may count as *resources* for (namely, inputs an agent can use to construct) information, and hence for knowledge, rather that *sources*, leads to constructionist arguments against mimetic theories that interpret knowledge as some sort of picture of the world. [...] Whether empirical or conceptual, data make possible only a certain range of information constructs at a given level LoA for a particular purpose, and not all constructs are made possible equally easily.

The distinction between resources and sources of information both leads to constructionist views and forges a link between constructionism and responsibility, because the informational, epistemic agent cannot have a passive attitude towards data: the agent is not a passive receiver of information; data are inputs that need to be processed to construct information. However, this construction is not made from scratch, since data are not only affordances, but also constraints. Informational, epistemic agents bear responsibility for their constructions, and this is mostly made visible through the idea of a web of questions and answers, i.e., through a representation of knowledge as a *network of account* (Floridi 2011a, chap. 12; 2011b, 295).

At the end of our analysis, we begin to see why informational constructionism is an epistemic attempt to amend the dichotomy between subjective and objective dimensions of knowing (Floridi 2011b, 285). Floridi states (2011a, 78):

> From this perspective, the world is neither discovered nor invented, but designed by the epistemic agents experiencing it. This is neither a realist nor an anti-realist but a *constructionist* view of information.

Floridi's *constructionist* view of information provides a conceptual vocabulary that enables us to understand why both (information and communication) technology and epistemology may be said, in a certain sense, to *construct* (or *design*) the world in which we make decisions and behave, without dictating to us how to decide or to behave (Floridi 2011b, 285):

> So our difficulty is complex, because it consists in being radically moderate: we need to identify and follow the middle course, represented by the *design* of the world. This hardly thrills young minds, smacks of compromise to older ones, and, worst of all, cannot escape the constant risk of being confused with either Scylla or Charybdis, *discovery* or *invention*. [...] Equilibrium requires more energy than resolution, so we can hardly hold firm the view that *constructionism* is neither *realism* nor *constructivism*, because knowledge neither *describes* nor *prescribes* how the world is but *inscribes* it with semantic artefacts.

In contrast, this construction makes us responsible for the *creative responses* (Durante 2011) we formulate within the *constraining affordances* that design our environment at different levels of abstraction, e.g., technological, epistemological and informational. The normativity of constraining affordances is consistent with both human indeterminacy (freedom) and accountable behaviours (responsibility). What this approach enables us to grasp is that such normativity is not just a matter of code (as suggested by Lessig 2006), law or social norms, but is already concerned with the relational nature of data. Hence, it underlies the *construction* of information, which in turn *constructs* us as epistemic, informational agents experiencing the world in terms of well-formed, meaningful and veridical data (Floridi 2011b, 283). This is also why philosophy is ultimately a normative investigation about how things should be, as we will try to argue more extensively in the second part of the book.

1.6 Conclusions

We have sought to demonstrate that Floridi's epistemic constructionism is normative in what it articulates about human freedom and responsibility by adopting a notion of informational resources (made of well-formed, meaningful and veridical data) conceived as *constraining affordances*. This is just one of the ways in which the philosophy of information may be said, according to Floridi, to be a *philosophia prima*, i.e., a philosophy whose conceptual vocabulary provides us with a broader understanding of our world.

This result is accomplished by Floridi's philosophy of semantic information in three key moves that we would like to sum up here. First, *data are conceived as relata*, relational entities, that cannot be accessed per se, but only through a given level of abstraction: this posits a plurality of observers and observations that may transform into relativism or perspectivism, if some sort of unity fails to be associated with plurality and if both the constraining nature of data and the orienting nature of purposes is disregarded. Secondly, *all levels of abstraction are informational*: it is the informational construction of an object (here, in the semantic terms of data + meaning) that allows epistemic agents to *vary* the levels of abstraction at which they can experience the object. Thirdly, it is the semantic treatment of informational resources as *constraining affordances* that forges the *unity* of the irreducible plurality of observers and observations, and bridges the philosophies of technology and epistemology, thanks to a normative conception of *epistemic constructionism*. However carefully Luciano Floridi attempts to delineate and distinguish his philosophy of information from his ethics of information, some fundamental tenets of his ethics (such as, for instance, the informational treatment of agents, patients and messages, the flourishing of the infosphere, or the direct relation between availability of information and level of responsibility) are deeply rooted in his *constructionist* view of semantic information.

References

Bateson, G. 1973. *Steps to an Ecology of Mind*. Frogmore, St. Albans: Paladin.

Benkler, Y. 2006. *The Wealth of Networks: How Social Production Transforms Markets and Freedom*. New Haven CT: Yale University Press.

Ceruti, M. 2009. *Il vincolo e la possibilità*. Milano: Raffaello Cortina Editore.

Deleuze, G., and F. Guattari. 1994. *What Is Philosophy?* New York: Columbia University Press.

Durante, M. 2010. The Value of Information as Ontological Pluralism. *Knowledge, Technology & Policy* 23 (1): 149–161.

———. 2011. Rethinking Human Identity in the Age of Autonomic Computing: The Philosophical Idea of the Trace. In *Law, Human Agency and Autonomic Computing. The Philosophy of Law Meets the Philosophy of Technology*, ed. M. Hildebrandt and A. Rouvroy, 85–103. London: Routledge.

Floridi, L. 2003. On the Intrinsic Value of Information Objects and the Infosphere. *Ethics and Information Technology* 4 (4): 287–304.

———. 2007. A Look into the Future Impact of ICT on Our Lives. *The Information Society* 23 (1): 59–64.

———. 2008a. Information Ethics, Its Nature and Scope. In *Moral Philosophy and Information Technology*, ed. J. van den Hoven and J. Weckert, 40–65. Cambridge: Cambridge University Press.

———. 2008b. Information Ethics: A Reappraisal. In Ess, C. (ed.). Luciano Floridi's Philosophy of Information and Information Ethics: Critical Reflections and the State of the Art. *Ethics and Information Technology*, 10(2–3): 189–204.

———. 2008c. The Method of Levels of Abstraction. *Minds and Machines* 18 (3): 303–329.

———. 2010. *Information. A Very Short Introduction*. Oxford: Oxford University Press.
———. 2011a. *The Philosophy of Information*. Oxford: Oxford University Press.
———. 2011b. A Defence of Constructionism: Philosophy as Conceptual Engineering. *Metaphilosophy* 42 (3): 282–304.
Kallinikos, J. 2011. *Governing Through Technology. Information Artefacts and Social Practice*. Houndmills, Basingstoke: Palgrave Macmillan.
Lessig, L. 2006. *Code: And Other Laws of Cyberspace, Version 2.0*. New York: Basic Books.
MacKay, D.M. 1969. *Information, Mechanism and Meaning*. Cambridge, MA: MIT Press.
Moor, J.H. 1985. What Is Computer Ethics? *Metaphilosophy* 16 (4): 266–275.
Prigogine, I., and I. Stengers 1981. Vincolo, Enciclopedia Einaudi, Einaudi, Torino, vol. 14, 1064–1080.
Taylor, M. 2001. *The Moment of Complexity: Emerging Network Culture*. Chicago: Chicago University Press.
Wellman, B., et al. 2003. The Social Affordance of the Internet for Networked Individualism. *Journal of Computer-Mediated Communication* 8 (3.), available online.

The Informational Environment

2

Abstract

Our world is technological. According to a longstanding philosophical tradition, the conceptual core of technology can be understood as being based on the relation between two main philosophical categories: the subject and the object (e.g. the relation between 'culture' and 'nature'). This tradition mainly conceives technology as a set of means that can be used to control and manipulate nature (*the object*), in order to achieve some end (culture) established by human beings (*the subject*). Consequent to the ICT revolution, this scenario must now be devised in terms of an informational world or environment. This requires a change of paradigm in the study of technology and in the comprehension of our world that displaces the presumed 'central' role of the subject. This happens in ways and for motives that have nothing to do with the philosophical hitches that ensue from the post-modern relativistic or nihilistic *death* of the subject. In the present chapter, we expound the meaning of this scenario, by focusing our attention upon the informational nature of the environment in which we live and act.

2.1 Introduction

Many scholars recognize the manifold impact of ICTs on our society, aptly dubbed the information society (Castells 1999; Benkler 2006). Such an impact is widely assumed to be social, economic, legal, moral, political and so forth, and poses two main questions that will be the core of present and future agendas: i.e., the question of the convergence between physical and virtual reality (Fernandez-Barrera et al. 2009) and the question of technological normativity, that is, to what extent the technological impact determines or shapes our own society (Hildebrandt 2008). However, few scholars recognize that both the convergence and the technological impact are, first and foremost, *epistemic*. We shall focus our attention on the first question in Chap. 5. Let us make three remarks regarding the second question,

M. Durante, *Ethics, Law and the Politics of Information*, The International Library of Ethics, Law and Technology 18, DOI 10.1007/978-94-024-1150-8_2

namely the impact of ICTs on our society, which is the topic of the present chapter, by availing ourselves of some of Floridi's observations.

Floridi points out that this impact brings about both benefits and risks (Floridi 2010, 6–7), not just in the rather common sense that technological application is for the good and for the bad, but in the sense that the ICT revolution raises questions that challenge the epistemic premises upon which our knowledge of the nature of reality is based and it might generate *policy vacuums* (Moor 1985), meaning the lack of clear guiding principles in the management of new ethical, legal, political, and social questions:

> ICTs have been changing the world profoundly and irreversibly for more than half a century now, with breath-taking scope and at a neck-breaking pace. On the one hand, they have brought concrete and imminent opportunities of enormous benefit to people's education, welfare, prosperity, and edification, as well as great economic and scientific advantages. [...] On the other hand, ICTs also carry significant risks and generate dilemmas and profound questions about the nature of reality and of our knowledge of it, the development of information-intensive sciences (e-science), the organization of a fair society (consider the digital divide), our responsibilities and obligations to present and future generations, our understanding of a globalized world, and the scope of our potential interactions with the environment.

Secondly and accordingly, he suggests that the impact of ICTs, which indeed concerns the whole life-cycle of information, is mainly of an epistemic nature that has to do with both our understanding of the world and our comprehension of ourselves (Floridi 2010, 8):

> ICTs have made the creation, management, and utilization of information, communication, and computational resources vital issues, not only in our understanding of the world and of our interactions with it, but also in our self-assessment and identity.

Then, on this account, Floridi reminds us that a theoretical lack of balance affects the information society and leads us to mistake ICTs for merely *enhancing* or *augmenting* technologies, for we fail to recognize how profoundly the ongoing information revolution is transforming our understanding of reality and of ourselves. This lack of balance calls for a viable philosophy of information (Floridi 2010, 7–8):

> The information society is like a tree that has been growing its far-reaching branches much more widely, hastily, and chaotically than its conceptual, ethical, and cultural roots. [...] The risk is that, like a tree with weak roots, further and healthier growth at the top might be impaired by a fragile foundation at the bottom. As a consequence, today, any advanced information society faces the pressing task of equipping itself with a viable philosophy of information.

What is in question is whether an informational approach provides us with a philosophical language capable of dealing with the aforementioned lack of balance. The answer requires a three-step conceptual analysis aimed at understanding: (1) how ICTs construct a different comprehension of reality and of ourselves; (2) how the informational turn is to be epistemically interpreted, in order to show that there is one level of explanation of reality and of ourselves consistent with the technological rendition of reality and our technologically-driven self-assessment; (3) what it means to be an informational epistemic agent and what sort of environment these new agents inhabit.

2.2 The Infosphere

We live in a world made up of information. We tend either to underrate or to overrate this idea. Those who underestimate it believe that the information revolution is mainly, if not only, a quantitative phenomenon: more information, more outlets of information and communications, more data, more links and so forth. Accordingly, they also believe that technology is a set of (powerful) tools and means that can be harnessed by human beings, at least until their quantitative dimension turns into new problems (e.g. information overload). Those who overestimate it believe that the information revolution affects the ultimate nature of reality, which is made up of information. This pancomputationalist view fails to acknowledge that the thrilling conceptual core of epistemology is not the description of the ultimate nature of reality (i.e. the *noumenal* reality, which is out of reach), but, rather, it is the understanding of how an epistemic agent experiences the *phenomenal* reality. Floridi's *epistemic constructionism* (see Chap. 1) is directed towards this notion. It rests on the idea that, at a certain point, quantity becomes quality, to put it in Hegelian terms, and that what really counts in the epistemological work is not the description of the nature of reality but, rather, the experience of reality, which does not bind us to any presumed ultimate account of the world, but allows us to responsibly construct our *own* world. As already pointed out (see Chap. 1), Floridi's epistemic constructionism is the theoretical foundation and counterpart of the ethical conception of *homo poieticus*, i.e., the demiurgic attitude of an informational agent.

This means that the practical (social, legal, ethical, political, etc.) impact of ICTs on the world at large should never be separated from their epistemological impact, i.e. how an epistemic agent experiences the reality constructed by informational objects. Too often, studies on digitalisation have treated the impact brought about by the evolution of ICTs simply as a quantitative phenomenon or one of many organizational devices, rather than conceptualizing the information revolution as a truly innovative qualitative phenomenon, which entails an epistemological *re-ontologization* of the entire reality and of the world, thus conceived as an *infosphere*. This aspect has been highlighted in Floridi's philosophy of information (Floridi 2007, 61; see also Floridi 2003):

> In order to grasp the ICT scenarios that we might witness and experience in the near future, it is useful to introduce two key-concepts […], those of "infosphere" and of "re-ontologization". *Infosphere* is a neologism I coined years ago […]. It denotes the whole informational environment constituted by all informational entities, their properties, interactions, processes and mutual relations. It is an environment comparable to, but different from cyberspace (which is only one of its sub-regions), since it also includes off-line and analogue spaces of information. *Re-ontologizing* is another neologism that I have recently

introduced in order to refer to a very radical form of re-engineering, one that not only designs, constructs or structures a system (e.g. a company, a machine or some artifact) anew, but that fundamentally transforms its intrinsic nature […]. Using the two previous concepts, my basic claim can now be formulated thus: digital ICTs are re-ontologizing the very nature of (and hence what we mean by) the infosphere, and here lies the source of some of the most profound transformations and challenging problems that our information societies will experience in the close future, as far as technology is concerned.

In the present chapter, we will focus on the notion of infosphere; that of re-ontologization will be dealt with in Chap. 5. The infosphere is defined as the informational environment viewed as a whole and constituted by: (1) informational entities; (2) their properties; (3) their interactions; (4) their processes; and (5) their mutual relations. This list, which qualifies the attitudes of informational entities (in terms of properties, interactions, processes and relations), is much more important to the definition of infosphere than may appear at first glance. It specifies not only how dynamically informational entities constitute the infosphere – which is not the static description of a state of things, but the dynamic account of how an environment is structured and evolves – but it will also help us later in this chapter to elucidate the philosophical notion of space that underlies the notion of the informational environmental viewed as a whole. Infosphere is, in fact, an *all-encompassing* category that includes the analogical and the digital space as well as the offline and the online spaces of information. They are all sub-regions of the infosphere, which can still be understood according to their own terms (i.e., continuous vs. discrete states of being). However, their informational construction and conceptual treatment also allow us to conceive them in more unified, if not universal, terms. This requires us to understand the philosophical notion of *space* that underlies the infosphere.

Let us turn our attention here to the conceptual category of space, which plays a central role in the modern philosophical tradition. This role is twofold. In the modern philosophical tradition, space is both the horizon of the object and the horizon of politics, as will emerge in the second part of this book. It is the horizon of the object, since it enables us to place an object within a given perspective (*rectius*: a level of abstraction, see Chap. 1) in which we can perceive it, we can describe it and know its features, and we can manipulate it. Therefore, space is the *subjective*, phenomenological or epistemological, horizon of objectivity, that is, of what can be held to be objective (i.e. the objective reality) by an epistemic agent, as for instance in Kant:

> Space does not represent any determination that attaches to the objects themselves, and which remains even when abstraction has been made of all the subjective conditions of intuition. […] It is the subjective condition of sensibility, under which alone outer intuition is possible for us. […] If we depart from the subjective condition under which alone we can have outer intuition, namely, liability to be affected by objects, the representation of space stands for nothing whatsoever.[1]

[1] I. Kant, *Critique of pure reason* [1781], trans. N. Kemp Smith, Palgrave Macmillan, Hampshire, 2003, p. 42.

If the configuration of space changes, then the way in which we conceive objectivity and understand reality must be updated, notably in relation to the very notion of epistemic agent. Space is also the horizon of politics, since it regulates how the objects placed within it can interact, or in other words, how they can coexist:

> I may only conceive of something as placed outside me by representing it as in a place which is different from the place in which I am myself; and I may only conceive of things outside one another by locating them in different places in space.[2]

In this perspective, space may be understood as the political horizon of coexistence, telling us how entities interact with one another, have mutual relations, and to what extent their claims can be made compatible. This means that every change that radically affects space also concerns the way objects are represented and coexist, and this is exactly what Floridi suggests is going to happen as the evolution of ICT redesigns, in informational terms, the space we inhabit.

Now let us focus our attention on the philosophical idea of space as regards the infosphere. We have already mentioned Kant, whose notion of space is central to the modern philosophical history of the concept. However, "Kant worked out his own position by reflecting on the opposed positions of these two thinkers [Newton and Leibniz]" (Dicker 2004, 28). Let us briefly recall the philosophical positions of Newton and Leibniz as well as that of Kant (as expounded in Dicker 2004, who concentrates his analysis precisely on Kant's theory of knowledge):

> According to Newton, space is *both real and absolute*. Space for Newton is real in that it exists independently of any mind (except possibly God's mind: Newton refers to space as 'God sensorium'). It is absolute in that it also exists independently of any objects in space, so that space – empty space – would still exist even if there were absolutely nothing in it (Dicker 2004, 28).

According to Newton, space is therefore real and absolute in the sense illustrated above: i.e., independence from the mind and from any object. Leibniz holds the opposite view, as Dicker points out:

> According to Leibniz, on the other hand, space is *both ideal and relative*. [...] space is ideal: it is merely something that appears in the perceptions of the monads, rather than something that really exists. For Leibniz, this does not mean that space is totally unreal, for even an appearance has some degree of reality. [...] Furthermore, for Leibniz space is also relative, rather than absolute, as for Newton. This means that for Leibniz space is nothing but a set of relations between the things that are said to be in space (Dicker 2004, 28).

According to Leibniz, space is thus a "'well-founded phenomenon', meaning that although it is merely an appearance, it has a foundation in the (perceptions of) the non-spatial monads, somewhat as the coloured bands in a rainbow have their foundation in transparent droplets of water" (Dicker 2004, 28). Moreover, space is a set of relations, somewhat as "the space in a room is nothing over and above a set

---

[2] See Kant 1992, 395.

of relations between the various pieces of furniture and other objects said to be in the room" (Dicker 2004, 28).

Newton's and Leibniz's positions are of crucial importance for Kant, whose notion of space is a kind of compromise between the previous views. However, this compromise is essential for Kant's theory of knowledge, since "it also served as the stimulus or springboard for the famous 'Copernican Revolution in Philosophy'" (Dicker 2004, 28). Let us see how this compromise is achieved:

> Kant's position on space (and on time too; he treats these in the same way) is as follows: space is *ideal and absolute*. Thus Newton is wrong in holding space to be real but right in holding it to be absolute, and Leibniz is wrong in holding space to be relative but right in holding it to be ideal (Dicker 2004, 28–29).

For our present purpose, we have to overlook, for a moment, Kant's criticism over the relative dimension of space and to focus our attention upon what Kant means by saying that space is ideal. Actually, "when Kant asserts that space is ideal, he means something much stronger than that space is something that appears rather than something fully real", as Dicker properly points out (2004, 30):

> Kant gives Leibniz's theory a new twist that radically transforms its significance. For Kant, to say that space is ideal (or 'transcendentally ideal', as his complete expression goes) means that it is *a permanent, built-in feature of the human knower, as opposed to something that exists independently of the knower* (Dicker 2004, 30).

Therefore, according to Kant, space is ideal and absolute: it is ideal (in a transcendental sense different from that of Leibniz), since space it is not only something that appears, but is a condition of possibility for knowing reality, namely, a condition which is inherent to the human knower and thus is not independent from the mind. This idea has been explained, by means of analogy, by Kant's English commentator, H.J. Paton, who said "a man has a pair of blue-tinted glasses permanently and irremovably affixed to his head. On the one hand, it is obvious that the man does not create or even alter the things he sees through the glasses. On the other, it is obvious that he can never see anything than except as blue" (Dicker 2004, 30). Space is absolute, since it exits independently from any object in space, in the sense that it cannot be derived from the relations between objects, which are perceived by means of experience and are thus a posteriori. On the contrary, according to Kant, space is conceived as an a priori intuition (a subjective condition of intuition or a general form of outer sense), since it is not derived from experience, as the empirical or a posteriori intuition, the content of which is always a single instance (unlike a class of instances that requires the mediation of a concept).

In the first chapter, we have already seen that Floridi's method of levels of abstraction resembles Kant's transcendental approach, even if there is a difference between them that can be further highlighted in the present context. Let us briefly recall what we have said on this point. Floridi's epistemological method of levels of abstraction resembles Kant's *transcendental* approach, as he himself notes (Floridi

2011a, 58; 2011b, 293) by stating where his assessment agrees with Kant's (Floridi 2011a, 59):

> The attempt to strive for something unconditioned is equivalent to the natural, yet profoundly mistaken, endeavour to analyse a system (the world in itself, for Kant, but it could also be a more limited domain) independently of any (specification of) the level of abstraction at which the analysis is being conducted, the questions are being posed and the answers are being offered, for a specific purpose.

Floridi endorses Kant's transcendental approach, "which considers the conditions of possibility of the analysis (experience) of a particular system", whilst he "does not inherit from Kant any mental or subject-based feature" (Floridi 2011a, 60). This has already been pointed out in the first chapter, where we also learned that the method of levels of abstraction allows us in the present context to overcome the Kantian distinction between a priori and a posteriori intuitions, precisely because of the notion of observable (interpreted as a *typed variable*) endorsed by the method of levels of abstraction, and to give a *constructionist* twist to Kant's transcendental idealism. We are now provided with all the information necessary in order to understand the informational idea of space that underlies both Floridi's notion of infosphere and his theory of knowledge.

According to Floridi's construction of the notion of infosphere, the space of information may be said to be *ideal* and *relative*. It is ideal in the Kantian sense, even if the meaning of transcendental idealism is slightly revised by Floridi. It is relative in the sense that Leibniz confers to this term. Therefore, the space of information is ideal for two main raisons: firstly, because it is the condition of possibility of the analysis (experience) of a particular system (*the transcendental aspect*). Secondly, because it does not exist independently of the mind (*the idealistic aspect*). However, this dependence should not be conceived in any strict subjective sense, as meaning a permanent, built-in feature of the human knower. A human being "might know that *p* better than his dog does because he can provide an account for it, not just hold an implicit account of it" (Floridi 2011a, 287). Such dependence should be conceived in an informational, *evolutionary* sense, since the meaning of information is always dependent upon an informee; however, relevant semantic information has to be correctly accounted for, in order to upgrade to knowledge. In this perspective, it is crucial to remark that at all times knowledge "comes in degrees" (Floridi 2011a, 287), since it depends on a specific ability (i.e. '*knowing how*'):

> For it seems clear that knowing that *t* relies on knowing how to build, articulate and defend a correct account for *t*. [...] The informational analysis of knowledge is engineer-friendly. According to it, the production of knowledge that *t* relies, ultimately, on the intelligent mastery of the practical expertise (including modelling or, more mundanely, story-telling) required to produce not only *t* but also its correct account *A*. 'Knowing that' is grounded on 'knowing how', hardly surprising from an evolutionary perspective" (Floridi 2011a, 287).

The space of information is relative, since it does not exist independently from informational objects: i.e., from the relations between the informational objects an agent may *experience* at any given level of abstraction. As already remarked, the specific and fundamental meaning that Floridi confers to the notion of experience makes him depart from an absolute conception of space (based on a priori intuitions). Since informational objects are constructed, in Floridi's epistemological perspective, on data, which are thus "*resources* for (namely, inputs an agent can use to construct) information, and hence for knowledge" (Floridi 2011a, 77), and data are understood as *constraining affordances* ("answers waiting for the relevant questions" (Floridi 2011a, 77), the relativity of the informational space is understood as the set of relations between informational objects, that is, as the tension between the constraints and the affordances of the informational resources made out of data. The ways informational objects may be related to each other and therefore may be experienced by an epistemic agent at a given level of abstraction specify the spatial characters of the infosphere.

The ideality and relativity of the infosphere, as we have defined them in the present context, let us understand that the space of information conceived by Floridi is an *ordered space* based on the relatedness between informational objects. This means that the infosphere is a space governed by laws, whose ideality (i.e. their 'ought to be') is grounded upon the respect we owe to the relational existence of informational objects, which is both an expression of the richness of the infosphere and a condition of possibility of the informational space itself in which we live. Therefore, the laws of the infosphere, which we will turn our attention to in the next section, are neither positivistic norms established by some authority nor they are natural laws, if these are intended as laws that preside over a pre-existing, fixed and immutable nature. They are *evolutionary laws* that are conceptually co-extensive with the conception of the informational space, the existence and evolution of which (i.e., the *flourishing of the infosphere*) these laws are meant to assure and protect. If we lose sight of the evolutionary aspect of the laws of the infosphere, we are also likely to overlook the *dynamic* dimension of the ontology of informational objects. Let us turn our attention to those laws of the infosphere.

2.3 The Laws of the Infosphere

Before introducing the analysis of the normative aspect of information ethics, concerning the four ethical principles or laws governing the infosphere, let us recall some basic moral tenets of Floridi's information ethics, which we have already pointed out in the Introduction. It is Floridi himself who poses a fundamental question that relates the moral situation of an informational entity to that of the infosphere in general (Floridi 2013):

> What is good for an informational entity and the infosphere in general? This is the moral question asked by IE. We have seen that the answer is provided by a minimalist approach to what Being deserves: any informational entity is recognised to be the centre of some basic ethical claims that deserve recognition and should help to regulate the implementation of any information process involving it. Approval or disapproval of any information process is then based on how the latter affects the essence of the informational entities it involves

and, more generally, the well-being of the whole infosphere, i.e. on how successful or unsuccessful it is in respecting the claims attributable to the informational entities involved and, hence, in enriching or impoverishing the infosphere. More analytically, IE determines what is morally right or wrong, what ought and ought not be done, and so the duties of a moral agent are, by means of four basic moral principles.

This extensive quote, coupled with what was said in the previous section about Floridi's conception of information space, we believe, gets us to the conceptual core of Floridi's understanding of the moral status of any informational entity. The moral status is not merely concerned with listing what ought and ought not to be done (which is certainly necessary at some point). In other words and making use of Stanley Cavell's moral distinction (1991, 2005) between *legislators* and *perfectionists*, Floridi may not qualify as a pure legislator. He does not believe that ethics consists *primarily* in the capacity of enacting moral standards, principles and rules. According to IE, the moral situation first and foremost concerns the *relation* of a part (i.e. the informational entity) to a whole (i.e. the infosphere), so that the part can neither be absorbed within the whole (objectivism or historicism) nor can it absorb the whole (subjectivism or idealism). This relatedness structures the moral situation, which is the *envelope* (Floridi 2013) of the moral agent, even before the agents and the patients are involved in the information processes that are governed by moral standards, principles and rules. In other words, it is precisely in the light of this relatedness that the following four ethical principles (Floridi 2013) are to be understood and appreciated:

0) entropy ought not to be caused in the infosphere (null law)
1) entropy ought to be prevented in the infosphere
2) entropy ought to be removed from the infosphere
3) the flourishing of informational entities as well as of the whole infosphere ought to be promoted by preserving, cultivating, and enriching their well-being

Floridi also specifies three criteria that explain how those four principles apply and serve as moral standards of one's actions and, more generally, of a responsible and caring life in the infosphere:

First criterion: *the moral progression.*

Floridi (2013) states the following in regards to the inbuilt possibility of a moral progression in the responsible and caring life in the infosphere: "the principles are listed in order of increasing moral value", so that "a process is increasingly disapprovable and its agent-source is increasingly blameworthy, the lower is the number index of the specific law that it fails to satisfy". On the contrary, "a process is already approvable and its agent-source praiseworthy, if it satisfies the *combination* of the null law with at least one other law, not the *sum* of the resulting effects". What is really at stake in this ethical perspective based on the idea of a moral progression? Here lies a fundamental point in Floridi's IE that has not been sufficiently underlined: a moral action can be evaluated both *statically*, i.e., in relation to a *single moral situation* (the agent's envelope), and *dynamically*, i.e., in relation to a *responsible and caring life* (the possibility for an agent to go through a moral progression). The distinction between negative and positive laws cannot be understood by reducing it to the negative or proactive attitude of a moral agent. It means something more. The moral discourse is not merely concerned with the blameworthiness or praiseworthiness of a single action in a moral situation; it is first and foremost concerned with the construction of one's entire life (which alone fully entails the idea of a moral progression).

Second criterion: *the moral balance*.

As Floridi (2013) remarks, "the best moral action is the action that succeeds in satisfying all four laws at the same time. Most of actions we judge morally good do not satisfy such a strict criterion, for they achieve only a balanced positive moral value, that is, although their performance causes a specific quantity of entropy, we acknowledge that the infosphere is in a better state after their occurrence". At the same time, "moral mistakes may occur and entropy may increase because of a wrong evaluation of the impact of one's actions – especially when local goodness, i.e. the improvement of a region of the infosphere is favoured to the overall disadvantage of the whole infosphere – because of the conflicting or competing projects – even when the latter are aiming at the satisfaction of IE moral laws" (Floridi 2013). What is truly relevant in the idea of a moral balance? At first sight, it is important to remark that the moral agent, who acts in the *presupposition* of performing a good action, may discover to have increased the entropy of the infosphere, because of an incorrect evaluation of the impact of that action. More profoundly, the idea of a moral balance suggests that local goodness does not suffice to entirely define a moral situation, that is, to make an agent comply with the requirements of the moral laws. Goodness requires time, because of its epistemic foundation (namely, the degree of predictability of a course of action) or, in other words, because of its intrinsic resilience. This leads us to the third and final criterion: the resilience of goodness.

Third criterion: *the resilience of goodness*.

Floridi (2013) remarks that "the advantage of IE is that, like our moral intuition, it attributes a non-monotonic nature only to goodness: unlike evil, goodness can, in principle, turn out to be less morally good and sometimes even morally wrong unintentionally, depending on how things develop, that is, on what new state the infosphere enters into, as a consequence of the process in question. This seems at least to be what people have in mind when talking about the fragility of goodness". However, the progression of time, which makes goodness fragile because of its non-monotonic nature, also provides goodness with "the property of being *resilient*, both in the sense of *fault tolerance* […] and in the sense of *error-recovery* […]. Resilience – what we often describe by terms such as tolerance, forbearance, forgiveness, reconciliation, or simply other people's positive behaviour – makes goodness much more robust than its non-monotonic nature may lead one to conclude at first sight. It explains the presence and possibility of entropic balance in the infosphere" (Floridi 2013). It is Floridi himself that links together the presence and possibility of entropic balance in the infosphere with the progression of time that underlies both the fragility and the resilience of goodness. Any moral situation is necessarily local, and precisely defined in time and space. However, goodness (and thus the moral experience) is not entirely local, being entrenched in the progression of time and the relatedness to the whole.

What emerges from the analysis of the four ethical principles that constitute the normative aspect of IE is a more general and unexpected characterization and comprehension of the ethical discourse. In our interpretation, this discourse (and thus the moral experience that is its own subject) is structured along two basic axes: the *vertical* and the *horizontal*. The *vertical* axis is a synchronic axis concerning the moral dimension of a determined agent that is called upon to comply with the moral requirements of the four ethical principles. Along the vertical axis, the emphasis of the ethical discourse is put on the notions of blameworthiness and praiseworthiness, which define the agent's moral attitudes towards the patient, i.e., any informational entity. However, the ethical discourse is not only concerned with a vertical axis that highlights the *here* and *now* of a moral situation. There is also a *horizontal* axis, which is a diachronic axis, concerning the moral progression (i.e., the entire caring and responsible life) of a particular agent called upon to revise and deepen its knowledge of the possible outcomes of the course of action undertaken, in relation to the patient's life. The horizontal axis calls attention to the *learning process* that diachronically structures the ethical discourse, which has an epistemic foundation. From a practical standpoint, recognizing what is right does not yet amount to behaving rightly, although, from an epistemic standpoint, it is a necessary condition for doing so. The horizontal axis is an essential complement and potentially a permanent rectification of the vertical one: for instance, we will never be able to fully understand the ethical complexity of the *homo poieticus* (to be investigated in the next chapter) and its radical involvement in the infosphere if we do not consider its moral dimension along these two axes. Their interplay can be further highlighted by analysing the fundamental principle of ontological equality that governs the infosphere and is the theoretical foundation of Floridi's ethics (or, in other words, of Floridi's possible philosophy of law).

2.4 The Principle of Ontological Equality

As usual, we shall present and illustrate this principle starting from reference to Floridi's formulation of it (2013):

> IE holds that every informational entity, insofar as it is an expression of Being, has a dignity constituted by its mode of existence and essence, defined here as the collection of all the elementary properties that constitute it for what it is. This dignity *prima facie* deserves to be respected and hence may place moral claims on any interacting agent. It ought to contribute to the constraint and guidance of her ethical decisions and behaviour, even if only

> initially and in an overridable way. This ontological equality principle [...] means that any form of reality – that is, given the structuralist approach defended by IE, any instance of information – simply for the fact of being what it is, enjoys an initial, overridable, minimal right to exist and develop in a way appropriate to its nature.

Thus, according to Floridi, any form of reality (i.e., any informational entity) deserves some respect, simply for the fact of being what it is (i.e., *qua* informational entity). This principle of ontological equality may and often does raise many epistemic and ethical questions and objections[3]: what is the mode of existence and essence of an informational entity? What does dignity mean in the context of information ethics? Does this meaning coincide with the Kantian idea of dignity? Why should the collection of all the elementary properties that constitute an informational entity for what it is deserve respect? What is thus appropriate to the nature of an informational entity? Is this principle of ontological equality a dogmatic justification of what already exists and, therefore, a form of conservationism? Do all informational entities deserve the same level of moral respect?

We will try to provide a workable answer to these questions in the first chapter of the second part of the book, where (in addition to examining Floridi's replies to the mentioned objections), we seek to demonstrate that Floridi's principle of ontological equality may serve as a theoretical foundation of an ontological pluralism. At present, we have to clarify some philosophical presuppositions and features of the principle of ontological equality that may shed more light on the two moral axes of Floridi's IE. Let us start again by quoting Floridi, since he makes a crucial distinction between what application of the principle of ontological equality presupposes (*a parte ante*) and what it is supposed to bring about (*a parte post*), when its application is achieved:

> The conscious recognition of the ontological equality principle presupposes, *a parte ante*, a disinterested judgement of the moral situation from an absolute perspective, i.e. a perspective that is patient-oriented. Indeed, moral behaviour is less likely without this epistemic virtue. At most, we can only act to the best of our knowledge concerning the options available, the likely consequences and implications of the action undertaken, and so forth, yet this is hardly sufficient to ensure that our moral actions will be morally right, if our knowledge is either limited or biased towards the agent and what is best only for her and does not include a wider degree of attentiveness to the patient as well (Floridi 2013).

Floridi helps us realize that recognition of the ontological equality principle involves, *a parte ante*, the existence of a horizontal axis of the ethical discourse, based on knowledge, which may serve as a form of rectification (that is, of generalisation) of the contingency of the vertical axis, with this rectification being the possibility of a disinterested judgement of the moral situation from an absolute

[3] For criticism and discussion of the issue at stake see, for instance, Himma 2004, Capurro 2008, Brey 2008, Doyle 2010. In the present book, we cannot address each criticism analytically, which would take too much space and Floridi has already taken on the task in several articles and books. Instead, we try to treat and discuss any critical points in more general terms, in order to provide the reader with a broad conceptual framework of Floridi's approach to ethical issues.

perspective, i.e., a perspective which is patient-oriented. This disinterestedness is made possible only by considering knowledge as both an epistemic and an ethical virtue or, in other words, by acknowledging that ethics involves two fundamental epistemic conditions:

(1) *re-orientation of the moral perspective* (from the agent to the patient); and
(2) a *lifelong learning process*, which thus becomes our primary moral duty.

Nonetheless, while the contingency of the vertical axis can be rectified, it can never be excluded: we are constantly called upon to act in a determined moral situation "in the dim light of uncertainty" and always lacking "a full ethical competence" (Floridi 2013). For this reason, it is not only a matter of the right interpretation of the ontological equality principle, but also of its correct application (namely, how to choose between several available options in the course of action to undertake). When is this principle correctly applied? "The application of the ontological equality principle is achieved, *a parte post*, whenever actions are impartial, universal and caring" (Floridi 2013). This means that the re-orientation of the moral perspective not only represents a shift from the agent's to the patient's perspective, but it is first and foremost a way to submit *both* the agent *and* the patient to the principles of impartiality, universality and carefulness while, at the same time, understanding the reference to the otherness of the other (which is implicit in the principles of impartiality, universality and carefulness) no longer as an abstraction, but as a concrete reference to the situation of the patient. For this reason, according to IE, our actions are impartial, universal and caring whenever those actions (Floridi 2013):

- are independent of the position we enjoy in the moral situation [i.e., along the vertical axe], as patient or agent. We would make the same choice and behave in the same way even if we were at the receiving end of the action (impartiality);
- can in theory regulate the behaviour of any other agent placed in any similar moral situation. Anyone else would make the same choices and behave in the same way in a similar situation (universality);
- take care of the well-being of both the agent and the patient (carefullness). Our choices and behaviour are equally agent-oriented and patient-oriented, insofar as the interests of both agent and patient are taken into account.

Impartiality tells us that information ethics endorses the idea of symmetry (or the ethics of reciprocity) that is apparent in the Golden Rule (and "its subsequent refinements such as the Kantian moral imperative or Rawls' choice in a state of ignorance", Floridi 2013) and that serves as the foundation of liberalism. However, it is important to stress that the *independency* of the position along the vertical axis (i.e., whether it is the agent or the patient in the moral situation) is not based on any *sympathetic* relation between agent and patient (such as the capacity of understanding and sharing the feelings of another). This independency is not anthropocentrically biased, since it is based on the *informational* treatment of both the agent and the patient (namely, the capacity to understand and share information with another). The independency of the *position* we enjoy in the moral situation (i.e., being *that* agent or *that* patient) also means that information ethics is never aimed at preserving a *predetermined* situation (that is, it is not a protection of the *status quo*), precisely because of the *universality* of the ontological equality principle, according to which no informational entity is in principle biased in relation to its position in the moral situation. This is what the requirement of universality tells us about information ethics. Finally, the requirement of carefulness tells us something important about information ethics, which is constantly subject to misinterpretation in terms of the ontological equality principle. If this principle affirms that any informational entity deserves a *minimum* level of respect (i.e., a right to exist and develop), this does not mean that every informational entity deserves the *same* level of respect. The effective level of respect that any informational entity concretely receives is a matter of carefulness, according to which the well-being of both the agent and the patient is to be taken into account. This also means that the level of respect that an entity deserves may *vary* according to the informational status it acquires. A stone deserves a minimal level of respect as part of nature, for instance. However paradoxical it may seem, a stone, which has been used to kill someone, may deserve a special kind of legal protection, as it is necessary evidence for someone to be found guilty, that is to say, because of its *different* informational status (note: not because of its utilization but because of its status).

In closing this section, we wish to make some further remarks on the interplay between the vertical and the horizontal axes that structure the infosphere understood as a moral envelope or situation. This seems to be a key point that not only marks the originality of Floridi's moral approach, but makes it fully comprehensible: both the normative aspect of information ethics (i.e. *the four ethical principles*) and its fundamental tenet (i.e. *the ontological equality principle*) can be better appreciated only if we take into consideration the diachronic epistemic dimension of ethics. The emphasis on the blameworthiness and praiseworthiness of actions in a moral situation (i.e., the vertical axe) should not prevent us from recognizing that this situation is always traversed throughout a lifelong learning process (i.e., the horizontal axe) that may revise the contingency of our actions. The self-reflective attitude of a lifelong ethical learning process is so important to information ethics that it helps explain why Floridi's information ethics is meant to endorse a *rule-ethics* rather than an *act-ethics* approach: "IE relies on human understanding for the implementation of the right action" (Floridi 2013). A rule-ethics approach emphasizes the dependence of action upon information: namely, it emphasizes the role of information as a rule of action, i.e., how information upgrades to knowledge and how knowledge may be transmitted through time as a constraint and guidance of ethical decisions and behaviour. In Floridi's own words (2013):

> IE relies on moral education and the transmission of whatever past generations have been able to grasp about the nature of the world, and its intrinsic value, thus adopting a rule-ethics rather than an act-ethics approach. Yet it must also acknowledge the fact that even a good will acts in the dim light of uncertainty and that, as human beings, we shall always lack full ethical competence. This is why our first duty is epistemic: whenever possible, we must try to understand before acting. This also explains why moral education consists

primarily in negative principles and a fundamental training not to interfere with the world, to abstain from engaging in positive actions and tampering with reality.

2.5 Conclusions

While it is important to highlight the originality of Floridi's philosophy of information, which has generated new theoretical notions such as that of the infosphere, we believe that it is perhaps even more important that these notions be inscribed and understood within the history of philosophy. This is not akin to saying that philosophy offers new answers for old questions. On the contrary, it means that philosophy, according to Floridi, is always *problematic*: it attempts to provide questions with answers. In other words, philosophical answers cannot be new if the questions have not already been structured in a different, original way, since the answers can only be understood within the scope of their questions. The theoretical task fundamentally starts from an understanding of the differences in how current questions are structured, and this always requires a confrontation with the philosophical tradition.

For this reason, we have set out in this chapter to demonstrate that the idea of infosphere should not be misinterpreted as synonymous with the digitization of the world. It is a much more sophisticated notion that includes a novel account and understanding of the analogical and the digital, the offline and the online spaces of information. They are all sub-regions of the infosphere: this has required an understanding of the philosophical idea of the information space that characterizes the infosphere. According to Floridi's philosophy, the information space can be interpreted as being ideal and relative. It is ideal in the Kantian sense (even if the meaning of transcendental idealism has been slightly revised by Floridi), since it is the condition of possibility of the analysis (experience) of a system (the transcendental aspect), and it does not exist independently of the mind (the idealistic aspect). It is relative in the sense that Leibniz confers to this term, since it does not exist independently from the relations between the informational objects an agent may experience at any given level of abstraction.

According to these characteristics (ideality and relativity), the information space is understood by Floridi as an *ordered space* based on the relatedness between informational objects. This means that the infosphere is a space governed by laws (the four ethical principles), whose ideality (i.e., their *ought to be*) is based on the respect we owe to the relational existence of informational objects. The ontological *right to exist* that any informational entity enjoys is entrenched in the very notion of space itself, which informational objects do not merely inhabit but are *part* of. This is why we have underlined that, according to information ethics, the relatedness structures the moral situation, which is the envelope of the moral agent; in other words, the moral situation concerns the *relation* of a part (i.e., the informational entity) to a whole (i.e., the infosphere), such that the part can neither be absorbed within the whole nor it can absorb the whole. Analysis of the four ethical laws that govern the infosphere allows us to make a crucial point, namely that the moral experience described by Floridi's information ethics is structured along two necessary axes: a *vertical* one and a *horizontal* one.

The *vertical* axis is a synchronic axis concerning the moral situation of a determined agent called upon to comply with the moral requirements of the four ethical principles. Along the vertical axis, blameworthiness and praiseworthiness define the agent's moral attitudes towards the patient. However, the moral experience is not only concerned with a vertical axis that highlights the *here* and *now* of a moral situation. There is a *horizontal* axis, which is diachronic, that concerns the entire caring and responsible life of an agent always called upon to revise and deepen its knowledge of the possible effects of a course of action undertaken, in relation to the patient's life. The horizontal axis calls attention to the *lifelong learning process* that structures the moral experience, by providing it with an epistemic foundation. Moral agents do not live in some sort of eternal present that seems to affect our contemporary society, but, according to a constructionist perspective in the articulation between a past and a future. Only that which is derived from a past can aspire to have a future.

It is within this perspective that the pivotal notion of the ontological equality principle underlying the entire project of information ethics must be interpreted and understood. The fundamental right to exist, which characterizes Floridi's informational ontology of law, is to be conceived neither as a mere protection of the *status quo* of a given informational entity nor as the mere tension *(entelechy)* of the entity towards the full realization of its own being. It has to be understood as the minimal, overridable protection of *both* the existence (included the expectation of existence) *and* the evolution of an informational entity *qua* informational entity, namely, as a relational entity, i.e., an entity capable of interaction in space and across time with other informational objects as well as with the infosphere as a whole. When examining and reflecting upon the philosophical tenets of information ethics, we should never lose sight of what the criterion for existence is according to Floridi (2010, 12):

> The criterion for existence – what it means for something to exist – is no longer being actually immutable (the Greeks thought that only that which does not change can be said to exist fully), or being potentially subject to perception (modern philosophy insisted on something being perceivable empirically through the five senses in order to qualify as existing), but being potentially subject to interaction, even if intangible. To be is to be interactable, even if the interaction is only indirect.

Here lies a new commencement for an ontology of law that is aware of the conceptual underpinnings of a mature information ethics. In the next chapter, we will investigate how this ontocentric perspective overcomes the limits of anthropocentrism while simultaneously reinforcing the role of human responsibility, since it extends the class of subjects that we are responsible for.

References

Benkler, Y. 2006. *The Wealth of Networks: How Social Production Transforms Markets and Freedom*. New Haven CT: Yale University Press.

Brey, P. 2008. Do We Have Moral Duties Towards Information Objects? *Ethics and Information Technology* 10 (2–3): 109–114.

Capurro, R. 2008. On Floridi's Metaphysical Foundation of Information Ecology. *Ethics and Information Technology* 10 (2–3): 167–173.

Castells, M. 1999. *The Information Age: Economy, Society, and Culture*. Vol. 1–3. Malden, MA: Wiley-Blackwell.

Cavell, S. 1991. *Conditions Handsome and Unhandsome: The Constitution of Emersonian Perfectionism*. Chicago: University Of Chicago Press.

———. 2005. *Cities of Words: Pedagogical Letters on a Register of the Moral Life*. Cambridge, MA: Belknap Press of Harvard University Press.

Dicker, G. 2004. *Kant's Theory of Knowledge. An Analytical Introduction*. Oxford: Oxford University Press.

Doyle, T. 2010. A Critique of Information Ethics. *Knowledge, Technology and Policy* 23 (1–2): 163–175.

Fernandez-Barrera, M., N. Gomes de Andrade, P. de Filippi, M. Viola de Azevedo Cunha, G. Sartor, and P. Casanovas (eds.). 2009. *Law and Technology: Looking into the Future*, Florence: European Press Academic Publishing.

Floridi, L. 2003. On the Intrinsic Value of Information Objects and the Infosphere. *Ethics and Information Technology* 4 (4): 287–304.

———. 2007. A Look into the Future Impact of ICT on Our Lives. *The Information Society* 23 (1): 59–64.

———. 2010. *Information. A Very Short Introduction*. Oxford: Oxford University Press.

———. 2011a. *The Philosophy of Information*. Oxford: Oxford University Press.

———. 2011b. A Defence of Constructionism: Philosophy as Conceptual Engineering. *Metaphilosophy* 42 (3): 282–304.

———. 2013. *Information Ethics*. Oxford: Oxford University Press.

Hildebrandt, M. 2008. Legal and Technological Normativity: More (and Less) Than Twin Sisters. *Techné: Research in Philosophy and Technology* 12 (3): 169–183.

Himma, K.-E. 2004. There's Something About Mary: The Moral Value of Things Qua Information Objects. *Ethics and Information Technology* 6 (3): 145–159.

Kant, I. 1992. In *Theoretical Philosophy, 1775–1770*, ed. D. Walford and R. Meerbote. Cambridge: Cambridge University Press.

———. 2003. *Critique of Pure Reason* [1781]. Trans. N. Kemp Smith. Hampshire: Palgrave Macmillan.

Moor, J.H. 1985. What Is Computer Ethics? *Metaphilosophy* 16 (4): 266–275.

The Centre of the Universe

3

Abstract

Technology does not really displace the role of human beings, as many authors seem to believe. On the contrary, according to Floridi's constructionist view of *homo poieticus*, technology calls on the role of human responsibility as never before. It is precisely to fully respond to this call that Floridi proposes a new ethical approach that reconfigures the question of the moral subject by abandoning the unchallenged theoretical privilege accorded to anthropocentrism since the modern ages. Human beings are no longer considered standalone entities at the centre of the universe as the unique principle of measure and legislator of all things. Floridi proposes an ontocentric approach based on the notion of informational object, enabling us to take into account the role of agent and of patient in a non-anthropocentric perspective and to extend the class of what counts as a moral subject. In the present chapter, our specific aim is therefore to elucidate how a non-anthropocentric approach does not necessarily lead to anti-humanistic rhetoric fostered by post-modern philosophy but, on the contrary, strengthens the role of human responsibility.

3.1 Introduction

Philosophy has always sought to answer the question of the "subject", i.e., the fundamental idea of a centre of the universe or, in other words, the question of the fundament itself, on the basis of which the representation of the whole universe is constructed and therefore may be explained. In Greek philosophy, the question of the subject or fundament is literally referred to by the term *upo-keimenon*, which means precisely that which is placed at the foundation. The Latin word *subjectus* (i.e., that which is placed under) translates the same idea, and designates the term that will be used in the modern philosophical tradition, culminating in the figure of the Cartesian subject. However, the same term has been used at different times in

M. Durante, *Ethics, Law and the Politics of Information*, The International Library of Ethics, Law and Technology 18, DOI 10.1007/978-94-024-1150-8_3

reference to different conceptions of the subject. Hence, the subject has been variously interpreted as substance, form, and logos, or – during modernity – as the rational human being. The philosophical tradition of the philosophy of subject has therefore been characterised by a twofold attitude: on the one hand, the role of the subject has invariably been taken as the foundation of the philosophical discourse; on the other, the conception of the subject playing this role has varied over time (e.g., form, substance, logos etc.). From modernity to the present day, when the subject has been interpreted in reference to the human being, this twofold attitude has become more radical, since the philosophical tradition has either endorsed or rebutted the idea itself of a centre of the universe by supporting either a humanist or an anti-humanistic approach to the philosophy of the subject. In both cases, as already pointed out, this philosophical attitude has always entailed and rested upon strong anthropocentrism, either to affirm or to negate the philosophy of the subject.

The idea of a gradual decentring of the concept of subject can be accounted for first of all with reference to the ways science can change our self-understanding. As remarked by Floridi, science has in fact "two fundamental ways of changing our understanding. One may be called *extrovert*, or about the world, and the other *introvert*, or about ourselves. Three scientific revolutions have had great impact both extrovertly and introvertly. In changing our understanding of the external world they also modified our conceptions of who we are" (Floridi 2010, 8). Three scientific revolutions are understood to play a fundamental role in the construction of modernity (without mentioning either the process of secularization [*e.g.* Schmitt 2006, 2007, or Lowith, 1957] or the question of the legitimacy of modernity [*e.g.* Blumenberg 1985][1]). Let us recapitulate how this was accomplished (Floridi 2010, 8-9):

> After Nicolaus Copernicus (1473–1543), the heliocentric cosmology displaced the Earth and hence humanity from the centre of the universe. Charles Darwin (1809–1882) showed that all species of life have evolved over time from common ancestors through natural selection, thus displacing humanity from the centre of the biological kingdom. And following Sigmund Freud (1856–1939), we acknowledge nowadays that the mind is also unconscious and subject to the defence of mechanism of repression. So we are not immobile, at the centre of the universe (Copernican revolution), we are unnaturally separated and diverse from the rest of the animal Kingdom (Darwinian revolution), and we are very far from being standalone entities entirely transparent to ourselves, as René Descartes (1596-1650), for example, assumed (Freudian revolution).

The question is not merely whether or not to accept that human beings have been displaced from their central role; at issue in this context is not just a critique of anthropocentrism. What is at issue is the conjuncture between anthropocentrism and the question of the subject (i.e., of the *fundament*). At this conjuncture, human beings are not only considered to be at the centre of the universe, but their centrality is also meant to form the basis for *any* explanation of reality. This means that whatever is not a human being is demoted to the role of object (i.e., what *stands before*

[1] See on this Foessel M., Kervégan J.-F., Revault d'Allonnes M. (2007).

the subject) and can therefore be explained, manipulated and disposed of by human beings. Therefore, criticism of anthropocentrism does not aim to displace the role of human beings (which is, on the contrary, reinforced, as we will see at the end of the present chapter). In contrast, this criticism is, first of all, aimed at overcoming the dichotomy between subject and object that underlies anthropocentrism. It is this implicit philosophical strategy that enables Floridi to universalize the class of moral subjects. In this perspective, the following quotation from Floridi is enlightening and, in our opinion, likely to result in stronger and deeper theoretical consequences than one would be possibly inclined to acknowledge:

> Since the 1950s, computer science and ICTs have exercised both an extrovert and an introvert influence, changing not only our interactions with the world but also our self-understanding. In many respects, we are not standalone entities, but rather interconnected informational organisms or *inforgs*, sharing with biological agents and engineered artefacts a global environment ultimately made of information, the infosphere (Floridi 2010, 9).

This point is crucial. We are no longer faced with a dichotomy between a subject (i.e., someone who takes initiatives towards the object) and an object (i.e., something which is *there* to merely endure the subject's initiatives). The object is no longer conceived as the carrier of *reflected interests* that only belong to the subject. In other words, the object is not to be protected, morally and legally, because and insofar as it carries on and reflects an interest that is inherent to the subject: its *being there* (Floridi 2013) has a different meaning and a value of its own.[2] Both subjects and objects can be described and experienced at the informational level of abstraction as interconnected, informational organisms, or as a set of information. This informational representation of being thus has important and direct consequences not only on an ethics of information but also and perhaps primarily on epistemology and a political and legal philosophy. The first and most striking consequence of such an approach consists in abandoning a philosophically and morally rigid anthropocentric perspective by treating human beings as informational objects along with all other entities in the universe. However, the more profound and less obvious consequence of such an approach is that it overcomes the subject/object dichotomy that has grounded our entire epistemological and political-legal representation of the universe in modern times. A similar result has been obtained through the pancomputationalist theory of information recently investigated and stated in philosophical and political-legal terms by Michel Serres (2009). According to the French philosopher of science, the subject/object dichotomy can be overcome, since entities are no longer conceived as either a subject or an object, but as an informational system capable of accomplishing four basic operations: receiving, producing, storing and treating information. Floridi specifies it more precisely in standard computer

[2]The idea of *beingthereness* (Floridi, 2013) should be correctly understood starting from the Heideggerian idea of interest, that literally means *inter-esse*, namely, the idea that every subject and object are not standalone entities but entities *among* other entities (subjects and objects) in a relation. It is this relatedness, again, that makes both subjects and objects *interesting*.

science terms: agents can perform three kinds of operations: *read* (receive, store), *write* (produce) and *execute* (treat) information.

Any entity capable of carrying out these operations deserves to be considered an informational system, and thus that plays a crucial role in the universe. For when we alter or destroy an informational system, we are not simply altering or destroying a reflected interest of human beings, but part of the informational universe itself, with which we are in communication. We will return to this idea in Chap. 8. Also in the second part of this book, we will analyse the philosophical implications for law and politics of such an approach (which is at the foundation of a new social contract) and spell out the difference between Floridi's notion of informational organism, which is grounded in epistemological levelism (see Chap. 1), and Serres' notion of informational system, which is grounded in a pancomputationalist theory of information. At present, let us make a more detailed analysis of the ontocentric approach to ethics.

3.2 The Ontocentric Approach

Floridi maintains that any anthropocentric approach to ethics is necessarily limited. He promotes an ontocentric approach to ethics instead, in which information plays a decisive role in three different and complementary ways, as stated by Floridi (2013):

1) information ethics provides "an additional perspective that can further expand the ethical discourse in such a way that it includes the world of morally significant phenomena involving any aspect of *Being*": this establishes the universalistic, inclusive *ratio operandi* of IE, since it brings to ultimate completion the process of enlargement of the concept of what may count as a centre of moral claim;
2) the informational level of abstraction of information ethics represents "a threshold beyond which nothing of moral significance really happens": this establishes the *ratio essendi* of IE, since it individuates the extension of the concept of what may count as a centre of moral claim and therefore some limits of the ethical discourse itself;
3) "looking at reality through the highly philosophical lens of an informational analysis improves our ethical understanding": this establishes the *ratio cognoscendi* of IE, since the ontocentric approach has an epistemic foundation (i.e., the philosophical lens of an informational analysis) and an epistemic goal (i.e., to improve our ethical understanding).

If information ethics aims to develop a macroethical approach, it needs to satisfy a double condition: "it needs to be able to show that the agent-related behaviour and the patient-related status of entities *qua* informational entities can be morally significant, over and above the instrumental function that may attributed to them by other ethical approaches, and hence they can contribute to determining normative rights, duties, and courses of action" (Floridi 2013). From this dual condition, it follows that "IE's claim consists of two theses" (Floridi 2013):

> The first thesis states that all entities qua informational entities have an intrinsic moral value, although possibly quite minimal and overridable, and hence that they qualify as moral patients subject to some (possibly equally minimal) degree of moral respect.
>
> The second thesis states that *artificial* informational entities, in so far as they can be agents, can also be accountable *moral* agents.

These two theses constitute the philosophical core of IE. We will discuss the first in this chapter and the second in the next. Floridi overturns the philosophical structure of the ethical discourse, which is traditionally based upon the primacy of the (role of the) agent as the foundation of a moral situation and the centre of a moral claim. It is a profound *gestalt switch* in the understanding of ethics. In fact, Floridi adopts the point of view of the *patient*, conceived and interpreted in terms of the informational object, not as a theoretical preference, but as a new foundation for the ethical discourse. Ethics is no longer to be thought of necessarily from the standpoint of an agent conceived both as a human being and a *legislator* (Cavell 1991, 2005), capable of enacting moral standards in its full autonomy. Indeed additional autonomy, a quintessentially agent-oriented feature, becomes important only as a secondary response to the primary role played by moral value, that which characterizes the moral patient as such. The development of the information society, driven by the technological revolution and conceived in terms of a multi-agent system, has led to a crisis in the notion of a legislator (i.e., a moral or a legal conscience) capable of regulating the complexity of the whole society, often top-down. Ethics must thus be thought of from another standpoint, which, according to Floridi, is that of the patient. Furthermore, since the patient is an informational object, it includes any instance of Being that may be described and experienced at a given level of abstraction in informational terms. Herein lies the turning point: the structure of the ethical relation between questions and answers. Because of its vulnerability, the patient *asks* (in the sense that the patient is the source of the moral question) an agent to *account* for its behaviour. This requires the agent to be at least morally accountable towards the patient, and if possible, responsible and capable of accounting for the performed action (something that only intelligent beings can do). The *status* of the patient is the starting point of the ethical discourse; this is what Floridi calls a "patient-centric approach to ethical issues" (Floridi 2013). Such an approach is rich in theoretical consequences, the most important of which are grounded in this fundamental tenet of philosophy: ethics is no longer based on the *autonomy* of the agent, but, rather, on the *heteronomy* of the patient, not on highlighting the importance of the periphery, but in changing what lies at the centre of the ethical discourse. There are at least two decisive theoretical consequences of the patient-centric approach to ethical issues: (1) the process of universalization of moral worth; and (2) the construction of ethical discourse through the relation between questions and answers that overturns the relation between freedom and responsibility. The first is explicitly affirmed and investigated by Floridi. The second is fairly implicit, but it constitutes, in our interpretation, the most powerful theoretical and ethical tool for dealing with the consequences of the informational turn on law and ethics.

3.2.1 The Process of Universalization of Moral Worth

The moral value of an action is no longer appreciated and measured in relation to the *status* of the agent (namely, by making reference to the agent's conscience, will, intentions, motives, interests, and so forth), but with regards to the *status* of the patient (namely, by making reference to the intrinsic and scalable moral value related to its existence *qua* informational entity). This idea presupposes a critique to Kantian axiology (Floridi 2013), which we briefly sum up here.

As Floridi remarks (2013): "According to Kant, either some x can rightly function only as a means to an end other than itself, in which case it has an *instrumental* or *emotional* value (extrinsic value […]); or some x qualifies also as an end in itself, in which case has an *intrinsic*, *moral* value insofar as it is that x and it is valued and respected for its own sake. […] Note that 'intrinsic value' […] can mean 'non-instrumental value', as in Kant, or 'inherent value', that is, a value that something enjoys independently of the existence of any evaluating source". Floridi is indeed sensitive to this idea – namely, that there is a moral value that *something enjoys independently of the existence of any evaluating source* – and it is this he wants to take as a real foundation of the ethical discourse. However, doing so requires a shift away from an agent-centric moral perspective, since, as in the Kantian axiology, there is at all times an *agent-type* representation of moral value operating as an unspoken evaluating source. In other words, the point is to support the basic idea that something enjoys a moral value independently of the existence of any evaluating source, without tracing this value back (more or less implicitly) to some sort of agent-type based representation of morality. Let us see how this happens.

Floridi remarks (2013): "Kant argues that anything can have an instrumental value for the sake of something else, but that only human beings as rationally autonomous agents can also have an intrinsic and absolute moral value, which he calls *dignity*. This is because only rationally autonomous agents, understood as potential 'good wills', can be the source of moral goodness, thanks to their rational and free action". What is crucial here is that, according to Kant's axiology, moral value is not only intrinsic, but also absolute. The consequences are significant. As Floridi (2013) points out:

> The Kantian dichotomy, intrinsic vs. instrumental value, has at least three major consequences:
>
> K.1) the dichotomy justifies the coextension of (i) the class of entities that enjoy moral value, (ii) the class of entities capable of moral respect, and (iii) the class of entities that deserve to be morally respected. In Kant, the only type of entity that has moral value is the same type of entity that may correctly qualify as moral patient and that may in principle act as a moral agent;
>
> K.2) the dichotomy solves the communication problem between *A* and *P* in the following sense. Thanks to (K.1) *A* is immediately acquainted with the moral value of *P*, and hence can respect it, because both entities belong to the same type of class […];
>
> K.3) the dichotomy implies that an entity's moral value is a kind of unconditional and incomparable worth.

According to Floridi, the Kantian dichotomy is questionable, since it elevates the intrinsic moral value to an absolute one, by implicitly endorsing an *agent-type* representation of moral value. In Floridi's terms (2013):

> The Kantian dichotomy is questionable because (K.3) clashes with two reasonable assumptions [...]. First, it seems reasonable to assume that different entities may have different degrees of relative value that can constrain *A*'s behaviour, without necessarily having an instrumental value, i.e. a value relative to human feelings, impulses, or inclinations, as Kant would phrase it. Second, it seems equally reasonable to assume that life, biological organisms, or the absence of pain in sentient beings can all have a great deal of moral value and deserve a corresponding amount of respect. For example, one may argue that a human being who is even *inherently* [...] incapable of any intentional, rational and free behaviour still has some moral value, no matter how humble, which deserves to be respected, although not necessarily for instrumental or emotional reasons.

Floridi makes us understand (2013) that: "contrary to what Kant suggests in (K.1), 'having an absolute moral value (dignity)', 'being capable of respect' and 'being intrinsically respectable' do not range over exactly the same class of entities". This means that not only rational beings but also all informational entities are "capable of various degrees of respect to which there seem to correspond various degrees of moral value" (Floridi 2013). In other words, the notion of an *intrinsic* moral value may be consistent with that of a *relative* moral value, if our moral perspective is no longer *agent-centrically* biased. As Floridi puts it (2013):

> Kant seems unduly to restrict the sense of 'relative value' to meaning only 'contingent worth depending on the agent's interest', so that if some x can be rightly and appropriately used only as a means, then x has no absolute value (x has only a relative value), and x's value has no moral value whatsoever, because x's value is to be interpreted as depending only on the instrumental or emotional interest of the agent, which is a clear *non sequitur*, if one rejects the very controversial equation just spelt out.

This is the sense in which we have stated that the object (here: *the patient*) is no longer conceived as the carrier of *reflected moral interests*, which would only belong to the subject (here: *the agent*). Even if relative, the patient has a moral intrinsic value that deserves to be respected and protected, since 'relative value' does not mean a 'contingent worth depending on the agent's interest' but a minimal universal value, as shall be explained below (see *infra* Sect. 3.3.). For the moment, let us expound the second consequence of the patient-centric approach to ethical issues.

3.2.2 The Relation Between Freedom and Responsibility

As already noted, the adoption of an *object-oriented* and *patient-centric* approach to ethical issues is a turning point in the construction of the whole ethical relation and discourse, which enables us to supplant the limits of anthropocentrism, while reinforcing the role of humans as responsible constructors and stewards of their world (as we will see *infra* in Sect. 3.4). In a distributed and multi-agent society – where agents are no longer necessarily human beings and the end results of behaviours are increasingly more difficult to trace back to a single, centred and autonomous source of action – it has become necessary to adopt a more comprehensive and unequivocal ethical standpoint, which is no longer subjectively (anthropocentrically) centred on the status of the agent, but objectively centred on the status of the patient. However, this is not the only reason for adopting an object-oriented and patient-centric approach to ethical issues.

We are witnessing a progressive *naturalization* of ethics resulting from a variety of factors. Perhaps, the term "naturalization" itself is too imprecise and ambiguous in the present context and should simply be dropped. However, the general idea is that human behaviour (including moral behaviour) is increasingly being conceived as *over-determined*, such that the entire conceptual framework of the human agent (i.e., free will, freedom, autonomy and so forth) is being called into question. In other words, human behaviour (including moral behaviour) is explained by *reducing* it to the multiple factors that may have originally engendered it (such as, for instance, neurons or genes), before people become fully aware of such *over-determination*. Needless to say, it is impossible for us to illustrate how far and in what sense human behaviour (*especially* moral behaviour) may nonetheless be conceived and judged to be *compatible* with such forms of over-determination, according to numerous scholars.[3]

In the present context, the line of ethical reasoning expounded in the previous paragraph can help us deal with the question of over-determination, through reliance on the idea of an object-oriented and patient-centric ethical approach which is *primarily* grounded on a universal but minimal condition of moral worth. In other words, IE is fully equipped theoretically to deal with the hypothesis of over-determination (of human behaviour) *not only* because it visibly endorses an object-oriented and patient-centric approach to ethical issues, which displaces the role of agent in the assignment of moral worth, *but also* because it endorses a minimal condition for such an assignment of moral worth. What does this mean and imply?

From the patient's standpoint, however over-determined a (human) behaviour may be conceived, there is always a *minimal* (moral and legal) sense (and a more or less institutionalised practice) in which, in a society, we ask ourselves *who* may be held responsible, accountable or imputable for such a behaviour, *and to what extent*. This question is *unavoidable,* and the patient-centric approach to ethical issues is the inescapability of another, similar-sounding question: what may be held responsible, accountable or imputable for a morally relevant behaviour, and to what extent? This question cannot be dismissed, even if the hypothesis of over-determination may lead us to circumscribe the extent of human responsibility. The reason it cannot be dismissed is not (only) strategic or pragmatic: it does not depend primarily or solely on the social (moral and legal) necessity to account for the consequences of behaviour. The question cannot be dismissed for a more subtle reason, namely, because it is concerned with the very understanding of morality, once the point of view of the *patient* is elected as the standpoint and benchmark of the moral discourse.

[3] For an introduction to the issue, see McKenna 2009.

As one of the greatest moral philosophers of the twentieth century has remarked: "In order to hear justice […] – or, if you will, in order to hear the voice of conscience – it is not sufficient, nor it is relevant, to be in relation with a freedom and to perceive it in the other […]. For me to realize my injustice – for me to glimpse the possibility of injustice – a new situation is required: someone must ask me for an accounting" (Levinas 2006, 26). The possibility for justice begins when someone asks me to account for my own behaviour. In Floridi, as in Levinas, the asking is central, but it is the patient of the action that must pose the question, not the agent understood as the judging legislator. The moral subject need not be perceived as a free, autonomous agent, i.e., as a moral legislator of all things, but as a contested subject, one who has been accused and asked to give an accounting. This is a philosophy of the victim, not of the perpetrator. In such a perspective, the foundation of moral discourse no longer resides in the spontaneity of subjects understood as agents, but in the receptivity of patients or, to put it differently, in their vulnerability, which is the origin itself of the patient's claim directly or indirectly addressed to the agent, as affirmed by different philosophers such as Levinas (1998), Butler (2005), Cavarero (2010), and Floridi (2008). However, Floridi's ethics radically differs from the other approaches, since his patient-centric moral theory goes as far as to state that the subject of moral claim is not necessarily a human being. Floridi's approach to ethical issues endorses a universalistic stance, since the informational construction of moral subjects overcomes the anthropological constitution of moral subjects, which limits the class of who may be held morally responsible to human beings, in favour of their ontological constitution as informational objects, which extends the class of what may be held morally imputable, if not responsible, to non-human beings.

In the patient-oriented perspective, morality stems from *the patient's call* for accountability. This call is not always made by the patient itself, but can be formulated on behalf of the patient by someone else[4]: to speak *on behalf of* someone else's interest is evidence of the sensitivity of the moral discourse within a society. Furthermore, such a request calls me into question and forces me to respond to the patient: it urges me to be accountable for my actions and to be just. In this relation of responsibility, in which I am exposed to the patient, nobody can take my place. Where I am called upon to respond to the patient's call, there I can, paradoxically, recognize myself as *free*, *irreplaceable* and *autonomous*, since it is exactly in this response that:

1) I am thought to be *free* to the extent to which I may assume my responsibility towards the patient;
2) I constitute my subjectivity and experience myself as an *irreplaceable* subject in my personal responsibility towards the patient;
3) I am meant to be *autonomous* to the extent to which I can provide explanations, reasons and justifications for my own behaviour, because this answerability is "the most salient way to appropriate our actions as *our* actions" (Hildebrandt 2011, 154).

[4]The same is true for Michel Serres' philosophical perspective concerning the moral and legal need for a new natural contract. See, on this topic, Chap. 8, in the second part of the present book.

This is a turning point for the philosophical understanding of the minimal, universal conditions of morality, or in other words, for its theoretical foundation. It is the heteronomy of the patient's call that grounds the autonomy of the moral subject: autonomy is no longer based on the power of self-determination or self-imposition but in the *moral tension* of responsibility. This tension is measured along two moral axes (see Chap. 2), a synchronic one (i.e., the vertical moral situation of the subject, that is *objectively* called upon to account for the consequences of its behaviour) and a diachronic one (i.e., the horizontal dimension of reflectivity of the moral subject and especially, of the *homo poieticus*). This idea entails two main consequences, that represent a radical turning point for moral theory:

1. Responsibility precedes freedom: the moral subject is such not because it is anthropologically (namely, consciously, intentionally, etc.) situated at the beginning of the chain of causation as a free and rational human subject, but because is made, objectively (i.e., *qua* informational object), *subject* to a moral relation of responsibility,[5] by being called upon to be responsible, accountable or just imputable for the consequences of its behaviour. In this perspective, for instance, being at the beginning of the chain of causation is only part of the objective description of a morally relevant relation between informational objects at a given level of abstraction (where consciousness or intentionality may count for establishing the *type* and *extent* of responsibility of a determined moral subject, but they do not count as the foundation of morality). The universalizing extension of the class of what counts as a moral subject (which we will investigate in the next section) sparked by Floridi's information ethics, is not so much a matter of envisaging a new taxonomy, which leaves things unaltered, but, rather, of *accounting* for the multi-agent (whether human or artificial) moral impact determined by the ICT evolution and, more broadly, by the informational turn. Floridi's information ethics is the *sign* of a new moral sensitivity (i.e., the response to new ethical problems), according to which being responsible can no longer be founded on the subjective conditions of the agent but, rather, on the objective status of the patient, if we wish to morally account for many new morally relevant situations, which otherwise would escape from our moral evaluation. This perspective is not a mere strategic rearrangement of moral categories. On the contrary, it involves a new foundation of ethics, since it leads us to a different understanding of the moral categories.
2. Moral subjectivity is constituted in the response to the patient's call: people (and scholars as well) are, theoretically and psychologically, afraid to recognize that an informational object (whatever instance of being that is not necessarily a human being but can be experienced as an informational object at a given level of abstraction: a stone, an animal, a tree, a right, a society, and so

[5] We take here this notion in a wide sense that will be made more precise in Chap. 4. Needless to say responsibility has to be specified according to degrees and types, and to be distinguished from accountability or mere imputation, as it will be done in Chap. 4 with regards to information ethics.

forth) may be morally relevant (either as an agent or as a patient). The reason for this fear is that they believe moral subjectivity is concerned only with our capacity as human beings to provide our lives with (human) meaning, meaning that morality is just a human affair, and moral subjectivity is (a crucial part of) our humanity. However, when understood in the correct light, Floridi's information ethics strongly supports this idea. According to Floridi, if human beings were incapable of providing their lives with meaning and if there were no morality, the whole of life and reality would be totally *meaningless*. There would be no meaning without an intelligent informee, for whom something can mean something else. However, this does not mean that morality is merely a human affair and that moral subjectivity is the built-in property of free and autonomous human agents, already constituted in their prerogatives and rights as occupants of the centre of the universe, i.e., as *full legislators*. People provide their lives with moral meaning to the extent to which they are driven to respond to the patient's call (which issues from any instance of being), according to standards that are not fixed once and for all, but are dependent on epistemic conditions. These conditions imply informational awareness, for the growth of information determined by the evolution of ICTs progressively broadens the realm of responsibility (Floridi 2006); namely, the more informed people are, the more responsible they are asked to be. People are free and autonomous not only to the extent to which they *could have done something else* in a certain situation: this merely proves that their course of action is not entirely over-determined. On the contrary, we believe that freedom and autonomy should primarily be attached to the meaning people give to themselves and to the world. People are free and autonomous to the extent to which, through their relations of responsibility towards the patients, they co-construct a viable world. In this way, people can share with others the meaning they intend to attach to their own lives and to the world at large. The moral subject is a subject *to*, not a subject *of*, moral action. In this sense, moral subjectivity (which of course encompasses humanity) is never given, but is always constituted in the scalable response (synchronic and diachronic) to the patient's call. This may require an extension of the class of moral subjects and hence of the limits of responsibility (or of what one is responsible for). The time has come to direct our attention to this process of extension.

3.3 The Class of Moral Subjects

Floridi's ethics is thus not anthropologically but ontologically oriented: any instance of Being can be a moral subject *qua* informational object. This is a minimal, universal and *inclusive* condition of ethics. Floridi does not intend to free ethics altogether from reference to human beings; on the contrary, in a stance that seems rooted in the ancient Greek classical philosophical tradition, he intends to lay the conceptual foundations for as *hospitable* an ontology as possible. Even if *hospitality* does not belong to Floridi's moral lexicon, it is the term that best accounts for his moral theory. In Floridi's own words: "It would be a better world, one in which human moral agents could see themselves as guests in the house of Being" (2013).

In this perspective, it is important to stress that the aim of IE is not merely to defend what already exists (i.e., *conservationism*) but to render the ontological description of moral subjects as hospital as possible (i.e., *inclusiveness*). This implies that the extension of the class of moral subjects (i.e., there are *more* subjects we need to respect) is not just a matter of preference; however, it does require an ontological re-description of what a moral subject is. How does Floridi manage to carry out this task? We shall try to sum the answer to this complex question in as straightforward a manner as possible. Floridi formulates his notion of the moral value of an entity by taking Kant's anthropocentric axiology as his theoretical benchmark. Floridi agrees with Kant that moral value is neither merely instrumental nor merely emotional. Thus, Floridi remarks that (2013):

> When the value in question is neither instrumental nor just emotional, one can first distinguish between extrinsic and intrinsic value and, correspondingly, between two types of respect. An entity *x* has extrinsic value when it is respected as some *y*. For example, a piece of cloth may be respected as a flag, a person may be respected as a police officer, or a practice may be respected as a cult. This sense of relative respect is associated with a sense of value that is no longer instrumental or emotional and may be called *symbolic*.

However, Floridi's main interest is not extrinsic moral value, since it is "still utterly contingent, may be acquired or lost, and can be increased as well as reduced" (Floridi 2013). His main interest is the idea of an intrinsic moral value, understood in the following terms (2013):

> In order to capture in full the fact that an *x* has moral value in itself – a value that belongs to *x* in all circumstances (necessarily), not only under some conditions, and is not subject to modification unless *x* ceases to exist as that *x* – one needs to consider the case in which *x* deserves to be respected not just symbolically, as something else, but *qua x*. [...] What the entity is determines the degree of moral value it enjoys, if any, whether and how it deserves to respected, and hence what kind of moral claims it can have on the agent.

What an entity is determines the degree of moral value it enjoys. This raises the question of how to conceive what an entity is. By relying on the OOP methodology (which is object oriented), Floridi adopts a token/type perspective, which enables him to consider an entity as the sum of properties, whose specificity can be "increased or decreased as required, depending on the choice of LoA" (Floridi 2013). Let us refer to Floridi's terms to clarify this point (Floridi 2013):

> The specific nature (essence) of an object *x* consists in some attributes that (1) *x* could not have lacked from the start except by never having come into being as that *x*, and (2) that *x* cannot lose except by ceasing to exist as that *x*. This essence is a factually indissoluble, but logically distinguishable, combination of *x*'s *local* and *inherited* attributes. For example, if 'Person' is the descendant object, and 'Living Organism' is the ancestor object, we may say that 'freedom' is an essential and local attribute of 'Person', that is, a new property, not

previously implemented in any of the ancestor objects, while 'sentient animal' is an essential attribute inherited by 'Person' from its ancestor object 'Living Organism'.

This point is crucial and underlies the entirety of Floridi's work in ethics. If properly understood, it allows readers to avoid many potential misunderstandings concerning Floridi's approach to ethical issues. The essence of an object is a combination of *local* and *inherited* attributes: local attributes are properties, which are not previously implemented in any of the ancestor objects (i.e., they are more *specific* attributes of a member of a class); inherited attributes are properties previously implemented in some of the ancestor objects (i.e., they are more *general* attributes of a member of a class). This means that entities are conceived in terms of dynamic informational objects, namely, as changeable combinations of local and inherited attributes, according to the LoA at which they are experienced by an epistemic agent.

Contrary to initial appearances, Floridi's ontocentric approach to ethics does not grant moral relevance, value or protection to objects as such, *qua* mere objects (as it would if his *non-anthropocentric* approach truly entailed a non-human or post-human conception of ethics), but in that they are dynamic combinations of local and inherited attributes, which may vary according to the LoA at which an informational object is experienced. As affirmed in the first chapter, from an epistemological standpoint, this crucially implies that: *it is precisely thanks to their representation as informational objects (i.e., as dynamic combinations of local and inherited attributes) that entities may vary and enjoy* different levels *of moral relevance, value and protection*. The agent thus has the *epistemic* responsibility (the responsibility of adopting the right level of abstraction) to ensure not only that the patient is at the centre of the ethical discourse, but also that it can initiate it. By analogy, it is not just a matter of listening to the patient, but also of ensuring that the patient can communicate. Let us appreciate this point as formulated in Floridi's terms (2013):

> It is correct to say, with Kant, that *x*'s intrinsic value depends on its essence, or more generally on its ontology, but is also important to specify that this essence, and the corresponding intrinsic value, are both aggregates, i.e. they are the result of a specific [...] combination of *local* and *inherited* attributes, which in turn can be observed only at a given LoA. This makes a significant difference.

This makes a significant difference, Floridi remarks. What difference does it make? No one, including Floridi, believes that a stone is as morally relevant and valuable as a human being. However, this is not because a human being is morally relevant and valuable, whilst a stone is absolutely not. It is because a human being may contain a more comprehensive combination of morally relevant and valuable local and inherited attributes than to a stone. As already pointed out, the universalistic approach of information ethics "looks for the *minimal*, not the *maximal* conditions of moral worth" (Floridi 2013). This means that an entity can lose some of its local or inherited attributes, since it dynamically changes and transforms itself across time, but this does not amount to losing its whole moral worth. However *impoverished* the combination of local and inherited attributes an entity enjoys, the entity still deserves some moral respect. This combination may even be reduced to a single kind of attribute. An entity may possess an intrinsic moral worth either as a specific individual (because of its local attributes) or as an instantiation of a type (because of its inherited attributes). In the latter perspective, for instance, an entity enjoys "a degree of intrinsic moral worth because of its nature as an informational entity and, as such, it can still exercise a corresponding claim to moral respect" (Floridi 2013). The *informational nature* of an entity plays two fundamental roles, both as: (i) the upgrading condition of possibility for an entity to *vary and enrich* its combination of local and inherited attributes, according to different LoAs (which are always informational in their nature), thus enjoying different levels of moral value; and as (ii) the incomparable and non-equivalent, minimal degree of moral value, since a minimalist axiology does "accept only *one set* of inherited attributes as the minimal condition of possibility of intrinsic worth" (Floridi 2013). This means that the minimal intrinsic worth of an entity does not reside in some specific attributes that make it individual, i.e., separated from the rest of the world and occupying the centre of the universe. On the contrary, it resides in what may be referred to as its *ontological poverty*, which is not merely a defective dimension, but the condition itself of its incomparable uniqueness:

> The minimal intrinsic worth of an entity is incomparable because it is unique in the sense that it can be reduced no further, it is necessary shared universally by all entities that may have any intrinsic value at all, and it deserves to be respected by default yet only *ceteris paribus*, that is to say, it can be overridden in view of considerations involving degrees of moral value at lower LoAs (Floridi 2013).

Therefore, Floridi implicitly distinguishes between the foundation and the goal of morality: *ontological poverty* (what can be impoverished or reduced no further) is the foundation of information ethics, whereas the *enrichment* of the infosphere (its well-being and flourishing) is its own goal. The centre of the universe is no longer occupied by an isolated sovereign subject already instituted in its full prerogatives (i.e., local attributes, properties and rights); instead, there is an ontologically poor, moral subject concerned with the creation of its own world, according to the constructionist values of *homo poieticus*. It is to these constructionist values that we turn to in the next section.

3.4 The Constructionist Values of *homo poieticus*

Adoption of a non-anthropocentric approach of ethical issues is nonetheless consistent with a reinforcement of human responsibility, which underlies the constructionist values of *homo poieticus*. We have already seen how a non-anthropocentric approach to ethical issues entails an extension of moral responsibility. According to information ethics, not only are human beings moral patients, but so too is every entity understood informationally – and this is what is meant by an extension of the class of moral patients. In other words, there are *more* subjects towards which we may be held responsible. In addition, information ethics also extends the class of moral agents by recognizing that "artificial agents too can be involved in moral situations as interactive, autonomous and adaptable entities that may perform actions with good or evil impact on the infosphere" (Floridi 2013). This means that there are *more* situations in which a moral subject may be held either responsible or accountable for the consequences of a moral action. The result is that a non-anthropocentric approach to ethical issues does not restrict but, on the contrary, widens the realm of responsibility, including human responsibility. This happens along the *vertical axis* of morality, which concerns, as already pointed out, the synchronic moral situation in which moral agents and patients are enveloped. However, this is true, in an even more apparent way, also along the *horizontal axis* of morality that concerns the diachronic dimension of *homo poieticus*.

The *homo poieticus* is the individual constitutive part of a renewed conception of humanity, understood as a multi-agent system, that operates as a *demiurge* in the responsible construction of its own environment (Floridi 2013). Floridi's constructionist approach to epistemological issues is also declined in a moral perspective, which nourishes the idea itself of *ecopoiesis*, in the following terms (Floridi 2013):

> Humanity is clearly a very special moral agent. Like a demiurge, it has ecopoietic responsibilities towards the whole infosphere. The term 'ecopoiesis' refers to the morally-informed construction of the environment based on the patient- or ecologically-oriented perspective [...]. The more powerful humanity becomes as an agent, the greater its duties and responsibilities become to oversee not only the development of its own nature and habits, but also the well-being and flourishing of each of its ever expanding spheres of influence, including the whole infosphere. To move from individual virtue ethics to global values, an *ecopoietic* approach is needed that recognises humanity's *responsibilities* towards the environment (including present and future inhabitants) as its enlightened creators, stewards, or supervisors, not just as its virtuous users and consumers. So IE is an ethics addressed not just to 'users' of the world, but also to producers or demiurges, who are 'divinely' responsible for its creation and well-being. It is an ethics of *creative stewardship* in which responsibility for the whole realm of Being, that is, the whole infosphere, plays a crucial role.

The idea of ecopoiesis sums up and unifies three fundamental tenets of Floridi's IE, which we have already brought to light: (1) a moral situation is the relation of a *part* (the informational object as a moral subject) to a *whole* (the infosphere); (2) this *part's* responsibilities towards the *whole* increase to the extent to which that part becomes more morally-informed of its powers as creator or designer of the environment (moral intellectualism); (3) justice comes *through* time (as noted in Greek philosophy), since ecopoiesis is based both on careful prediction (information as resource and product) and on prudent self-reflexivity (information as target), which both require a duration of time for us to appreciate, evaluate and refine the relation between construction and responsibility (*creative stewardship*). As pointed out, morality is never entirely accomplished in the deployment of a single moral situation, but always entails a lifelong, all-consuming process: if we lose sight of this fundamental temporal dimension, we risk underestimating the complexity of the information ethics ecological approach. In fact, *ecological* does not just refer, in Floridi's terms, to space (the infosphere as a whole). but also to temporal duration (the entire life-cycle of information).

This notion, which lies at the basis of our distinction between the two moral axes characterizing Floridi's IE, can also be explained through the distinction between reactive and proactive macroethics. Floridi first sketches out what is an ethical reactive approach and seeks as well to suggest that the ethical discourse cannot be entirely reduced to such an approach, since it cuts off the very constructionist dimension of the *homo poieticus* (Floridi 2013):

> Alice is confronted by a moral dilemma and asked to make a principled decision by choosing from a menu of alternatives. Moral action is triggered by a situation. One may call such approach *situated action ethics*, to borrow an expression from AI. In a situation action ethics, a moral dilemma may give the false impression that the ethical discourse concerns primarily *a posteriori* reactions to morally problematic situations in which Alice unwillingly and unexpectedly finds herself parachuted from nowhere. The agent is treated as a world user, a game player, a consumer of moral goods and evils, a browser, a customer who reacts to pre-established and largely unmodifiable conditions, scenarios, and choices. Only two temporal modes count: present and future. The past seems irrelevant ('how did Alice ended up in such predicament in the first place'). At most, the approach is further expanded by a casuistry analysis. Yet ethics is not only a question of dealing morally well with a given world.

This last remark (*ethics is not only a question of dealing morally well with a* given *world*) is extremely important, since it clarifies two crucial points: (1) information ethics is not a merely conservatory approach that protects the *status quo*. Ethics is not only a question of the proper moral handling of a given world. It is not merely an adaptation of human beings to the world, not only because ethics is not thought of only from the standpoint of human beings, but first and foremost because ethics is not primarily a mere adaptation to the world as it is given. If we endorse an exclusively reactive approach to ethical issues, we risk transforming the ethical discourse into a form of conservationism; for this reason, we need to adopt a supplementary, yet fundamental, ethical standpoint: a proactive approach; (2) information ethics endorses a proactive approach to ethical issues. This point is essential for understanding why the ethics of responsibility is a mundane dimension based on actions, even though it is not a mere adaptation to the world. Rather, it is a life-consuming process that encompasses all the modes of temporality: only that which is rooted in the past can aspire to have a future. Let us see in what terms a proactive approach to ethics has thus been conceived by Floridi's information ethics (2013):

> [Ethics] is also a question of constructing the world, improving its nature, and shaping its development in the right way. This proactive approach treats the agent as a world owner, a game designer or referee, a producer of moral goods and evils, a provider, or a creator. I use the term 'proactive' technically here, to qualify policies, agents, processes, or strategies that
>
> 1. implement effective action in anticipation of expected problems, difficulties, or needs, in order to control and prevent them, at least partially, rather than merely reacting to them as they occur. In this sense an ethically proactive approach can be compared to preventive medicine, which is concerned with reducing the incidence of disease by modifying environmental or behavioural factors that are causally related to illness; or that
> 2. actively initiate good changes, promoting rather than merely waiting for something positive to happen.

This passage tells us much about information ethics. Two expressions are crucial, even if they may seem quite cursory: "as they occur" and "to happen". These expressions hide a precise relationship between ethics and history, which is already peculiar, for instance, to Hannah Arendt (2011, 118). When the notion of acting is replaced with that of happening, the idea of morality is destroyed, since the moral subject is transformed into a spectator and personal responsibility ends. The moral fabric of history is not based on mere succession of events but on actions (*res gestae*). Furthermore, the moral subject is not only a "game player", but first and foremost a "game designer". In a proactive scenario, the role of the agent acquires a central place, since "the agent is supposed to be able to plan and initiate actions responsibly, anticipating future events, in order to (try to) control their course of by making something happen or by preventing something from happening rather than waiting to respond (*react*) to a situation once something has happened, or merely hoping that something positive or negative will or will not happen" (Floridi 2013). Without pushing the analogy further, suffice it to observe that the term 'initiate' seems to be much more than a simple reference to Arendt's conceptual vocabulary. What really matters is going back to our starting point to remark that macroethics "that adopts a more proactive approach can be defined as *constructionist*" (Floridi 2013).

Floridi's meditation on the subject of constructionism is very subtle and deserves to be brought to light. As already noted, human responsibility is given new centrality, since human beings are conceived as demiurges, responsible for the construction of their own environment. This is the key point of constructionism, but it is not the only one. Often, constructionism is accused of promoting human arrogance and egotism. On the contrary, in the proactive perspective so far explored, constructionism reminds us not only that we are responsible creators, but also and above all that we are *created*, namely, that we are limited creatures (*creating and created entities*) that form part of the global and interactive co-creation. Self-construction is only part of a wider construction and cannot serve as a model for the ethical construction of society, since the global information society cannot be the simple and direct representation, generalization and progression of subjectivist and individualistic stances. It is precisely in this sense that Floridi states that "information ethics needs to be not just *egopoietic*, but, most important, *ecopoietic*" (2013) and "sociopoiesis is no longer reducible to egopoiesis alone" (2013).

Co-creation or, to put it in other words, complexity is an *emergent property* (Taylor 2001) of the contemporary global information society, according to which "some of the major new variables that govern its development are internal forces, emerging *holistically* from the actions and the decisions of its members" (Floridi 2013; our italics). This means that communal behaviours are not "immediately or directly explicable as mere aggregates of individual behaviours" (Floridi 2013) or, to put it differently, that complexity does not lie in opposition to simplicity but, rather, to over-determination (Pagallo 2006). We are creating and created entities, and, in both cases, in a non-deterministic way. At the very foundation of Floridi's ethical meditation, it is under-determination (i.e., the contemporary quest for freedom) that calls for a responsible ecopoietic approach that can account for the complexity of society or the mutual, interactive co-creation of a multi-agent system:

> The kind of ethical constructionism needed today goes well beyond the education of the self and the political engineering of the simple and closed cyberpolis. It must also address the urgent and pressing questions concerning the kind of global realities that are being built. This means decoupling constructionism from an agent-oriented approach (leading to subjectivism and then individualism) and re-orienting it to the patient, so that it might be applied *also* to society and the environment, the receivers of the agent's action. In short, what is needed is an ecopoietic approach to information ethics (Floridi 2013).

As remarked throughout this chapter, on the one hand, co-creation (being created and creating entities) defeats human narcissism. On the other, it requires us to bolster human responsibility, insofar as IE is confronted with the complexity of an under-determined (autonomous, interactive and adaptive) multi-agent system, where the 'scalability problem' (from individuals to societies) cannot be accounted for if not in an informational ecologically-oriented perspective.

3.5 Conclusions

(Western) morality since the modern age has mainly relied on classifying human beings separately from the rest of the world (animals, nature, etc.) and attributing to them a central role in the universe as full moral and legal legislators based on an agent-type representation. According to information ethics, as we have tried to argue, human beings cannot be separated from the rest of the world: they form part of the whole as interconnected informational entities. It is precisely this relatedness that underlies the moral tension between moral subjects (agents and patients) and which is placed at the centre of the universe, although the idea of relatedness itself seems to displace the notion of a fixed, permanent centre. Human beings are moral subjects (both as sources and as receivers of moral actions) *among* other moral subjects. We have tried to show that, however paradoxical it may seem, this idea strongly reinforces and extends the moral responsibility of human beings. This happens for three main reasons, which can be summed up as: (1) inclusiveness; (2) meaning; (3) constructionism.

1. Floridi's information ethics strives not for conservationism but for inclusiveness. Information ethics is the most hospitable ontology, not only because it aims to extend the class of moral subjects, but because it acknowledges both the poverty and the enrichment of Being as moral conditions. Ontological poverty is the foundation of ethics, whilst the enrichment of the infosphere is its goal. Thus, ontological poverty is certainly not the goal of ethics; nonetheless, it is not conceived as a merely defective condition, as in the longstanding philosophical tradition that views evil as deprivation of Being. Rather, evil, as Floridi indicates, is always dynamic (in a completely static world, there can be only the goodness of

Being), it is the *depriving* of Being. However deprived of local and inherited attributes, an informational object may still enjoy a *minimal* level of moral respect. This leads us to constantly search for the minimal, most inclusive, conditions of moral relevance. Thus, IE reinforces and extends human responsibility, since it makes human beings more responsible in that they are responsible towards a greater number of moral subjects (*ontological hospitality*) in a greater number of moral situations (*ethical inclusiveness*). For this reason, a non-anthropological approach cannot be said to displace the central role of human beings as moral subjects, insofar as it extends the domain of human responsibility. It only disentangles the *intrinsic* dimension of moral value from its *absolute* dimension, by renouncing the agent-type representation of moral value. This is made possible by the informational treatment of moral subjects, since *it is precisely thanks to their representation as informational objects (i.e., dynamic combinations of local and inherited attributes) that entities may vary and enjoy* different levels *of moral relevance, value and protection*. IE teaches us an important lesson for now and in the future: an intrinsic moral value may also be relative. This seems to us to be a crucial theoretical step towards pluralism (see Chap. 6) and a global, multicultural approach to ethical issues.

2. A non-anthropocentric approach to ethical issues therefore does not restrict but, on the contrary, widens the realm of responsibility, including human responsibility. As just underlined in the previous point, this occurs along the *vertical axis* of morality, which concerns the synchronic moral situations in which moral agents and patients are enveloped according to a reactive ethical approach. However, this process of extension of responsibility is even more apparent along the *horizontal axis* of morality, which concerns the diachronic dimension of ethical intellectualism according to a proactive ethical approach. Viewed from a diachronic standpoint, a moral situation is not the relation of a part (the informational object as a moral subject) *within* a whole (the infosphere) that assigns meaning to the part, which merely depends on the representation of the whole. It is the relation of a part *to* the whole, meaning that the *part's* responsibilities towards the *whole* increase as far as that part becomes more morally informed about its powers as creator or designer of the environment (ethical intellectualism). The ecological approach promoted by Floridi's IE means precisely that ethics (as well as law and politics) forms part of the life-cycle of information, according to the fundamental ethical and epistemic tenet that the more informed an entity is, the more responsibility it has. In this perspective, responsibility is not only aimed at restoring a fracture in the order of things; it is aimed at teaching us something new about ourselves and about the society we live in; it teaches us *to what extent* we can recognize ourselves as free agents. By means of an expanding set of networked relations of responsibility, we give meaning to our own world, since we conceive it as an informed space of interactions. Responsibility is traversed by freedom. It logically presupposes freedom, but actually reveals the ways in which we are socially recognized as free. According to IE this depends on the level of information we manage to deal with, when we assign (moral or legal) responsibilities.

3. Floridi's emphasis on the related group of concepts of *homo poieticus*, demiurge, constructionism, stewardship and ecopoiesis, is primarily aimed at making us understand that human beings as *creators* of their own world are also *created* entities. This teaches us an important philosophical lesson: *that which is created is the beginning of the creation*. There is no mystery or big bang that marks the beginning of moral life. To create (construct or conceptually design) our world requires us to shed new light on what is created, for what is created is in itself problematic. To create is to experience and understand one's own limits. Ethical intellectualism consists in transforming problems into questions and in providing questions with new answers. Only if we understand the structure of the fundamental relation between questions and answers, can we appreciate why the information-based constructionism promoted by Floridi's IE is actually "neither conservative nor revolutionary" (Floridi 2013). This final point can be explained by means of a formula. Answers are always given and comprehended within the scope of their own questions; however, for an answer to be a true answer, it has to generate something which is not already included in the question. This is the specific novelty that an information-based construction of the world can aspire to: it is neither construction from scratch nor conservation of what already exists. To conclude, it is worth reiterating the essence of the present chapter: only what comes from a creatively re-elaborated past can aspire to have a future. The notion of the human being as the sole moral legislator or axiological benchmark lying at the centre of the universe has been supplanted by the centrality of the human reflective "learning/teaching experience" (Floridi 2013) of both the synchronic and the diachronic moral life of a multi-agent system.

References

Arendt, H. 2011. *Quaderni e diari 1950–1973*. Trans. C. Marazia. Milano: Neri Pozza.

Blumenberg, H. 1985. *The Legitimacy of the Modern Age* [1976]. Trans. R.-M. Wallace from the 2ed ed. Cambridge, MA: MIT Press.

Butler, J. 2005. *Giving an Account of Oneself*. New York: Fordham University Press.

Cavarero, A. 2010. *Horrorism: Naming Contemporary Violence*. Trans. W. Mc Cuaig. New York: Columbia University Press.

Cavell, S. 1991. *Conditions Handsome and Unhandsome: The Constitution of Emersonian Perfectionism*. Chicago: University Of Chicago Press.

———. 2005. *Cities of Words: Pedagogical Letters on a Register of the Moral Life*. Cambridge, MA: Belknap Press of Harvard University Press.

Floridi, L. 2006. Information Technology and the Tragedy of the Good Will. *Ethics and Information Technology* 8 (4): 253–262.

———. 2008. Information Ethics, Its Nature and Scope. In *Moral Philosophy and Information Technology*, ed. J. van den Hoven and J. Weckert, 40–65. Cambridge: Cambridge University Press.

———. 2010. *Information. A Very Short Introduction*. Oxford: Oxford University Press.

———. 2013. *Information Ethics*. Oxford: Oxford University Press.

Foessel, M., J.-F. Kervégan, and M. Revault d'Allonnes. 2007. *Modernité et sécularisation: Hans Blumenberg, Karl Löwith, Carl Schmitt, Leo Strauss*. Paris: CNRS Editions.

Hildebrandt, M. 2011. Autonomic and Autonomous 'Thinking': Preconditions for Criminal Accountability. In *Law, Human Agency and Autonomic Computing. The Philosophy of Law Meets the Philosophy of Technology*, ed. M. Hildebrandt and A. Rouvroy, 141–160. London: Routledge.

Levinas, E. 1998. *Otherwise Than Being or Beyond the Essence* [1974]. Trans. A. Lingis. Pittsburgh: Dusquene University Press.

———. 2006. *Entre Nous: Thinking of the Other*. Trans. M. Smith and B. Harshaw. London/New York: The Athlone Press.

Lowith, K. 1957. *Meaning in History: The Theological Implications of the Philosophy of History [1949]*. Chicago: Chicago University Press.

McKenna, M. 2009. *Compatibilism, Stanford Encyclopedia of Philosophy*, (first published 2004; substantively revised 2009), online at: http://plato.stanford.edu/entries/compatibilism/.

Pagallo, U. 2006. *Teoria giuridica della complessità*. Torino: Giappichelli.

Schmitt, C. Der Gegensatz von Parlamentarismus und moderner Massendemokratie. 2006. *Political Theology: Four Chapters on the Concept of Sovereignty*. Trans. G. Schwab. Chicago: Chicago University Press.

———. 2007. *The Concept of the Political* [1932], (expanded edition). Trans. G. Schwab. Chicago: Chicago University Press.

Serres, M. 2009. *Temps des crises*. Paris: Editions Le Pommier.

Taylor, M. 2001. *The Moment of Complexity: Emerging Network Culture*. Chicago: Chicago University Press.

The Morality of Artificial Agents

4

Abstract

The informational approach has powerful practical and theoretical consequences on the notions of agency and responsibility. This chapter discusses one of the most crucial questions facing our networked information society today: who is the "who" that performs an action and may be held accountable for the (moral or legal) consequences of that action? It is increasingly likely that the agent is an artificial one, whose autonomous performance of tasks poses the risk of unexpected and potentially harmful effects. How are we to deal with consequences that cannot be traced back directly to a human being? Here we explore insights that IE might offer into the questions at hand. Investigation of the notions of agency and autonomy from an informational point of view is useful in shedding light on the moral experience of accountability and responsibility. As with patients of the moral experience, by extending the class of moral agents in the direction of non-human agents, we can better grasp the role of humans in moral (as well as in legal) responsibility, and are better equipped to deal with the novel theoretical and practical problems arising from our interaction with artificial autonomous agents.

4.1 Introduction

The infosphere is populated by different types of agents, whether human or artificial, individual or distributed. Each type of agent interacts with the others in novel and not entirely predictable ways, with the risk of potentially unforeseen and evil (and therefore undesirable) effects. Our traditional moral (and legal) categories, through which individual human agents are held accountable for the consequences of their actions, seems inadequate in accounting for these new types of interaction among agents. This is true even where ethics, and notably the law, have already allowed for forms of artificial and distributed agency, since their understanding and

M. Durante, *Ethics, Law and the Politics of Information*, The International Library of Ethics, Law and Technology 18, DOI 10.1007/978-94-024-1150-8_4

regulation of these forms of agency ultimately traces them back to their nuclear, human and individual components, as rightly noted by Floridi (2013, 117–118):

> In particular, the concept of 'moral agent' has been expanded to include both natural and legal persons, especially in business ethics. *A* has then been extended to include agents like partnership, governments, or corporations, for which legal rights and duties have been recognised. This more ecumenical approach has restored some balance between *A* [agents] and *P* [patients]. A company can now be held directly accountable for what happens in the environment, for example. Yet the approach has remained unduly constrained by its anthropocentric conception of agency. An entity is still considered a moral agent only if
>
> 1) it is an individual agent, and
> 2) it is human-based, in the sense that it is either human or at least reducible to an identifiable aggregation of human beings, who remain the only moral responsible sources of action, like ghosts in the legal machine.
>
> Limiting the ethical discourse to *individual* agents hinders the development of a satisfactory investigation of *distributed morality*, a macroscopic and growing phenomenon of global moral actions and collective responsibilities resulting from the 'invisible hand' of systemic interactions among several agents at a local level. Insisting on the necessarily *human-based nature* of the individual agents involved in any moral analysis means undermining the possibility of understanding another major transformation in the ethical field, the appearance of artificial agents (AAs).

Floridi goes on to suggest that, under certain circumstances, AAs should be considered as moral agents, or, in other words, as legitimate sources of moral and immoral actions. We can therefore expand the class *A* of moral agents to include AAs in the ethical discourse, not just with regards to information ethics, but also to ethics in general. As when extending the class of moral patients to include any instance of the universe conceived in terms of informational object, here, too, Floridi's radical, non-anthropocentric perspective often sparks strong objections and reactions. These are touched on briefly in section four[1] and readers can refer to Floridi's own more extensive responses to this theoretical dispute elsewhere (2013).

Floridi's non-anthropocentrism results in expansion of human moral responsibilities and a more inclusive and universalistic conception of ethics. The resulting debate concerning the relation between humans and technology is often structured and carried out in ideological terms. This is because it often fails to recognize that human beings are technologically constituted from the start, and that all of human experience is technologically mediated, even as when this text is being typed on keyboard. However, examination of this debate is less interesting for our present purposes. What is more interesting here is that the non-anthropocentric bent of Floridi's proposal provokes such strong reactions. These reactions are significant, since they provide evidence of how profoundly the concept of morality is embedded in the assignment of responsibility.

---

[1] Many of these criticism and remarks are of interest but it is impossible to analyze and deal with each of them in detail. See for instance Himma 2009.

There are very practical reasons for this. Without being able to establish a chain of responsibility, a society would be less free and secure, since the trajectories of agents' behaviours would not be decipherable or predictable (and thus would not be subject to blame and accountability). But this is not the end of the story. We assign responsibilities, in order to learn something about ourselves as part of a society, that is to say, to trace the distinction between what is acceptable (included) and what is not acceptable (excluded but somehow kept and preserved) in the society. The assignment of (moral or legal) responsibility is a human process that involves some degrees of inclusion while involving also some degrees of exclusion, not from, but within the society (see Chap. 9). The articulation of inclusion and exclusion is a normative process (as argued by Foucault 1988, in a different context), in the sense that it needs a parameter in order to establish what is an agent and thus a moral agent, namely, a legitimated source of morally qualifiable action. This parameter often plays the role of a "hidden parameter" (Floridi 2013, 118), since it already belongs to the well-established and widespread conception of what an agent and moral agent is. Paradoxically, it was sufficient to state that humans are the measure of all things to conceal the (requirement of a) parameter. For this reason, a non-anthropocentric approach seems to exclude, from the very start, human beings from their deep-seated role of being the (hidden) parameter of the whole moral experience: it is this sense of exclusion that raises strong reactions. However, this assumption is wrong and is the source of most of the theoretical confusion, since the necessity of a parameter is confused with the necessity of a human and individual agent as the real and exclusive parameter of the whole moral experience.

Floridi's non-anthropocentric approach does not deny that the moral experience is, first and foremost, a moral dimension through which human beings assign a significant, if not crucial, meaning to themselves and to their world. It only claims that choosing the parameters according to which we frame and regulate the moral game is part – indeed an essential part – of the moral life, and that this choice, too, should be subject to reflection and discussion. This is a key methodological point to which Floridi astutely draws our attention. As seen in previous chapters, the baseline of reasoning for Floridi's philosophy and ethics of information (Chap. 1) is the method of levels of abstraction, which finds application again in the present chapter. The next section deals with the choice of parameter (or level of abstraction) necessary in order to characterise agents and moral agents when assigning (moral or legal) responsibility. The analysis will show that non-anthropocentrism is not ideological, but methodological.

4.2 Characterisation of an Agent

In order to understand and characterise a moral agent, we need to understand and characterise in advance what exactly an agent is. The definition of the agent is extremely relevant in the fields of ethics and of law, given the numerous ethical and legal consequences. However, the problem cannot be approached as it were a mere question of clarifying or refining long-established ethical or legal categories, as pointed out by Floridi (2013, 118):

> Sometimes, the problem is addressed optimistically, as if it were just a matter of further shaping and sharpening whatever necessary and sufficient conditions are required to obtain a *definiens* that is finally watertight. Stretch here, cut there; ultimate agreement is only a matter of time, patience, and cleverness. In fact, attempts follow one another without a final identikit ever being nailed to the *definiendum* in question. After a while, one starts suspecting that there might be something wrong with this *ad hoc* approach. Perhaps it is not the Procrustean *definiens* that needs fixing, but the Protean *definiendum*.

The problem can be tackled more successfully if we apply the method of levels of abstraction to the process of characterising the *definiendum* at stake. Many relevant concepts in the field (mind, intelligence, conscience, intentionality, action and so forth) support different definitions and characterisations: this is not enough to let us be either optimistic (it is merely a question of revising our conceptual framework) or pessimistic (a single viable definition or characterisation cannot be found). These concepts do not come from nowhere; each of them is 'parameterised' by a relevant level of abstraction at which the concept becomes intelligible and plays its own role:

> Indeed, abstraction acts as a 'hidden parameter' behind exact definitions and makes a crucial difference. Thus, each *definiens* comes preformatted by an implicit LoA; it is stabilised, as it were, in order to allow a proper definition. An x is defined or identified as y never absolutely (i.e. LoA-independently), as a Kantian 'thing-in-itself', but always contextually, as a function of a given LoA, whether it be in the realm of Euclidean geometry, quantum physics, or commonsensical perception (Floridi 2013, 118–119).

This point is extremely important and must be stressed. The structure of signification (x is defined or identified as y) is never independent from the LoA at which x is predicated in terms of y. This does not entail any form of relativism, but helps us understand that, since levels of abstraction are always teleological, i.e., adopted for a reason, every concept is chosen and used for the specific reason underlying the adopted level of abstraction. In the end, "it is the reason determining their adoption that needs to be justified" (Floridi 2013, 126). This is a particularly relevant point in the assignment of responsibility, whether morally or legally. Let us briefly consider the two predominant approaches generally taken in assigning responsibility.

The assignment of responsibility is often studied and examined by means of a dichotomy. On the one hand, there are those who believe that assignment of responsibility is just a practical activity concerned with the legitimacy and social acceptability of the ways in which responsibility is attributed. On the other hand, there are those who believe that the assignment of responsibility is primarily a conceptual activity concerned with clarifying and refining the concept of responsibility (and the categories involved in the process of assigning responsibility). According to the former view, these concepts are a function of a basic practical need: to recognize some agents as the source of evil actions who need to be blamed and punished. These concepts are not useful in helping us construct a reality in which to elaborate the normative criteria enabling us to distinguish the agents who are to be blamed and punished from those who are not. In other words, according to this view, these concepts are already influenced by the normative criteria expressing current social preferences for blameworthiness and punishment. Instead, the latter view holds that the concepts involved in the process of attributing responsibility are a function of the scientific, cognitive and philosophical level of reflection attained regarding the issue at stake. These concepts allow us to construct a reality upon which to elaborate and discuss the normative criteria enabling us to distinguish agents who are to be blamed and punished from those who are not. In this perspective, the criteria are subject to examination and discussion, and are not merely vehicles of subjective preferences.

These positions closely parallel the pessimistic and optimistic stances mentioned above (for more details, see Santoni de Sio 2013). The former fails to take into account that the adoption of parameters (levels of abstraction or normative criteria for blameworthiness and punishment) is part of a wider epistemic process, which can be accounted for and needs to be justified. Furthermore, the very fact that a parameter is 'hidden' does not imply that is justified; it is the reason underlying its adoption that needs to be justified. The latter position fails to take into account that the adoption of parameters is a necessary component of the wider epistemic process of responsibility-attribution, since concepts (moral or legal categories) are never LoA-independent. The attribution of responsibility is a triadic structure, according to which the responsibility (for the consequences of the action) *x* is attributed to *y* for a reason *r*, which is reflected in the LoA that is adopted to parameterized *x* and *y*. Things are difficult to grasp when the adopted parameters are 'hidden' or 'transparent' to the users, but they get even messier when there is no prevalent LoA to apply. This brings us back to the issue of the *definiendum* from which we started. Again, let us refer to Floridi (2013, 119) on this point:

> When a LoA is sufficiently common, important, dominating, or in fact happens to be the very frame that constructs the *definiendum*, it becomes 'transparent' to the user, and one has the pleasant impression that *x* can be subject to an adequate definition in a sort of conceptual vacuum. [...] When no LoA is predominant or constitutive, things get messy. In this case, the trick does not lie in fiddling with the *definiens*or blaming the *definiendum*, but in deciding on an adequate LoA before embarking on the task of understanding the nature of the *definiendum*. [...] The conclusion is that some *definienda* come pre-formatted by transparent LoAs. They are subject to definition in terms of necessary and sufficient conditions. Some other *definienda* require the explicit acceptance of a given LoA as a pre-condition for their analysis. They are subject to *effective characterisation*.

Agency is one of the concepts requiring effective characterization. We therefore have to apply the method of levels of abstraction to its analysis, and this brings us back to our initial question: "whether *A* (the class of moral agents) needs to be expanded depends on what qualifies as a moral agent, and this, in turn, depends on the specific LoA at which one chooses to analyse and discuss a particular entity and its context" (Floridi 2013, 119).

Floridi is thus confronted with the task of choosing the specific and correct LoA at which one can analyse and characterize an agent. His choice is consistent with the general theoretical framework of his philosophy and ethics of information. Being is interpreted as being subject to interaction (Chaps. 1 and 2); thus, interactivity is not only a potential property, but a necessary characteristic of an agent that is rooted in the ontological dimension of any informational entity. The identity of any informational entity is constructed through a process of progressive detachment from the non-self (the world) (see Chap. 5); this means that agents not only interact with their environment but they also change themselves and evolve without direct response to external interactions. In this perspective, autonomy is not only a potential property, but also a necessary characteristic of an agent that is rooted in its capability of detachment from the non-self (the world). The proactive and constructionist dimension of agents (Chap. 3) tells us that agents may learn from experience and plan or initiate a course of action responsibly, anticipating future events, in order to (try to) control their course of action by making something happen or by preventing something from happening; this also means that agents not only interact with their environment or change their internal states, but they also adapt their courses of action through the correlation between experience and anticipation. In this perspective, adaptability is not only a potential property, but also a necessary characteristic of an agent that is rooted in its being-with-and-within the infosphere and provided with some self-reflective capacity (see Chap. 5).

This means that Floridi envisages three criteria (interactivity, autonomy and adaptability) as the basic, constitutive elements of the correct LoA at which to characterize an agent. Those criteria are, on the one hand, chosen parameters (other parameters could have been chosen); on the other hand, they are adopted consistently with the general theoretical framework in which any informational entity is rooted (other parameters could not have been consistent with Floridi's ontology). Let us analyse these criteria in more detail (2013, 120):

> In agreement with recent literature ((Danielson 1992), (Allen, Varner et al. 2000), (Wallach and Allen 2009), I shall argue that the right LoA is probably one that includes the following three criteria: (a) *interactivity*, (b) *autonomy*, and (c) *adaptability*:
>
> a) *interactivity* means that the agent and its environment (can) act upon each other. [...]
> b) *autonomy* means that an agent is able to change its state without direct response to interaction: it can perform internal transitions to change its state. So an agent must have at least two states. [...] and finally
> c) *adaptability* means that the agent's interactions (can) change the transition rules by which it changes state. Adaptability ensures that an agent might be viewed, at the given LoA, as learning its own mode of operation in a way that depends critically on its experience.

Other parameters or criteria could have been chosen and would have turned out to be more or less inclusive than those envisaged by Floridi (namely, the real extension of the class of agents depends on the adopted parameters). One must keep in mind, however, that Floridi chooses the criteria also in view of the further characterization of an agent as a moral agent. This means that, from the very start, Floridi takes into full account the tradition of moral philosophy in defining what an agent is. In other words, the criteria of interactivity, autonomy and adaptability not only define an agent; they also establish family resemblances with traditional moral concepts: namely, responsibility, freedom and self-reflectivity. In this perspective, interactivity implies the characteristic of acting and evolving in *direct response* to interaction; autonomy implies the characteristic of starting freely from oneself (*kath'auto*) rather than from someone else; and adaptability implies the characteristic of learning from experience (which expresses a certain degree of *self reflection*). In so doing, Floridi does not mean to anthropomorphize AAs. He attempts instead to consider how moral categories can be parameterized when they need to be applied to AAs, in such a way as to not set AAs apart from other moral agents, but to include them in a broader and all-encompassing class of moral agents. Once more, Floridi provides us with a deeper understanding of moral life, by decoupling it into two basic spheres: i.e., the moral experience, through which we give meaning to our associated life, and the moral game, through which we parameterize our moral categories and make them applicable to any instance of the universe considered at the proper LoA. While the moral experience requires an intelligent agent to whom the meaning of morality is accessible and relevant, the moral game is open to any type of agent to which moral categories are applicable thanks to the parameterization of categories at the proper LoA. This brings us to the next point in our investigation: namely, the characterization of a moral agent.

4.3 The Characterization of a Moral Agent

Whether systems may or may not count as agents depends on the LoA adopted and, "since LoAs are always teleological, i.e. chosen for a reason, in the end, it is the reason determining their adoption that needs to be justified" (Floridi 2013, 125–126). This leads to Floridi choosing three criteria (interactivity, autonomy, and adaptability), which allow us to parameterize and characterize what an agent is. This parameterization and characterization are accomplished in view of a further characterization (namely, that of moral agent): however, the above-mentioned criteria are not sufficient *per se* to tell us what a moral agent is. Floridi offers us a clear and instructive example. Let us consider two entities, call them H and W, which are able:

> i) to respond to environmental stimuli – e.g. the presence of a patient in a hospital bed – by updating their states (interactivity), for instance, by recording some chosen variables concerning the patient's health. This presupposes that H and W are informed about the environment through some data-entry devices, for example, some preceptors;
> ii) to change their states according to their own transition rules and in a self-governed way, independently of environmental stimuli (autonomy), e.g. by taking flexible decisions based on past and new information, which modify the environmental temperature; and
> iii) to change the transition rules, by which their states are changed according to the environment (adaptability), e.g. by modifying past procedures to take into account successful and unsuccessful treatment of patients (Floridi 2013, 126).

H and W certainly qualify as agents; however, we still do not know whether or not they also qualify as moral agents. Before answering this question, we need to further clarify what the criteria of interactivity, autonomy, and adaptability imply from a possible moral standpoint (or criterion of identification) that still needs to be recognized.

Interactivity presupposes that H and W are informed: being informed (and furthermore, being capable of processing information) is not only a precondition for interactivity; it is also a fundamental condition for moral accountability and responsibility. The more information one possesses (and furthermore, one is capable of processing), the more one is likely to be held accountable and responsible. This has two main consequences in both ethics and law. First, agents may be held accountable and responsible for information they could have accessed with a minimal effort but did not. Secondly, agents can be viewed simply as systems that process information at the proper LoA. This is mostly true in the field of law, where many subjective or objective circumstances which may count as legal excuses or justifications, are nothing but factors impairing or weakening an agent's capacity to correctly process information (an informational approach to the legal categories of excuses and justifications will often prevent us from sinking in the widely metaphysical quicksand of free will, consciousness, intentionality, and so forth).

Autonomy presupposes that H and W are sufficiently informed to take different and alternative courses of actions. Floridi's above-cited specification, according to which "flexible decisions" are "based on past and new information" (2013, 126), is a subtle, accurate way to refute Harry Frankfurt's argument (1969) that the practical counterfactual (i.e., the possibility to act differently) is no longer viewed as the foundation of freedom (or at least of autonomy), since agents cannot perceive (i.e., have complete information about) the specific factors that could have prevented them from acting, had they really chosen a different course of action. When choosing 'autonomy' as a parameter, Floridi assumes that an agent is sufficiently informed to take different and alternative courses of actions, which are parameterized not in relation to all hidden and supervening factors impeding a course of actions from occurring (this idea also tends to confound the lack of a capacity [to close a door] with a contingent inability [to close a door that is already closed]), but in relation to the agent's capacity to correctly process information, in order to represent and take different and alternative courses of actions. Again, we should distinguish between the question of the occurrence of circumstances that prevent the agent from autonomously or freely deliberating or acting (which concerns the characterization of what is an agent) and the question of those ethical criteria that allow us to evaluate whether an action can cause moral good or evil (which concerns the characterization of what is a moral agent).

Adaptability presupposes that H and W take into account successful and unsuccessful performances, in order "to change the transition rules, by which their states are changed according to the environment" (Floridi 2013, 126). Learning from experience is not only a precondition for adaptability; it is also a crucial precondition, in order to develop and improve relevant capacities. In this perspective, successful and unsuccessful performances (for instance, in the achievement of social goals, standards, and values) should be understood and treated, according to Amartya Sen's political and economical philosophy (1985), as part of agency and, therefore, included in the information basis of public choices. When choosing 'adaptability' as a parameter, Floridi reveals his belief that all agents so characterised are supposed to be able to develop themselves and to "take advantage of the available opportunities to improve their general behaviour" (2013, 126).

Floridi is fair in choosing parameters that are morally sensitive, since all LoAs are teleological. His choice is strategic and for good reason, since it establishes the premises upon which the criterion of identification of what is a moral agent may be adopted and justified. Once more, this criterion is adopted and justified according to a minimalist option. Floridi is interested in setting the minimal conditions at which an agent may qualify as a moral agent:

> (O) *An action is said to be morally qualifiable if and only if it can cause moral good or evil,* that is, *if it decreases or increases the degree of metaphysical entropy in the infosphere.*
>
> Following (O), an agent is said to be a moral agent if and only if it is capable of morally qualifiable action. Note that (O) is neither consequentialist nor intentionalist in nature. It is neither affirming nor denying that the specific evaluation of the morality of an agent might depend on the specific outcome of the agent's actions or on the agent's original intentions or principles (Floridi 2013, 126).

This definition tells us that an agent qualifies as a moral agent if and only if it *can* cause moral good or evil, or, in other words, if and only if it is *capable* of a morally qualifiable action (namely, an action decreasing or increasing the degree of metaphysical entropy in the infosphere, as explained in Chap. 2). Agents are characterised as moral agents with regards to the general and abstract capability of accomplishing moral good or evil, rather than with regards to intentions, or the particular and concrete outcome of their own actions. This means, for instance, that specific circumstances (which may count at times as moral or legal excuses or justifications) do not prevent an agent from qualifying as a moral agent as long as they concern the particular and concrete outcome of the agent's actions as opposed to the agent's general and abstract ability to carry out morally qualifiable actions. In contrast, an agent cannot qualify as a moral agent when, for instance, a specific impediment prevents the agent from processing the information that conditions its general and abstract capability of accomplishing moral good or evil. That is why Floridi remarks that his characterization of what is a moral agent is not consequentialist, as might appear at first glance. The morality of an agent does not depend directly and straightforwardly on the specific outcome of an action (the moral evaluation of which is to some degree contingent upon many concurring circumstances), but on the general and abstract possibility for the action to be qualified in moral terms: plausibly, the specific outcome of an action is a significant clue as to this possibility, as often happens; however, this is not always the case, and for this reason, Floridi is cautious when he states that (O) neither affirms nor denies that the specific evaluation of the morality of an agent might depend on the specific outcome of the agent's actions. This prevents Floridi's characterization of the moral agent from being tangled up in the intricacies of "moral luck" (Williams 1981), according to which the specific outcome of an agent's actions alters the evaluation of the morality of the action and, thereby, of the agent. (O) is not consequentialist in nature for another reason, which brings us back to the question of LoAs or parameters. A consequentialist approach, based on the evaluation of the outcome of an action, is often parameterized in utilitarian terms, which evaluate the outcome of an action in terms of the increase or decrease of utility. In its turn, utility is parameterized in terms of the decrease or increase of the (absolute [Pareto] or relative [Kaldor-Hicks]) happiness it brings about, which always refers to and is confined to human beings, thus frustrating, from the very start, any chance of qualifying AAs in moral terms.

Floridi also tells us that (O) is not intentionalist in nature. Contrary to a longstanding and traditional anthropocentric approach to morality, an action may be said to be morally qualifiable independently from the agent's original intentions and principles. The agent's original intentions and principles are essential in order to evaluate the moral experience (for human beings to give meaning to their world throughout their own moral life), but they are not strictly necessary to the moral game (for an action to be morally qualifiable as good or evil). Likewise, original intentions and principles impinge on two traditional but different (sometimes at variance with each other) anthropocentric approaches to morality. Intentions focus their attention on human inner life. According to this approach, morality ultimately depends on *who* we are (intentions may be traced back to our own personal history). Thus, becoming moral implies changing ourselves. Principles focus their attention on human outer life. According to this approach, morality ultimately depends on what *grounds* outer life is built (principles may be traced back to our collective history, that is, to the shared values we impinge on when justifying our actions). Thus, becoming moral implies sharing the values of the community we wish to be part of. This means that original intentions and principles are essential to human beings when they wish to reconcile themselves with their personal or collective history, but that they are not strictly necessary, in the moral game, for a minimalist characterization of what a moral agent is. Once again, intentions and principles may be a significant indication as to what is judged to be a moral action, but not in every case. Floridi is again cautious when he states that (O) neither affirms nor denies that the specific evaluation of the morality of an agent might depend on the agent's original intentions and principles. It depends again on the LoA at which moral life is considered, i.e., either as an experience through which we give meaning to our history (thus reconciling it with a collective narrative) or as a game through which we are called upon to identify the source of morally qualifiable actions in many different circumstances and contexts, which can no longer be accounted for in anthropocentric terms alone. Let us turn back to the example provided by Floridi and to his question: are H and W also moral agents?

According to Floridi's perspective, summarised in (O), we cannot "provide a definite answer unless H and W become involved in some moral action" (Floridi 2013, 126). Floridi invites us to make the following supposition:, H kills the patient and W cures her. This means that they are both involved in potentially morally qualifiable actions. Let us see whether these actions may qualify as moral, according to the parameters chosen and independently from the nature of the agents at play. Floridi (2013, 126) remarks that:

> They [H and W] both acted interactively, responding to the new situation with which they were dealing, on the basis of the information at their disposal. They both acted autonomously: they could have taken different courses of actions, and in fact we may assume that they actually changed their behaviour several times in the course of the action on the basis of new available information. They both acted adaptably: they were not simply following orders or predetermined instructions. On the contrary, they both had the possibility of changing the general heuristics that led them to make the decisions they did, and we may assume that they took advantage of the available opportunities to improve their general behaviour. The answer seems rather straightforward: yes, they are both moral agents.

Both agents, H and W, are moral agents, since their agency is consistent with the parameters adopted, and their actions qualify as moral actions, since they decrease (in the case of H) or increase (in the case of W) the degree of metaphysical entropy in the infosphere. Notably, H's actions disregard the null law or first ethical principle, according to which entropy ought not to be caused in the infosphere (see Chap. 2). By killing the patient, H destroyed at least two informational objects: the patient's existence and the patient's right to existence. Instead, if killing the patient means letting the patient die (euthanasia, for example), it might be excusable; and if killing the patient is motivated by the desire to free the world from a dangerous and threatening dictator (as in a renowned episode from the Doctor House television series), it might be justified. These cases are different, however, since they both concern the evaluation of the agent as a morally responsible agent (to be praised or blamed) and not its identification as the source of a morally qualifiable action (we shall return to this point below). In cases like these (euthanasia or as a preventative measure), the destruction of informational object is to be balanced against the promotion of other informational objects (i.e., the patient's right to die without suffering or the protection of other informational objects' existence). W's actions respect the third and possibly the fourth ethical principle (according to which entropy ought to be removed from the infosphere and the flourishing of informational entities as well as of the whole infosphere ought to be promoted by preserving, cultivating, and enriching their well-being). By curing the patient, W removed entropy from the infosphere; W most likely fulfilled its professional duties with care; and it potentially promoted the well being of the infosphere, since it enabled the patient once again to be a source of new informational objects. Whether W managed to fulfil its professional duties without using particular care; or whether the patient was likely to be the source of evil actions; these situations count for the evaluation of the agent as a morally responsible agent and not for the identification of the agent as the source of a morally qualifiable action. For these reasons, H and W may qualify as moral agents but, as Floridi remarks, one is a human being, and the other is an AA. Like in a Turing-like test, Floridi argues that, if we cannot distinguish between the cases of H and W, then we should agree that "the class of moral agents must include AAs like webbots" (Floridi 2013, 126). This argument may raise several objections. In the next paragraph, we will deal with at least some of them.

4.4 Objections to the Morality of AAs

It is important to stress that all the objections that Floridi foresees and deals with are conceived and formulated against the backdrop of the above-mentioned LoAs or parameters that underlie and preside over the characterization of what an agent is and, thereby, of what a moral agent is, as noted in the previous paragraph. It would be pointless to consider and discuss in the present context all of the different conceptions of morality that stem from very dissimilar theoretical or practical premises of agency, since they would never be (i.e., in no possible sense or world) predictable or referable to *any* conception of AAs. For this reason, Floridi envisages and deals with four main objections that include in their premises a broad and encompassing conception of agency, which deserves to be examined and discussed in the process of characterising what a moral agent is. According to Floridi (2013, 148), there are four main objections:

- *the teleological objection*: an AA has no goals;
- *the intentional objection*: an AA has no intentional states;
- *the freedom objection*: an AA is not free; and
- *the responsibility objection*: an AA cannot be held responsible for its actions.

The first three objections are mainly related to the underlying characterization of a moral agent as an agent: they mainly refer to the agents' stances, states or capacities that structure the general form and content of agency that preside over the characterization of their moral agency. Let us deal with them jointly, in order to focus our attention more extensively on the fourth and last objection, which, according to Floridi, is the most relevant, if not the only real, objection (2013, 150).

4.4.1 The Teleological, Intentional, and Freedom Objections

In Floridi's view, the "teleological objection can be disposed of immediately. For in principle LoA_2 [regarding the parameters of interactivity, autonomy and adaptability that ground the characterization of what is an agent] could readily be (and often is) upgraded to include goal-oriented behaviour (Russell and Norvig 2010). Since AAs can exhibit (and upgrade their) goal-directed behaviours, the teleological variables cannot be what make a positive difference between a human and an AA" (Floridi 2013, 148). A teleological condition is not included in the LoA_2, because "a non-teleological level of analysis helps to understand issues in 'distributed morality' involving groups, organizations, institutions, and so forth, that would otherwise remain unintelligible" (Floridi 2013, 148). This means that the goal of actions brought about by groups, organizations, or institutions, rather than being prearranged, is an 'emergent property' of distributed and complex forms of agency, which would require the analysis to widen and renew the traditional and familiar conception of teleology.

Let us refer again to Floridi's formulation of the second objection: "The intentional objection argues that is not enough to have AAs behave teleologically. To be a moral agent, the agent must relate itself to its actions in some more profound way, involving meaning, whishing or wanting to act in a specific way, and being epistemically aware of its behaviour" (Floridi 2013, 149). This objection seems to be more pertinent and consists in requiring the existence of a special link between the agent and its actions, conceived in terms of mental or intentional states, in order for an agent to qualify as a moral agent. According to Floridi, this objection is refutable for two reasons. Firstly, it is at variance with the method of LoA, which is phenomenologically based on what is observable (see Chap. 1). In fact, the intentional objection "presupposes the availability of some sort of privileged access (a God's-eye perspective from without, or some sort of Cartesian internal intuition from within) to the agent's mental or intentional states that, although possible in theory, cannot be easily guaranteed in practice" (Floridi 2013, 149). The method of LoA, which requires, as remarked, "a clear and explicit indication of the LoA at which one is analysing the system from without" (Floridi 2013, 149), "guarantees that one's analysis is truly based only on what is observable, and hence only on the available information" (Floridi 2013, 149). Since the agent's mental or intentional states are difficult to observe and assess from without, what is relevant (both from the agent's and the observer's side) is the available information processed both by the agent, when acting, and by the observer, when analysing the agent's actions: as in legal hermeneutics, the *animus operandi* is always inferred by the agent's words, actions or behaviours (i.e., *modus operandi*). Secondly, "agents (including human agents) should be evaluated as moral if they play the 'moral game'. Whether they mean to play it, or they know that are playing it, is relevant only at a second stage, when what we want to know is whether they are *morally responsible* for their moral actions" (Floridi 2013, 149). Floridi tells us that the existence of a link between the agent and its action (conceived in terms of mental or intentional states) hints at the maturity or self-awareness of the 'moral experience', but it does not concern the 'moral game' nor is it required by it. In a consequentialist perspective, for instance, "human beings would still be regarded as moral agents (sources of increased or diminished well-being), even if viewed at a LoA at which they are reduced to mere zombies without goals, feelings, intelligence, knowledge, intentions, or mental states whatsoever" (Floridi 2013, 149).

According to Floridi, the same "holds true for the freedom objection and, in general, for any other objection based on some special internal states enjoyed only by human and perhaps superhuman beings" (Floridi 2013, 149). The freedom objection involves a persistently tricky and problematic debate about determinism, compatibilism, free will, and so forth, where it becomes extremely difficult to envisage, assess and share clear and explicit LoAs. Moreover, AAs may be said "free in the sense of being non-deterministic systems. This much is uncontroversial, scientifically sound, and can be guaranteed about human beings as well" (Floridi 2013, 149). At variance with the moral experience, the moral game does not necessarily require us to be trapped with the above-mentioned debate involved by the freedom objection. "All one needs to do is to realize that the agents in question satisfy the usual practical counterfactual: they could have acted differently had they chosen differently, and they could have acted differently because they are interactive, informed, autonomous, and adaptive" (Floridi 2013, 149). The practical counterfactual, which Floridi makes reference to, is conceived and measured with regards to the available information that are expected to be processed by the agent, and not with regards to the absolute and actual alternate possibilities that may or may not exist (and which would require, yet again, a God's-eye perspective from without, to be all at once fully processed). After having examined the first three objections, we now turn our attention to the most difficult objection, namely, the responsibility objection.

4.4.2 The Responsibility Objection

This objection affirms that an AA cannot be held responsible for its action, since responsibility "means here that Alice, her behaviour, and actions, are assessable in principle as praiseworthy or blameworthy, and they are often so not just intrinsically, but for some pedagogical, educational, social or religious end" (Floridi 2013, 150). Against the backdrop of this definition, Floridi immediately concedes that "it would be ridiculous to praise or blame an AA for its behaviour, or charge it with a moral accusation" (Floridi 2013, 150). However, Floridi contends that this objection does not prevent us from considering AAs as sources of morally qualifiable actions. This would happen for three different reasons: the first two are proposed and described by Floridi, while we add the third.

Firstly, Floridi remarks that "the whole conceptual vocabulary of 'responsibility' and its cognate terms is completely soaked through anthropocentrism. […] The anthropocentrism is justified by the fact that the vocabulary is geared to psychological and educational needs, when not to religious purposes. We praise and blame in view of behavioural purposes and perhaps a better life and afterlife" (Floridi 2013, 150). This remark is important. Floridi tells us that anthropocentrism (i.e., the anthropocentric conception of moral responsibility) functions here as a 'hidden parameter' that associates normative evaluations (formulated in terms of praiseworthiness or blameworthiness) with behavioural purposes (psychological, educational, or religious purposes that point to a better life and afterlife). Again, this means that this parameter is adopted for a reason (and, remember, it is the reason determining its adoption that needs to be justified), which, in reality, "says nothing about whether an agent is the source of morally charged action" (Floridi 2013, 150). According to Floridi, the fact that an AA lacks, for instance, a psychological component makes it pointless to blame it, but it does not logically impede any further moral consideration based on parameters adopted for different reasons. In this perspective, "given the appropriate circumstances, we can rightly consider them [i.e., AAs] sources of evil, and legitimately re-engineer them to make sure they no longer cause evil". This way of reasoning perfectly applies to the field of law, and explains why it is so important to be able to consider AAs accountable (namely, sources of harm), given the appropriate circumstances, since, for instance, this allows us to re-engineer them to make sure they no longer cause harm. Therefore, AAs can be called upon, in many circumstances, to directly bear the consequences of their actions, even if this involves neither a psychological component nor a pedagogical, educational or religious purpose. This brings us to the second reason why AAs may be considered sources of morally qualifiable actions. This reason is more analytical and enables Floridi to distinguish between the idea of moral accountability and that of moral responsibility. Let us see how.

Floridi remarks that the responsibility objection assumes that "agents are moral agents only if they are responsible in the sense of being prescriptively assessable in principle. An agent *A* is a moral agent only if *A* can be put on trial" (Floridi 2013, 151). This assumption goes too far. Not only does it confuse the *identification* of *A* as a moral agent, according to which we state who or what is the moral source of (and hence is accountable for) a moral action, with the *evaluation* of *A* as a morally responsible agent, according to which we assess, prescriptively, whether and how far the recognized moral source is also morally responsible for that action; it also reduces (and here lies its crucial mistake) "all prescriptive discourse to the analysis of responsibility" (Floridi 2013, 151). This reduction involves "an unacceptable assumption, a juridical fallacy", since "there is plenty of room for prescriptive discourse that is independent of responsibility assignment and hence requires a clear identification of moral agents. Good parents, for example, commonly engage in practices involving moral evaluation when interacting with their children, even at an age when the latter are not yet responsible agents, and this is not only perfectly acceptable, but something to be expected. This means that parents identify children as moral sources of moral action, although, as moral agents, they are not yet subject to a process of moral evaluation" (Floridi 2013, 151). With a different language, law comes to a similar conclusion: namely, law can identify children as sources of harm, whilst only their parents can be put on trial (i.e., called upon to be responsible for their children's actions). The identification of a morally charged action and, thereby, of an agent as the source of that action is an act logically separate from the evaluation of the same agent as morally responsible for that action. For this reason, as already remarked, AAs may well be involved in a moral game as major players, even if they cannot be involved in the moral experience (which includes the responsibility assignment). This brings us to consideration of a third reason why the distinction traced by Floridi between the identification of *A* as a moral agent (moral accountability) and the evaluation of *A* as a morally responsible agent (moral responsibility) is indeed important.

Such a distinction prevents us from reducing the moral discourse to the analysis and the assignment of responsibility. This is important precisely because the analysis and the assignment of responsibility have been mostly construed in normative terms as an assessment of praiseworthiness or blameworthiness, i.e., as an attribution of praise and blame leading to rewards and punishments. This attribution always involves, more or less visibly, an enormous risk for morality (even a reversal of morality), since, historically, it is often the stronger one (power, authority, group, tradition, and so forth) that governs the attribution of praise and blame (rewards and punishments) or, at least, has the power to establish the criteria by which praise and blame (rewards and punishments) are attributed. The moral inquiry (and hence the discourse on morality) has to be, first and foremost, concerned with how such criteria are identified and asserted and only thereafter with the concrete assignment of responsibility. In plain terms, morality is primarily concerned with this inquiry, not with the desire not to be blamed. Otherwise, morality risks turning into the commitment to values and the criteria of the stronger. For this reason, the peak of morality is, paradoxically, its own crisis, because, in the crisis of morality, moral criteria are tested, verified and rethought in the light of the incessant evolution of history, which does not necessarily change the values underlying these criteria, but may alter the context in which such criteria are to be applied. This is precisely what Floridi's EI invites us to do: to test, verify and rethink, against the backdrop of the information revolution, the reasons for which specific criteria (parameters, and so forth) are identified and asserted. This draws us to the topic of the next section concerning why Floridi judges it important to extend the class of moral agents.

4.5 Why Extend the Class of Moral Agents

The very fact that we continuously and increasingly interact with AAs appears to be a sufficient theoretical and practical justification for the class of moral agents to be extended, in order to include some AAs in the moral discourse. This inclusion allows the moral discourse to apply to many cases that otherwise would escape any moral assessment: namely, cases in which "human programmers" cannot be held accountable for the actions performed by AAs; users may have "no access to the code and its provenance with resulting execution of anonymous software" or "software may be probabilistic (Motwani and Raghavan 1995); adaptive (Alpaydin 2010); or may be itself the result of a program (in the simplest case a compiler, but also genetic code (Mitchell 1998))" (Floridi 2013, 154), and so forth. However, this is not the only reason why it is so important to extend the class of moral agents as to include AAs. The aforementioned reason, however crucial, remains confined to the appraisal and generalization of cases (which concern the content of moral discourse), but does not yet affect the process of universalization of morality (which concerns the statute of moral discourse). For this reason, Floridi proposes three additional reasons for extending the class of moral agents.

Firstly, this moral approach is more universalistic, since it provides us with "a terminology that applies equally to all potential agents that populate our environment, from humans to robots and from animals to organizations" (Floridi 2013, 158). This is made possible by the theoretical choice of analysing all entities that populate the infosphere in non-anthropocentric terms. Renouncing anthropocentrism is a philosophically strategic move that, once again, is meant not to displace the role of human beings in technologically-driven societies but, on the contrary, to enrich it with new moral relations and dilemmas that make us test, verify and rethink our deep-seated moral standards and criteria. In a sense, the philosophical inquiry on morality is to Floridi what poetry was to J.D. Salinger, who claimed that "poetry, surely, is a crisis, perhaps the only actionable one we call our own" (Salinger 1963).

Moral inquiry is perhaps as well the only actionable crisis we call our own. This may sound paradoxical, for it implies that the true path to universalism today passes through a non-anthropocentric approach to morality, even if the quest for universalism has been one of the crowning achievements of humanism. The first important reason to expand the class of moral agents is thus deeply philosophical and concerns the quest for universalism (in the wider sense of inclusiveness) that should characterize the statute of moral discourse. In line with his ontocentric approach to morality, Floridi's ontology is hospitable (and thus inclusive) on the side of both patients and agents. Again, this is not necessarily at variance with the philosophical tradition, since the entire development of ontology has been concerned with the progressive redefinition of its 'hospitality' (namely, the extension of what counts as an entity).

Secondly, Floridi manages to expand the class of moral agents by applying the method of abstraction. As Floridi remarks: "Whether an entity forms an agent depends necessarily (though not sufficiently) on the LoA at which the entity is considered; there can be no absolute LoA-free form of identification" (2013, 158). This point is important, since it implies that the identification of agents counting as sources of morally qualifiable actions is never *absolute* but, on the contrary, always dependent on the LoA at which the agent is considered. This means that the expansion of the class of moral agents is achieved by adopting a non-absolutist conception of moral agency. In contrast, it is precisely the method of abstraction that allows us to vary our conception of moral agency without having to endorse either an absolutist position (because there is not only one correct LoA) or a merely relativistic one (given that LoAs can be compared thanks to different gradients of abstraction: see Chap. 1). This also means that the expansion of the class of moral agents necessarily involves a moral discussion that inherently concerns the identification of the correct LoA at which agents are to be considered and examined. Hence, no LoA (parameter, standard, criterion, and so forth) can be taken for granted or assumed (and thereby justified) as a 'hidden' factor. All LoAs are to be examined, discussed and justified, including both the new and the deep-seated, traditional ones. This shows us that the identification of agents counting as sources of morally qualifiable actions lies in a specific choice (i.e., the adoption of a LoA), which nonetheless does not depend on merely subjective or value preferences, but on the range of observables (that is the quality and quantity of information available about a particular system) that we have access to at each LoA, as Floridi himself remarks:

> Since I have considered entities from the world around us, whose properties are vital to my analysis and conclusions, it is essential that we have been able to be precise about the LoA at which those entities have been considered. We have seen that changing the LoA may well change our observation of their behaviour and hence change the conclusions we draw. Change the quality and quantity of information available on a particular system and you change the questions that can reasonably be asked and the scope of plausible conclusions that could be drawn from its analysis (Floridi 2013, 158).

This also allows us to parameterize the analysis with regards to the type of agents at hand and the nature of the context in which such agents behave. This approach (namely, the method of abstraction applied to the analysis of the morality of AAs) has already proved to be fruitful outside the domain of moral inquiry. For instance, in the field of law it has fruitfully been applied by Ugo Pagallo (2013a) to analysis of the laws of robots (against the backdrop of three different and specific legal contexts: crimes, contracts and torts). As Pagallo remarks:

> Each level of abstraction […] can be grasped as an interface made up by a set of features, that is, the observables of the analysis. […] By changing the interface, the analysis of the new observables and variables of the model should strengthen our comprehension of the legal phenomenon, casting further lights on the challenge of today's laws of robots (Pagallo 2013b, 28–29).

On this methodological assumption, Pagallo may endorse and make use of Floridi's distinction between moral accountability and responsibility, by applying it to an understanding of the legal phenomenon (the identification of robots as AAs at a given LoA, characterised by interactivity, autonomy and adaptability) and to the assessment of particular robots as morally and legally accountable. Let us refer again to Pagallo:

> Accordingly, we can extend the class of morally accountable agents so as to include the artificial agency of robots and still reject the idea that they are either morally responsible or criminally accountable […]. By distinguishing the source of relevant moral actions from the evaluation of agents as being morally responsible for a certain behaviour, *i.e.*, the aforementioned cases of children's actions or the behaviour of animals, we can assess that defendants have to have essential psychological qualities, such as consciousness, moral understanding and free will, to be both morally and legally responsible. Otherwise, by blurring the notions of accountability and responsibility, we are forced back to the days when criminal trials were commonly performed against animals (Pagallo 2013b, 39–40).

This observation leads us back to the third reason why expanding the class of moral agents is such a significant move: namely, the distinction itself between moral accountability and responsibility. We have already focused on this point (Sect. 4.4.2), but let us revisit it here in Floridi's words:

> Morality is usually predicated upon responsibility. The use of LoAs and thresholds enables one to distinguish between accountability and responsibility, and formalize both, thus further clarifying our ethical understanding. The better grasp of what it means for someone or something to be a moral agent brings with it a number of substantial advantages: we can avoid anthropocentric and anthropomorphic attitudes towards agency and rely on an ethical outlook not necessarily based on punishment and reward but on moral agency, accountability, and censure; we are less likely to assign responsibility at any cost, forced by the necessity to identify a human moral agent; we can liberate technological development of AAs from being bound by the standard limiting view; and we can stop the regress of looking for the *responsible* individual when something evil happens, since we are now ready to acknowledge that sometimes the moral source of evil or good can be different from an individual or group of humans (Floridi 2013, 158–159).

Distinguishing between accountability and responsibility assures a wider range of analysis and inquiry for the moral discourse, which is hence not limited to praiseworthiness and blameworthiness (with all the aforementioned risks that this brings about). However, some scholars may raise, at present, a further objection, no longer concerned with responsibility, but with accountability. For some ethicists, the idea of accountability involves a dialogical relation, in which one accounts for one's actions before someone else. If, for instance, a teacher asks who was responsible for the harm that came to Alice, there would be a key difference between being recognized as the source of the action (moral accountability in Floridi's sense) and standing before the class, in order to undertake the responsibility of what happened (moral accountability in a dialogical sense). In the latter case, moral accountability would be intrinsically characterised by this explicit assumption of responsibility. In this case, the moral threshold of accountability (i.e., the level at which one can be considered as morally accountable) would be circumscribed to human beings, who alone can stand and speak before someone else. Indeed, Floridi endorses such a position, but in a different, epistemological context, when he refers to accountability in terms of 'providing an account' and then uses it as the condition that needs to be satisfied by someone who is informed that p, in order to qualify as someone who knows that *p* because she can account for *p* (Floridi 2011, ch. 12). However sharp and reasonable this distinction (between dialogical and Floridi's conception of accountability) might appear, it is misleading. It is misleading, not only because dialogical accountability presupposes Floridi's conception of accountability (for one to publicly recognize oneself as accountable, one has to recognize oneself as the source of the morally qualifiable action), but for another reason: namely, because once again it does not properly distinguish between the moral experience and the moral game (both of which are constitutive factors of the moral life). To stand before someone and to assume full responsibility for the morally qualifiable action is part of one's moral experience: namely, it is a way to give meaning to what happened (either because this makes what happened more socially acceptable, or it reinforces our moral subjectivity, appeases our sense of guilt or shows immediate repentance, or for whatever other reason concerned with our capacity to provide our associated life experience with meaning). However, none of this is required by the moral game, whose only fundamental concern is that of identifying the sources of the morally qualifiable actions, short of which there would be no moral experience at all.

4.6 Conclusions

Today's world is populated by different types of agents, whether human or artificial, individual or distributed. Each type of agent interacts with the others in novel and not entirely predictable ways, introducing the risk for unforeseen and undesirable or even evil consequences. In these circumstances, our traditional moral and legal categories, through which agents are held accountable for the consequences of their actions, no longer seem sufficient in order to acknowledge and account for the changed scenario of agency. The problem is that these categories were developed on the sole basis of an individual and human-based conception of agents. Floridi's information ethics deals with this theoretical and practical problem by re-examining the characterization of the notions of agents and of moral agents within an informational approach, and thus extending the class of moral agents to include artificial agents.[2] The focus on AAs is not intended to display the role of human beings in moral affairs. On the contrary, extending the idea of agency and of the class of moral agents in the direction of non-human agents allows us a better grasp on the role of human beings in moral responsibility; it also provides a more adequate framework for tackling the new theoretical and practical problems stemming from our interaction with artificial autonomous agents. Floridi's informational approach to agency may therefore also be useful in the legal field, when dealing with artificial autonomous agents (*e.g.* robots) or even when representing the mental stances of human agents as guided by the capacity to correctly process information.

Floridi's extension of the idea of moral agency has provided us with a deeper and more comprehensive understanding of moral life, by decoupling it into two fundamental spheres: i.e., the moral experience, through which we give meaning to our associated life, and the moral game, through which we parameterize our moral categories and make them applicable to any instance of the universe considered at the proper LoA. Whereas the moral experience requires an intelligent agent to whom the meaning of morality is available and relevant, the moral game is accessible to any type of agent to which moral categories are applicable through the parameterization of such categories at the proper LoA. This is methodologically sound, since it is based on a delimited and controlled theoretical claim. Floridi's ontocentric approach does not deny that moral experience is essentially concerned with how human beings give meaning to themselves and to their world. It only claims that choosing the parameters, according to which we frame and regulate the moral game, is part – indeed a basic part – of the moral life, which should also be subject to reflection and discussion. This is a key methodological point to which Floridi draws our attention: it is based on the correct application of the method of levels of abstraction and is achieved through the consequent distinction between accountability and responsibility, that is to say, between the identification and the evaluation of a moral agent. This approach enables us to distinguish between the identification of *A* as a moral agent, according to which we state who or what is the moral source of (and hence is accountable for) a moral action, and the evaluation of *A* as a morally responsible agent, according to which we assess, prescriptively, whether and how far the recognized moral source is also morally responsible for that action. This distinction has a further merit that is often overlooked or underestimated. It prevents us from reducing all prescriptive discourse to the analysis of responsibility, and it assures a wider range of analysis and inquiry to the moral discourse, which is hence not limited to praiseworthiness and blameworthiness. Morality is not merely a commitment to the currently asserted values and criteria on which one is praised or

[2] In the present chapter, there was no enough room to analyze the related topic of distributed morality, elaborated by Floridi (2013), which accounts for the morality of non-individual agents. In many different respects, Floridi is currently directing his attention to the non-individual dimension of some relevant topics (ranging from morality to privacy), which have been traditionally treated as based on strict methodological individualism.

blamed. On the contrary, the peak of morality is, paradoxically, its own crisis, because, in the crisis of morality, moral values and criteria are called into discussion and therefore tested, verified, rethought, and eventually justified. As remarked, by paraphrasing Salinger, moral inquiry to Floridi is a crisis, perhaps the only actionable one we call our own.

However, to endure and experience this sort of crisis, which we cannot reductively interpret as a mere radical non- or anti-anthropocentrism, is a novel and unexplored way to strive for a more universalistic conception of morality. In line with consideration in the previous chapter about moral patients, Floridi's ontocentric approach to the morality of artificial agents is based on an ontology that is hospitable (i.e., it expands the class of agents that count as moral agents) and thus more inclusive (i.e., it expands the number of situations in which agents can behave morally). Again, this approach disentangles the *intrinsic* dimension of moral value from its *absolute* dimension, by relinquishing any agent-type representation of moral value. This can be achieved by characterizing agents using parameters adopted according to the method of level of abstraction, an approach made possible by the informational treatment of moral agents, since it is precisely their representation as informational objects that allows different types of entities to enjoy different levels of moral agency and relevance. In this sense, IE also teaches us another important lesson regarding artificial agents as we move into the future: intrinsic moral value may also be relative. This concept has already been touched on in the previous chapter and seems to be a promising, first theoretical step towards pluralism (see Chap. 6) and a global, multiagent approach to ethical, political and legal issues (see Chaps. 9 and 10).

References

Alpaydin, E. 2010. *Introduction to Machine Learning*. II ed. Cambridge, MA: MIT Press.

Floridi, L. 2011. *The Philosophy of Information*. Oxford: Oxford University Press.

———. 2013. *Information Ethics*. Oxford: Oxford University Press.

Foucault, M. 1988. In *Power/Knowledge: Selected Interviews and Other Writings 1972–1977*, ed. C. Gordon. New York: Pantheon Books.

Frankfurt, H. 1969. Alternate Possibilities and Moral Responsibility. *Journal of Philosophy* LXVI: 829–839.

Himma, K.-E. 2009. Artificial Agency, Consciousness, and the Criteria for Moral Agency: What Properties Must an Artificial Agent Have to Be a Moral Agent? *Ethics and Information Technology* 11 (1): 19–29.

Mitchell, M. 1998. *An Introduction to Genetic Algorithms*. Cambridge, MA/London: MIT Press.

Motwani, R., and P. Raghavan. 1995. *Randomized Algorithms*. Cambridge: Cambridge University Press.

Pagallo, U. 2013a. *The Laws of Robot: Crimes, Contracts, and Torts*. Dordrecht/Berlin: Springer.

———. 2013b. What Robots Want: Autonomous Machines, Codes and New Frontiers of Legal Responsibility. In *Human Law and Computer Law: Comparative Perspectives*, ed. M. Hildebrandt and J. Gaakeer. Dordrecht: Springer.

Russell, S., and P. Norvig. 2010. *Artificial Intelligence: A Modern Approach*. III ed. London: Pearson.

Salinger, J.-D. 1963. *Raise High the Roof Beam, Carpenters and Seymour: An Introduction.* New York: Little, Brown and Company.

Santoni De Sio, F. 2013. *Per colpa di chi. Mente, responsabilità e diritto.* Milano: Raffaello Cortina Editore.

Sen, A. 1985. Well-Being, Agency and Freedom: The Dewey Lectures 1984. *Journal of Philosophy* LXXXII: 169–221.

Williams, B. 1981. *Moral Luck: Philosophical Papers 1973–1980.* Cambridge: Cambridge University Press.

The Informational Construction of the Self

5

Abstract

The information revolution engendered by the evolution of digital ICTs in our current information societies confronts us with a specific and peculiar problem: how to conceive of our personal identity as it is constructed in the information age. First and foremost, this presupposes that personal identity is constructed. The self (or personal identity) is not a fixed, built-in entity to which one can gain immediate access with no regard to context or purpose. Access to the self (or self-knowledge) is constantly mediated, context-dependent and goal-oriented. In this perspective, the self is constructed through the progressive encapsulation of data and their transformation into meaningful information. Personal identity may therefore be described as the sum of information experienced by an epistemic agent at a given level of abstraction. This implies that the informational construction of the self has to do with the human faculty of imbuing with meaning a reality fashioned from the constraining affordances of data that concern us. This process of the semanticization of reality is not merely idealistic; it is already part of our adaptation to the informational environment.

5.1 Introduction

We live in a digital era characterized, if not dominated, by the development of big data. The resulting impact is so great that it may lead to a tipping point in the construction of the self. Floridi holds that the advancement of ICTs marks the emergence of a new historical age called *hyperhistory*: "In prehistory, there are no ICTs; in history, there are ICTs, they record and transmit data, but human societies depend primarily on other kinds of technologies; in hyperhistory, there are ICTs, they record, transmit and, above all, process data, and human societies are vitally dependent on them" (Floridi 2012, 2014a, b; on this point see Chap. 9). Yannis Kallinikos and Niccolo Tempini (2012) believe that this inaugurates a *post-material* age, whereby

M. Durante, *Ethics, Law and the Politics of Information*, The International Library of Ethics, Law and Technology 18, DOI 10.1007/978-94-024-1150-8_5

"contemporary living is embedded in dense information environments in which a growing number of contingencies, problems or situations are increasingly framed in terms of data availability and the technologically based operations of algorithmic reasoning and statistical data crunching by means of which data are assembled to meaningful structures and categories. [...] Placed in wider historical purview, these trends are underlain by the prominence of cognition *qua* computation and the concomitant retraction of perception as an axial principle of human conduct, tied to palpable reality and situated encounters". Jim Gray has argued, as noted by Michael Nielsen (2011), that this historical change involves a new paradigm in scientific discovering: "The world of science has changed, and there is no question about this. The new model is for data to be captured by instruments or generated by simulations before being processed by software and for the resulting information or knowledge to be stored in computers. Scientists only get to look at their data fairly late in this pipeline. The techniques and technologies for such data-intensive science are so different that is worth distinguishing data intensive science from computational science as a new, *fourth paradigm* for scientific exploration" (Hey et al. 2007).

All of these scholars acknowledge that the "data intensive paradigm" is a double-edged sword. On the one hand, it allows "trend analysis, statistical clustering, and discovering global patterns in the data" (Hey et al. 2007). Furthermore, "It certainly opens up a vast horizon of opportunities, all essentially driven by the data-processing power of ICTs. From synthetic biochemistry to neuroscience, from the Internet of things to unmanned planetary explorations, from green technologies to new medical treatments, our activities of discovery, invention, design, and control would be not only unfeasible but unthinkable in a purely mechanical, historical context" (Floridi 2012). On the other hand, "Data tokens as carriers of cognitive or cultural content is involved in the redefinition of personal living, including personal identity, in less conspicuous ways that necessitate the deconstruction of the commercial and institutional contexts within which data are gathered and assembled to digital content and services. Nowhere is this shown more clearly than in what is called profiling, that is, the assembly of personal data drawn from the Web into coherent patterns that reveal specific behavioural profiles" (Kallinikos and Tempini 2012).

We must therefore learn to operate within dual faces of reality, where personal identity – our own self – appears to be based either on an offline reality (mediated by "palpable reality and situated encounters" [Kallinikos and Tempini 2012]) or on an online reality (mediated by a "computational rendition of reality" [Kallinikos and Tempini 2012]). This opposition may threaten the 'unity of the self', and involve social classifications, abstract profiles, identity and privacy issues potentially posing legal and moral dilemmas. Nonetheless, the solution does not lie in considering the self as reducible to one of these dimensions, for online and offline realities today often overlap or even converge.

Here we investigate how a databased construction of the self might be able to account for a conception of personal identity that is consistent with the information revolution. Sensitive to the challenges that technological progress brings, Floridi's philosophy (2011a) and ethics of information (2013) provides an up-to-date approach to understanding our world in informational terms, and may provide guidance as to how to reconcile the dual offline and online realities.

In particular, Floridi's investigation into the informational nature of the self (2013) seems theoretically equipped to provide: (1) synchronic and diachronic accounts of the unity of the self; (2) a criterion for the individualization and identification of personal identity over time; and (3) a renewed conception of the self in terms of informational structure. Floridi's analysis and critique of the history of philosophy (Hume, Spinoza, Kant, and notably Aristotle) sheds light on the complex, theoretical crux of the intertwining issues affecting the question of identity, evincing an innovative perspective based on the overall informational treatment of human beings.

5.2 The Synchronic and Diachronic Unity of the Self

Throughout modernity, most political and legal philosophies have been based on a specific anthropology or, in more general terms, on a particular conception of the human being. This conception has always gone hand in hand with reflection on the spatial and temporal realm in which human beings are embedded. The current technological evolution (time) requires us to rethink the conception of the self as part of the informational environment (space), since it is this renewed self-understanding that will guide us, in the second part of the book, in the comprehension of a number of legal and political issues and consequences driven by the informational turn:

> Human life is quickly becoming a matter of onlife experience, which reshapes constraints and offers new affordances in the development of our identities, their conscious appropriation, and our personal as well as collective self-understanding. Today, we increasingly acknowledge the importance of a common yet unprecedented phenomenon, which may be described as the construction of personal identity in the infosphere (Floridi 2013, 175).

This quotation is significant, not only in introducing the question of the informational construction of the self, but also in clarifying what Floridi means when he suggests that human beings are informational structures made up by their own information. A specific expression (*onlife* experience: see Floridi (ed.), 2014b) leads us back to a particular philosophical view that may help explain this point: Kant's distinction between noumenal and phenomenal reality. Only phenomenal reality may be subject to human experience in a spatial and temporal dimension, which are the a priori conditions for sensibility. Nothing – not even the self – can be experienced in its ultimate, inner reality, as it is; on the contrary, it can only be experienced as it appears to an epistemic agent representing it at a determined level of abstraction. In this perspective, the self is "no one", to adopt Thomas Metzinger's philosophical vocabulary (2004): it is just a phenomenal representation displayed by epistemic agents experiencing it. To say that we are informational beings does not amount to saying that we can have access, in informational terms, to the ultimate and inner reality or nature of the self. In contrast, it means that human beings can be experienced, described and known in terms of information, i.e., as entities whose phenomenal representation is constructed of a sum of well-formed and meaningful data (information). Expressed as a formula, we can say that the self is not, noumenically, made *of* information but, constructively, *by* information. Although sometimes Floridi himself uses the expression made *of* information, he means, as we will see *infra* in § 5.3.2., that there would be no identity at all without providing data with meaning: see Floridi 2013, 179).

However, this epistemic representation is not just a description but, more significantly, serves as an interface with the world. It is a matter of construction that is driven by evolutionary and pragmatic factors, and nowadays is influenced, if not brought about, by ICT technologies:

> […] ICTs are, among other things, *egopoietic technologies* or technologies of construction of the self. They significantly affect who we are, who we think we are, who we might become, and who we think we might become, once our philosophical anthropology is updated to take into account an informational ontology. […] ICTs, as egopoietic technologies, deeply influence our ethical relations with ourselves, offering new opportunities and risks in the ethical developments of our selves and our lives (Floridi 2013, 175).

Criticism of Floridi's informational approach to the conception of human beings often derives from a persistent misunderstanding. The informational construction of the self does not concern a pretended reality or nature of the self (essentialism), nor it is a mere depiction of the self (descriptivism). It instead concerns the *experience* that we make of both ourselves and others and that mediates the experience of the world we live in, namely, of how to live *together*. For this reason, this experience is not only epistemic but also greatly affects our ethical, political and legal relations with others. This crucial point is based on Floridi's technological interpretation of Plato's conception of the soul as a chariot:

> We will liken the soul to the composite nature of a pair of winged horses and a charioteer. […] the charioteer of the human soul drives a pair, one of the horses is noble and of noble breed, but the other quite the opposite in breed and character. Therefore in our case the driving is necessarily difficult and troublesome (Phaedrus 246a-254e).

Floridi (2011b, 551) remarks that Plato allows us to conceive the self as a *multi-agent system* (MAS), namely, as a complex and engineered artefact made up of three components or agents, whose technological nature "invites a shift from a phenomenological or descriptive approach to the self to a constructionist or design-oriented approach, one that considers what it means to create (or at least what it means for something to constitute) such a chariot or multi-agent system" (Floridi 2011b, 551). What is of great interest in Floridi's technological interpretation of Plato is the very simple but fundamental notion, for any philosophy of politics or of law, that the conception of self includes in itself the idea of a multi-agent system or "society of agents" (Minsky 1988): that is, the notion that the self not only interacts with the environment and with others but that it is, first and foremost, progressively and necessarily constructed by means of this interaction, and through the communication, coordination and collaboration between agents, with the counterintuitive but noteworthy result that the self is not something already constituted or presupposed but what only emerges as "the last step" (Floridi 2013, 558) in the process of self-construction. This means that "good engineering of the self is good virtue ethics" (Floridi 2013, 176). Needless to say, self-engineering techniques entail no reference to selective or eugenic techniques. They refer to the notion that selves are informational structures, i.e., semantically structuring structures, namely, entities that are constantly in the process of providing both the world and ourselves with meaning:

> Their special nature lies not in what they are – in their physics and biochemistry, to use a different level of abstraction – but in what they can do. For they are *structuring structures*, the ultimate defence against entropy/evil. They are the *loci* where the flow of information reaches its maturity and becomes self-conscious, capable of self-determination, and able to decouple itself from the rest of the fabric and reflecting on its own nature and status (Floridi 2010a).

As pointed out at the beginning of this chapter, the unity of self is an issue: "what makes such a complex MAS a coherent unity and source of action, and keeps it as such?" (Floridi 2013, 176). Floridi refers to this critical question for any informational-based theory of the self as *the problem of the chariot*, because "it is the chariot and the tack that, in Plato's analogy, represent the *fourth*, hidden component that guarantees the unity and coordination of the system, thus allowing the self to be, persist and act as a single, coherent, and continuous entity in different places, at different times, and through a variety of experiences" (Floridi 2011b, 552; emphasis mine). It is remarkable that Floridi makes reference to the philosophical issue of the 'fourth' quite in the same sense[1] in which it is referred to by Rainer Brandt (1991) when interpreting Kant's well-known three tasks, according to what Kant himself suggested in a letter, as Brian Jacobs reminds us (2003, 116):

> In a letter to Carl Friedrich Stäudlin dated May 4, 1793, Kant writes: The plan which I have held myself to for a long time consists in working out the field of pure philosophy toward the solution of three tasks: 1) what can I know? (metaphysics); 2) what I ought to do? (morals); 3) what may I hope? (religion); from which the fourth question ought to follow: what is the human being? (anthropology, on which I have held an annual lecture for more than 20 years).

The question of the fourth is therefore the question of anthropology, or egology, (which concerns what the human being is or can do), which is conceived, from modernity onwards, in ontological terms, by wondering about "the unity, identity, and continuity of the I, or self" (Floridi 2011b, 552), understood as an entity that exists both in space (synchronically) and through time (diachronically). In the present context, a meditation on the ontology of the self is characterized by and based

[1] We said *quite in the same* sense, because Floridi's conception of the 'fourth' as meaning the question of anthropology should be also analyzed and put into relation with Heidegger's interpretation of Kantian anthropology (Heidegger, 1997), since the German philosopher radicalizes Kant's question (what is the human being?), by transforming it into the following question: what can the human being do? This idea could be rephrased in the already mentioned Floridi's terms: "Their special nature lies not in what they are [...] but in what they can do" (Floridi, 2010b, [replies to Durante]).

on the perspective of a synchronic and a diachronic axis, which we have so far recognized as the theoretical foundation of Floridi's method of conceptualization.

5.3 The Identification and the Individualization of the Self

Modern egology, understood as an ontology of the self, may be constructed and studied along two axes, one diachronic and the other synchronic:

> *Diachronic* egology, understood as an ontology of personal *identity*, concentrates on the problems arising from the *identification* of a self through time or possible worlds, progressively moving towards metaphysics. *Synchronic* egology, understood as an ontology of *personal* identity, deals with the *individualisation* of a self in time or in a possible world (Floridi 2011b, 552).

Both axes are crucial to an understanding of what the personal identity of the self is from the standpoint of moral and legal philosophies. Consider from the diachronic perspective, for instance, the role played by "time" in the current dispute between the online virtues or vices of remembering and forgetting in the digital age (Mayer-Schonberger 2009; Pagallo and Durante 2014). The same dispute is also concerned, from a synchronic point of view, with the issue of individualization of a self in time or in a possible (real or virtual) world, since the identity of the self is often grounded in the continuity of memory or in the narrative construction of autobiography. The moral and legal debate about the right to be forgotten is a clear example of how relevant the informational understanding of personal identity is at present.

Let us deal separately with the questions of identification and of individualization before turning to the issue of the informational structure of the self.

5.3.1 The Diachronic Identification of the Self

Floridi focuses on two main theories concerning the issue of the identification of the self: (1) the theory of "endurantism" and (2) the theory of "perdurantism".

> *Endurantism* argues that a self is a three-dimensional entity that wholly exists at each moment of its history, and the same self exists at each moment. *Perdurantism* argues that a self is a four-dimensional entity constituted by a series of spatial and temporal parts, somewhat like the frames of a film (Floridi 2011b, 553).

The fragmentation of the self into a series of spatial and temporal parts distinguishes the latter theory from the former. More importantly however, these theories have something in common. They share an ontology of the self, "by presupposing some form of direct realism, according to which the model (description, theory, representation, analysis etc.) of the system (the referent of the model, in this case the self, the I, or whatever is intended by personal identity as a feature of the world) can be developed through non-mediated access to the system in itself" (Floridi 2011b,

553). In other words, both theories hold the view that the self is ultimately anchored to some (material or procedural) entity that underlies and permeates all manifestations of the self. This view is at odds with Floridi's idea of constructionism, which is based on levels of abstraction and always requires mediated access to the system under examination. In this perspective, the self itself should be de-emphasized and treated like any other system, which "is always accessed and hence modelled at a given level of abstraction" (Floridi 2011b, 553). This notion allows Floridi to suggest an alternative approach, according to which:

> the analysis of self 'identity' (*a* is this) and 'sameness' (this is the same *a* as that *a*) relations should be developed in terms of the relevant kinds of information (observables) that, once fixed, provide the referential framework required to satisfy the specific epistemic goals in question (Floridi 2011b, 553).

The identification of a system – its identity – is never independent from the specific framework within which it is being investigated. It is this referential framework, with its relative set of questions, which causes us to identify a system *as* such. "The illusion that there might be a single, correct, absolute answer, independently of context, purpose and LoA, leads to paradoxical nonsense" (Floridi 2011b, 553). Floridi's informational approach to identity enables us to emancipate ourselves from the philosophical overload of the ontology of the self, which is always susceptible to interpretation in ideological or political terms. What we are depends on the level of abstraction at which we are being investigated, and "this depends of the purpose for which, and the context in which the question is asked" (Floridi 2011b, 553). This is true no matter what system, including the self, is being examined.

In political, moral and legal philosophy, the question of identity is particularly troublesome, since it often conceals political, moral and legal strategies or value-choices under the heading of the realistic and ontological account of the self. The best way to disclose such a strategic dimension and to unfold the possible value-choices included in the description of identity is make it clear that the issue of identity is always a teleological 'question', and that this happens for very pragmatic and adaptive reasons:

> Identity and sameness relations are satisfied according to the LoAs adopted, and these, in turn, depend on the goals being pursued. This is not relativism: given a particular goal, one LoA is better than another, and questions will receive better or worse answers. [...] Questions about diachronic identity and sameness are really teleological questions, asked in order to attribute responsibility, plan a journey, collect taxes, attribute ownership or authorship, trust someone, authorize someone else and so forth (Floridi 2011b, 554).

Identification is thus a context-dependent and goal oriented process, experienced and displayed at a certain level of abstraction, and is free from ideological burden. Now let us turn to the issue of individualization.

5.3.2 The Synchronic Individualization of the Self

In truth, the issue of individualization has logical precedence over that of identification, since to establish whether this system is the same as *that* system, we first need to know what the system is in the first place (Floridi 2011b, 554). However, we deal with this question after that of identification for two reasons: (1) because it serves to introduce us to Floridi's understanding and treatment of the self as an informational structure, and (2) because it is thus more fundamental, from an information viewpoint, than that of identification.

According to Floridi, there are at least two main theories concerning the issue of the individualization of the self: (1) the "Lockean" theory and (2) the "narrative" theory about the nature of the individual self. Let us see what they hold:

> According to the Lockean approach, the identity of the self is grounded in the unity of consciousness and the continuity of memories. According to the Narrative approach (Schechtman 1996), the self is a socio- or (inclusive) autobiographical artefact (Floridi 2011b, 554).

It is beyond our scope to deal with and account for these two approaches in full detail here. Both emphasize the human capacity to rebuild identity in the sphere of reflexivity by means of internal or external memory. Nonetheless, it is important to note what both approaches presuppose: both require us to be able to have access to data, to process such data (by elaborating output from input), and to transform the data into information, by providing it with meaning. It is a sort of informational ability (more than an in-built competence) that over-determines the issue of individualization and, hence, of personal identity:

> Now, in both cases, *individualisation* – the characterization or constitution of the self – is achieved through forms of information processing: consciousness and memory are dynamic states of information, but so is any kind of personal or social narrative. So both the Lockean and the Narrative approach presuppose the existence of individual agents endowed with the right sort of informational skills (Floridi 2011b, 555).

This also means that while the ongoing information revolution (Floridi 2010a) sheds light on the informational understanding and treatment of the self, it does not create it ex novo. There is a problem arising from this type of informational understanding and treatment of the self, which brings us back to the issue of the chariot and the tack (i.e. the unity of the self):

> If the self is made of information (perceptions or narratives, or any other informational items one may privilege), then a serious challenge is to explain how that information is kept together as a whole, coherent, sufficiently permanent unity (Floridi 2011b, 556).

If the unity of the constitution or self-narration of the self is not assured on the part of the object (i.e., a fragmented and miscellaneous sum of data), it has to be guaranteed on the part of the supposed subject of narration. Floridi suggests that the first, partial answer to this problem is offered by Kant, who advances the idea that "the unified coherence of the information about the external world, synthesized by the epistemic agent, could be guaranteed only by the unity of the very agent's self", that is, the information's source (Floridi 2011b, 556). In other words, the unity of constitution or self-narration can be assured by presupposing and representing the self as the unitary source of information that prevents the dispersion and fragmentation of data by committing them to the unity of a meaningful narration. However, this amounts to presupposing the existence of what has to be accounted for: that is, the unity of the self as the unitary source of information (data plus meaning). This would require further study:

> The semanticization of the world requires a unity of perspective, so presence of the former guarantees the presence of the latter. How such unity and coordination come to be there in the first place and have those features is not the issue addressed. It is part of the question left unanswered (Floridi 2011b, 556).

This means that one cannot simply account for the unity of the self in terms of mere presupposition. The understanding of the informational unity of the self "may be achieved, or at least described, through a three-phase development of the self" (Floridi 2011b, 557). The self is does not come with a complete set of characteristics, properties and prerogatives; it only emerges as the last step in a process of self-constitution, which is context-dependent, goal-oriented and contingent upon the "questions" one is called on to answer (see supra § 5.3.1).

5.4 The "Three Membranes Model"

At this point it may be useful to examine the development of the self by making reference to Floridi's "Three Membranes Model" (Floridi 2011b, 557). Floridi suggests that selves structure themselves progressively in a three-stage development process, which can be likened to three membranes: the corporeal, cognitive, and consciousness membranes. At each stage, selves encapsulate and process data, which is transformed into information, thus allowing selves to gradually detach themselves from the environment and to be constituted into autonomous entities. These encapsulations of data constitute three fundamental evolutionary dimensions of the self: the organic, the cognitive, and the mental dimensions:

> Selves emerge as *the last step* in a process of detachment from reality that begins with a corporeal membrane encapsulating an organism, proceeds through a cognitive membrane encapsulating an intelligent animal, and concludes with a consciousness membrane encapsulating a mental self or simply a mind (Floridi 2011b, 558; emphasis mine).

Again, let us stress the importance of the notion that selves emerge as "the last step" in the process that constitutes their identities. Selves do not come with a prefabricated set of characteristics, properties and prerogatives, but are gradually formed through a process of detachment from reality, that is, from the surrounding environment. This also means, in contrast with the widespread notion to the contrary, that personal identity is not trapped in and stuck to the surrounding environment; on the contrary, it emerges as the last step of a process of detachment from it. The idea of a membrane suggests both the idea of a permeable interface between the constituting self and reality and of a form of protection against the environment itself:

> Each membrane is a defence of the structural integrity of what it encapsulates, against the surrounding environment. Of course, in moving from the corporeal, to the cognitive to the consciousness membrane, there is an increasing process of virtualization (Floridi 2011b, 558).

What is more, against the backdrop of this process of detachment, personal identity does not represent idealistically an "inside" opposed to the "outside" of the environment; on the contrary, it is the very process of progressive detachment (the auto-assembly and the auto-organization of selves in several steps) that generates at each stage "a new divide, within the old environment, between a new inside and a new outside" (Floridi 2011b, 558). Let us examine in greater detail how the self develops through these three stages.

During the first, corporeal stage, data are physical patterns (signals) broadcast by other structures in the environment (also considered to be informational systems), which are captured and encapsulated by means of the membrane of the organism, whose bodily dimension "protects the stability of the living system" (Floridi 2011b, 559). At this stage, the corporeal membrane functions as a "hardwired divide" (Floridi 2011b, 559), which delineates the biotic structure of the organism, the new inside, from the surrounding environment, the new outside. There is one particularly important aspect to note about the first stage, even if it applies to all steps of the development of the self. The self is an informational structure among other informational structures, which can be also experienced and described, at a given level of abstraction, by an epistemic agent as informational objects and, to some extent, as systems that collect, process, and share data with other informational systems. This establishes a sort of continuity between informational structures, which are distinguished from each other only because of their specific forms of encapsulating data, i.e., because of the particular functioning, development and interconnection of their membranes.

At the second, cognitive stage, data are encodable resources, or resources that can be formatted as some sort of code to be exploited "by organisms through some language broadly conceived (sound, visual patterns, gestures, smells, behaviours etc.)" (Floridi 2011b, 559). At this stage, the aim of encapsulation is to store, process and communicate data by means of the cognitive membrane. Data are committed to short and long-term memory. Since we are evolutionary informational structures, is not surprising that over time we have developed increasingly sophisticated and resourceful methods of committing data to forms of external memory, ranging from script to images, recordings and the world wide web), which distinguish us from less adaptive informational structures. At the cognitive stage, the encapsulation of data thus has a different and more complex function:

> The stream of data, which were before quantities without direction (scalars), broadcast by sources not targeting any particular receiver (e.g. the sun generating heat and light, or the earth generating a magnetic field), acquire a direction, from the sender to receiver (vectors), and an interpretation (e.g. noises become sounds interpreted as alarms) (Floridi 2011b, 559).

In this perspective, the cognitive membrane can be considered as a "semi-hardwired divide" (Floridi 2011b, 559), which detaches the cognitive system from the surrounding environment, by allowing it to encode and store data (i.e., to commit data to internal [and external] memories), to process (i.e., to elaborate output from input by means of language), and to communicate this data to other informational structures (i.e., to share encoded and interpreted data).

At the third, consciousness stage, data are not only formatted in code, but become "repurposable information" (Floridi 2011b, 559), which also comprises conventional meaning. At this stage, selves appropriate and unify the data gradually encapsulated at the first and second stage as their experiences, and they transform them into new information that may be subject to further reflection and redirection. In this sense, the self becomes self-aware and capable to undergo increasing degrees of self-reflection, which allows the self or conscious mind to become an I. At this stage, the consciousness membrane can be considered as a "softwired (programmable)" divide (Floridi 2011b, 559), which makes the body become "the outside environment for an inside experience" (Floridi 2011b, 559).

Therefore, the self gradually emerges over a three-stage developmental process by means of its evolutionary capacity to encapsulate and manipulate data and hence to transform this data into information and to provide it with meaning. This allows individual selves to detach themselves from the world. In this sense, the self is an egopoietic force that constructs itself from a series of progressive transformations: the three-stage development through which data are encapsulated and transformed into signals, codes and meanings. However, the self is not merely the by-product of this transformation, but is the actual experience, or appropriation through self-reflection, of these transformations. In this view, the self is primarily an epistemic agent engaged in its constructive and reflexive self-experience. This experience – which is a means of distancing oneself from the world and of emerging from this detachment as an individual – is thus made possible "by a specific, auto-reinforcing, bonding force" (Floridi 2011b, 559). Here is Floridi's description of the membranes as the bonds and orientations that provide the self with its unity and coordination:

> The corporeal membrane relies on chemical bonds and orientations. The cognitive membrane relies on bonds and orientations provided by what is known in information theory as mutual information, which is the (measure of) the interdependence of data […]. And, finally, the consciousness membrane relies on the bonds and orientations provided by semantics (here narratives provide plenty of examples), which ultimately makes possible a stable and long-lasting detachment from reality. At each stage, corporeal, cognitive and consciousness elements fit together in structures (body, cognition, mind) that owe their unity and coordination to such bonding forces. The more virtual the structure becomes, the more it is disengaged from the external environment in favour of an autonomously

> constructed world of meanings and interpretations, the less physical and more virtual the bonding forces can be (Floridi 2011b, 560).

The problem of the chariot and the tack - which in Plato's analogy represents the *fourth*, hidden component that guarantees the unity and coordination of the system - is solved by the coordinated function of the different bonding forces (at the stages of the corporeal, cognitive, and consciousness) that prevents data from being dispersed and fragmented by converting them into information. This process of construction is gradual, and a single stage alone is not sufficient to drive it. The semantic bonding force emerges out of the three components, because it enables the self to appropriates and unify all the data encapsulated at the three stages by means of self-awareness. For this reason, the self may be said to be deeply characterized by its informational capacity to progressively transform data into meaningful information.

This capacity does not spring into existence fully formed, but emerges gradually at each stage by means of the healthy development of the three membranes, which may in turn be affected by the development ICTs. The consequences are many and far-reaching, as Floridi describes:

> Any technology capable of affecting any of them is *ipso facto* a technology of the self. Now, ICTs are the most powerful technologies to which selves have ever been exposed. They induce radical modifications (a re-ontologization) of the contexts (constraints and affordances) and praxes of self-poiesis, by enhancing the corporeal membrane, empowering the cognitive membrane, and extending the consciousness membrane (Floridi 2011b, 561).

This means that the development of ICTs affects not only the environment in which selves are embedded and from which they gradually detach, but also self-poiesis, by enhancing the body, the empowerment of cognition, and the extension of mind. Of course, this development may also give rise to side effects or adverse consequences. What is clear is that enhancement, empowerment, and extension (and their negative counterparts) raise numerous moral and legal issues concerning the self as an individual and as part of a community. We shall limit ourselves here to briefly describing three of them.

Firstly, ICTs increase the phenomenon of "tele-presence" (Floridi 2011b), which etymologically means "presence from a distance" and characterizes the distinction between the presence and the location of the self. Selves may be cognitively present (that is, aware of the information processes in which they are engaged) while being located elsewhere. This means that being embedded in a physical context no longer accounts entirely, or even primarily, for the information processes in which selves are engaged. This also implies that this type of disembeddedness not only affects the consequences of our actions, which may be transnational or even global, but also the information processes in which we are engaged, which may be transcultural or even multicultural.

Secondly, ICTs increase the commitment of personal data to external memory as well as the distribution of such data outside our ordinary standards of proximity by means of digitized interactions that bridges the divide between online and offline realities. This requires us "to be thriftier with anything that tends to fix the nature of the self, and more in handling new or refined self-poietic skills. Capturing, editing, saving, conserving, managing one's own memories for personal and public consumption will become increasingly important not just in terms of protection of informational privacy, but also in terms of construction of one's personal identity" (Floridi 2011b, 562). This means that people in information societies need to become increasingly aware of the fact that the construction of one's personal identity is also a hetero-construction. There are two main reasons for this: (1) personal data are more easily decontextualized and recontextualized when they have been committed to external memory and (2) the process of semanticization of reality is hardly ever a purely individual and private activity, but a collective and public one.

Thirdly, ICTs amplifies the phenomenon and the salience of the "digital gaze" (Floridi 2011b, 563), which consists in the fact that "the self tries to see how others see itself, by relying on ICTs that greatly facilitate the gazing experience" (Floridi 2011b, 563). According to Floridi, this phenomenon can affect the construction and development of personal identity in four ways: (1) the self "uses the digital imaginary concerning itself to construct a virtual identity through which it seeks to grasp its own personal identity […], in a potential feedback loop of adjustment and modifications leading to an equilibrium between the off-line and the online selves" (Floridi 2011b, 563), with the result that this "ontic feedback – the tendency of the gaze to re-ontologize (change the very nature of) the self that is subject to it – becomes a permanent feature of the *onlife* experience" (Floridi 2011b, 563); (2) through the digital gaze, the self is encouraged to see itself from a third-person perspective, which is always conditioned by the nature of the medium through which it is perceived: this allows the self to have only a partial and preformed self-reflection; (3) the growing experience of the digital gaze made possible by the widespread and pervasive employment of ICTs may cause the self to lose sight and awareness of its own identity, becoming mesmerized and seduced by the false perception of oneself attributed by others; (4) through the medium of the digital gaze, social pressure may negatively lead the self to re-ontologize itself heteronomously, by letting the hetero-construction of the self prevail over the self-construction of personal identity.

This is the backdrop against which the self is called upon to progressively construct its personal identity in the infosphere. It is hence crucial to call attention to this dimension, since it will continue to have an increasing effect on the protection of informational privacy, as already remarked, and – even more importantly - on the right to the self-construction of personal identity. The divide between online and offline realities has been significantly eroded and the infosphere is becoming the whole environment in which we grow up and live. The right to narrative self-construction of personal identity is increasingly important may even take precedence over all other rights as a sort of precondition for inhabiting the infosphere. There is one key exception: the right to access data (to be transformed into information) is also paramount. The right to narrative self-construction and the right to access will always need to be carefully counterbalanced, as they mutually influence each other. This is evident once we recognize that the self is constitutively characterized by its capacity to encapsulate and transform data into information by providing it with meaning.

5.5 Conclusions

The self (our personal identity) is not a fixed and built-in entity to which one can gain immediate access with no regard to context or purpose. Access to the self, namely, self-knowledge, is always mediated, context-dependent and goal-oriented. In this perspective, the self is constructed through the progressive encapsulation of data and its transformation into information; it may be described as the sum of information experienced by an epistemic agent at a given level of abstraction, like any other informational object. In this sense, we have remarked that the self is not the direct result but the re-elaborated experience of such transformations (the three stages of self-development). To paraphrase Aldous Huxley (1932) ("Experience is not what happens to a man; it is what a man does with what happens to him"), we may say that experience is not just the sum of the data one encapsulates. It is the meaning one creates out of the available data. Hence, this construction is neither arbitrary nor over-determined. The self is free in that it gives meaning to reality within the constraining affordances provided by data. This is the why the process of progressive detachment of the self "from the non-self (the world)" (Floridi 2011b, 563) is so significant for the construction of personal identity. The self emerges as the last step of this process, insofar as it becomes aware of its profound involvement in the course of its self-recognition:

> The process itself, however, is also part of the narrative through which we semanticise reality, i.e., through which we make sense of our environment, of ourselves in it, and of our interactions with and within it. In other words, the process of progressive detachment of the self from the non-self is always and inevitably reconstructed by the self from the self's perspective (Floridi 2011b, 564).

This means that "a later stage in the information flow (the acquisition of new information) forces the correct reinterpretation of the whole information flow (all information previously and subsequently received)" (Floridi 2011b, 564). Floridi refers to this later stage in the process of self-recognition as "realization," which is a possible translation of Aristotle's concept of *anagnorisis*. Newly acquired information does not render previous information false (i.e. falsified), but it enables us to resituate and reinterpret it so as to provide it with new meaning, such that "information becomes self-aware" (Floridi 2011b, 564). Floridi's example is instructive: at some point (B) in time Alice loves Bob. At a later stage (R), it is still true that Alice used to love Bob (at B), but now (at R) Alice realizes that it is only fraternal love, and that this is not going to change. This newly acquired information does not make previous information false, but it does enable Alice to reinterpret the whole information flow (i.e. her story) according to a meaningful account, which is not going to change at a later point (A). This means that R affects both information at point B and information at point A that is not yet available (Floridi 2011b, 564).

In other words, the self is able to "recount the story of its own emergence in terms of a progressive detachment from external reality", which grows out of newly acquired information (and misinformation) about itself. This can be compared to Rorty's conception (whose influence can be seen in Davidson's theory 1984) of self-recognition understood as self-narration (1989), which is always and inevitably charged with the role of recapitulating and recounting the story of its own character. As in Floridi, this story is constructed 'by the self from the self's perspective'. Unlike Floridi, this narration does not entail a progressive detachment from reality, since narration is not anchored to reality of any sort (that is, reality stems only from the narration); this means, in other words, that data are not constraining affordances, as they instead are in Floridi's philosophy of information. Floridi's conception of realization may be also said to entail and amount to a new form of idealism: the self is in fact progressively detaching itself from the non-self, by means of a comprehensive account that integrates both the self and the non-self within the same narration. In a sense, this is indeed true. However, there is a slight, yet crucial difference with any idealistic account of the self. The process of progressive detachment of the self from the non-self (i.e., the auto-assembly and auto-organization of selves in several steps) generates at each stage "a new divide, within the old environment, between a new inside and a new outside" (Floridi 2011b, 558), and this happens for evolutionary reasons. The narrative, "through which we semanticise reality, i.e., through which we make sense of our environment, of ourselves in it, and of our interactions with and within it" (Floridi 2011b, 563), is no longer a grand narrative (Lyotard 1984) or an egological story: it is a form of adaptation to the informational environment itself. To put it in Floridi's terms, we are called upon to take care of other informational structures and to move "from the egology to the ecology of the self" (Floridi 2011b, 564).

ICTs contribute, through erosion of the divide between offline and online realities, to the construction of an ever-larger infosphere, that is, the environment in which we live and construct our personal identities. The informational construction of personal identity is thus a way to interact *with* and *within* the infosphere: this is the crucial ecological (and not egological) aspect of the informational constitution of the self. Self-poiesis modifies the environment, since it enriches the infosphere *with* new informational objects while also enacting an adaptive and creative response to the environment, i.e.. to other informational structures, organisms and agents, *within* the infosphere. The informational personal identity of the self is thus characterized by its *being-with-and-within* the infosphere. The relation dimension of the self is, for this reason, twofold: it is directed both towards others (including itself) and towards the world. The dichotomy between others and the world is resolved in an informational perspective. Both directions contribute to the construction of the self, united by the informational constitution and understanding of all entities. The ecology of the self resides precisely in the 'and' of its being-with-*and*-within the infosphere, which also entails a moral relation of care:

> There are still only informational structures. But some are things, some are organisms, and some are minds, intelligent and self-aware beings. Only minds are able to interpret and take

care of other informational structures as things or organisms or selves. And this is part of our special position in the universe (Floridi 2011b, 565).

The shift from the egology to the ecology of the self marks our moral engagement with-and-within the environment, increasing our awareness of the egopoietic role of ICTs, which contribute to structuring the infosphere "with new affordances, constraints and challenges" as well as "with still unknown and largely unassessed risks and rewards" (Floridi 2011b, 565). In this perspective, selves are informational structures that occupy "a special position in the universe", since they are called upon to interpret (that is, to semanticise reality) and take care of other informational structures (that is, to be morally accountable for the wellbeing and flourishing of the infosphere or of regions of it). Because of their active role in the universe, selves are not only informational structures but, more accurately, "the final stage in the development of informational structures, for they are the semantically structuring structures conscious of themselves" (Floridi 2011b, 565).

References

Brandt, R. 1991. *D'Artagnan und die Urteilstafel. Über ein Ordnungsprinzip der europäischen Kulturgeschichte*. Stuttgart: Franz Steiner.

Davidson, D. 1984. *Inquiries into Truth and Interpretation [1974]*. Oxford: Clarendon Press.

Floridi, L. 2010a. *Information. A Very Short Introduction*. Oxford: Oxford University Press.

———. 2010b. Information Ethics. In *The Cambridge Handbook of Information and Computer Ethics*, ed. L. Floridi, 77–99. Cambridge: Cambridge University Press.

———. 2011a. *The Philosophy of Information*. Oxford: Oxford University Press.

———. 2011b. The Informational Nature of Personal Identity. *Minds & Machines* 21: 549–566.

———. 2012. Hyperhistory and the Philosophy of Information Policies. *Philosophy and Technology* 25: 129–131.

———. 2013. *Information Ethics*. Oxford: Oxford University Press.

———. 2014a. *The Fourth Revolution. On the Impact of Information and Communication Technologies on Our Lives*. Oxford: Oxford University Press.

———. (ed.). 2014b. *The Onlife Manifesto. Being Human in a Hyperconnected Era*, Dordrecht: Springer.

Heidegger, M. 1997. *Kant and the Problem of Metaphysics*, 5th ed. enlarged, Trans. R. Taft. Bloomington: Indiana University Press.

Hey, T., S. Tansley, and K. Tolle. 2007. *Jim Gray on eScience: A Transformed Scientific Model*, accessible online at: http://research.microsoft.com/en-us/collaboration/fourthparadigm.

Huxley, A. 1932. *Texts & Pretexts: An Anthology with Commentaries*. London: Chatto & Windus.

Jacobs, B. 2003. Kantian Character and the Problem of a Science of Humanity. In *Essays on Kant's Anthropology*, ed. B. Jacob. Cambridge: Cambridge University Press.

Kallinikos, Y., and N. Tempini. 2012. Post-material Meditations: On Data Tokens, Knowledge and Behavior. Accessible online at: www.tigair.info/docs/kalltemp_egos11.pdf.

Lyotard, J.-F. 1984. *The Postmodern Condition: A Report on Knowledge* (1979). Trans. G. Bennington and B. Massumi. Manchester: Manchester University Press.

Mayer-Schonberger, V. 2009. *Delete: The Virtue of Forgetting in the Digital Age*. Princeton: Princeton University Press.

Metzinger, T. 2004. *Being No One: The Self-Model Theory of Subjectivity*. Cambridge, MA: MIT Press.

Minsky, M. 1988. *The Society of Mind*. New York: Simon & Schuster.

Nielsen, M. 2011. *Reinventing Discovery: The New Era of Networked Science*. Princeton: Princeton University Press.

Pagallo, U., and M. Durante. 2014. Legal Memories and the Right to be Forgotten. In *Protection of Information and the Right to Privacy – A New Equilibrium?* Law, Governance and Technology Series, ed. L. Floridi, vol. 17, 17–30. Dordrecht: Springer.

Rorty, R. 1989. *Contingency, Irony, and Solidarity*. Cambridge: Cambridge University Press.

Part II

Normative Implications and Challenges

The Value of Information as Ontological Pluralism

6

Abstract

Pluralism is not a secondary, derivational offshoot that follows on from the fragmentation of Being. In other words, pluralism is not a degradation of Being, as has been understood and portrayed in a large part of the history of philosophy. Floridi's informational perspective, which characterizes his ontological approach to ethical issues, allows us to give an ontological foundation to pluralism, thus understood in informational terms. An ontological foundation of pluralism or, to put it differently, a pluralistic conception of Being, is indeed important from a philosophical standpoint, not only because it provides us with a deeper understanding of Floridi's ontological approach to ethical issues (concerned not only with the requirements of the ethos of hospitality and universalism but with pluralism as well), but also and above all because it offers us a way out of the quicksand of a relativistic approach to the crucial notion and fundamental value of (respect for) difference in our pluralistic societies.

6.1 Introduction

Information plays an ever increasingly decisive role in all spheres of today's globalized world, ranging from social and political to cultural, legal, economic and moral. (Castells 1996, 1997, 1998; Benkler 2006; Floridi 2010). Our networked digital reality is made up of information that provides the basis upon which we formulate expectations, make evaluations, take decisions, and act in the world. What is more, our moral and legal responsibility tends to vary in proportion to the degree of information we are given (Floridi 2008a; Durante 2009). The evolution of ICTs is constantly redefining the limits of information societies and posing unprecedented ethical, political and legal questions and issues. Notably, the ongoing process of globalization, coupled with the digitization of our information societies, calls up the issue of pluralism. The widespread flow of shared information has brought vastly

M. Durante, *Ethics, Law and the Politics of Information*, The International Library of Ethics, Law and Technology 18, DOI 10.1007/978-94-024-1150-8_6

different people, cultures, languages, values and perspectives together, compelling them to confront one other as never before. This may give rise either to communication, by favouring several forms of integration and inclusion, or to conflict, by favouring separation and exclusion. The issue may be framed and accounted for in many ways, using terms such as *multi-culturalism*, *inter-culturalism*, *relativism* and so forth. But labels are not so important to us. What matters is whether an ontological conception of information might prove to be consistent with pluralism. The information turn seems not only to be consistent with a pluralistic conception of society, but also to promote and support such a conception. Nonetheless, we know that any informational approach that points out the inescapable intertwinement of different people, cultures, languages, values, perspectives and so forth runs the risk, on the one hand, of sinking in the quagmire of multi-culturalism, inter-culturalism, relativism etc., or, on the other, of disguising and concealing a belief in the superiority of the Western (philosophical, moral, political and legal) tradition under cover of contrived universalistic formula often devoid of a solid philosophical basis. For this reason, an informational approach requires an ontological foundation, in order to rigorously account for universalistic claims by reconciling a construction of information with a pluralistic conception of Being. It is with this perspective in mind that we focus our attention in this chapter on one of the main theoretical and practical issues of Luciano Floridi's information ethics. As we see it, Floridi's approach has a particular methodological merit: namely, it provides an understanding and interpretation of the information revolution with a solid philosophical basis (concerning the nature of data and the meaning of information), the philosophical roots of which deserve careful examination. To this end, we will analyse a crucial question that is essential not only from a theoretical but also from a practical (moral, political and legal) standpoint, i.e., whether or not Floridi's construction of information is consistent with a pluralistic conception of Being. This analysis may also shed further light upon the criticism that has been levelled at the principle of ontological equality (that is, all informational objects deserve a minimal level of moral respect *qua* informational objects) which underlies Floridi's information ethics.

Floridi's construction of information may pave the way to an ontological foundation of pluralism on the basis of a previous informational understanding of Being (*Esse est information*). This would be at variance with a longstanding philosophical tradition that conceives of Being in a monistic way and, as a result, thinks of pluralism as contradicting any ontological description of the world.

6.2 The Ontological Foundation of Information Ethics

Let us recall what has already been said in Part I of this book regarding the ontological foundation of Floridi's information ethics, as it provides the theoretical foundation necessary for understanding what we will argue in the present chapter about 'ontological pluralism' (which sounds very much like a philosophical contradiction in terms). Information ethics is an ontocentric, patient-oriented, ecological macroethics that encourages a shift in perspective from rigid methodological anthropocentrism to a wider perspective that accounts for a different understanding of the interaction between agents and patients or reagents, reshaping those notions on more solid ontological bases (Floridi 2008a, 21):

> All entities, *qua* informational objects, have an intrinsic moral value, although possibly quite minimal and overridable, and hence can count as moral patients, subject to some equally minimal degree of moral respect understood as a *disinterested, appreciative and careful attention.*

This approach illustrates not only how interacting agents and patients communicate by means of positive or negative messages, but thanks to its ontocentric perspective, it offers a distinct, unified perspective of the status and mode of being of all entities that inhabit the new informational environment: the infosphere. On the basis of the ontological equality principle, those entities are informational entities that should be treated morally and respected as part of the informational environment to which they belong as informational systems. In other words, all entities deserve a minimal, overridable level of moral respect *qua* informational objects. Consequently, the ontocentric and infocentric convergence suggests, methodologically, what the general aims of Floridi's information ethics are.

The first ontological commitment of information ethics is to be "impartial and universal because it brings to ultimate completion the process of enlargement of the concept of what may count as a centre of moral claim" (Floridi 2008a, 12). Secondly, as a result of its characters of impartiality and universality, this perspective offers a field-independent macroethics that "rectifies an excessive emphasis occasionally placed on specific technologies, by calling attention to the more fundamental phenomenon of information in all its varieties and long tradition" (Floridi 2006, 256). Thirdly, the enlargement of the concept of what deserves a minimal level of moral respect requires us to extend the limits of our own care and responsibility towards all the informational objects that inhabit the infosphere.

A comprehensive normative framework is therefore able to regulate the life cycle of information within the infosphere in an impartial, universal, field-independent way. This framework is based, on the one hand, on the moral analysis of the concept of informational entropy as the most ominous form of evil and, on the other hand, it is structured according to four moral laws that regulate the level of entropy in the infosphere. Whereas informational entropy makes reference to any kind of destruction or corruption of informational objects, that is, any form of impoverishment of being (Floridi 2008a, 11; Floridi 2010, 84), the four moral laws command that (Floridi 1999, 2003):

> 0. Entropy ought not to be caused in the infosphere (null law); 1. Entropy ought to be prevented in the infosphere; 2. Entropy ought to be removed from the infosphere; 3. The flourishing of informational entities as well as the whole infosphere ought to be promoted by preserving, cultivating, enhancing and enriching their properties.

What is important to note about this framework is that entropy refers to informational objects (and not only to information as such), while the four moral laws do not always refer to informational objects but, notably, to the infosphere as a whole: "The duty of any moral agent should be evaluated in terms of contribution to the sustainable blooming of the infosphere, and any process, action or event that negatively affects the whole infosphere –not just an informational object– should be seen as an increase in its level of entropy and hence an instance of evil" (Floridi 2008a, 24). The ontological perspective allows us to perceive of the infosphere as a comprehensive environment, where, despite the contrived division into real and virtual domains, all of reality can be accounted for in moral terms.

6.3 The Informational Dimension of the Ontological Equality Principle

According to our analysis, as discussed in Chap. 2 of Part I, the ontological equality principle plays a decisive role in Floridi's IE, since it sets the construction of the notion of information within an ontological perspective that provides us with a philosophical basis for an ethical theory At first glance, this principle seems to contain a provocatory statement, since it says that *all* entities deserve a minimal level of moral respect, for the very simple fact that all entities are entities (*informational objects*). As already seen in Chaps. 2 and 3, this principle has been subject to several criticisms: (1) not all entities deserve to be respected; (2) entities are not to be respected *qua* entities but for other, different reasons; (3) the moral equation between entities is disturbing and untenable; (4) the ontological equality principle is likely to be transformed into an indiscriminate protection of the *status quo*; (5) the attribution of moral value to all entities violates the dictate of Moore's law, which separates the sphere of Being from that of value (Moore 2004).

We will not deal here with all these forms of criticism analytically. Floridi has already done so effectively several times (Floridi 2008b, 2013), always within the limits of the issue at stake, that is, against the backdrop of his information macroethical approach. We would therefore like at present to focus our attention on some implicit but fundamental philosophical premises implied in such critiques. This attitude can lead us, at the end of the present examination, to bring to light a philosophical dimension, which is implicit in Floridi's IE but has been too often been overlooked or underestimated by other scholars: namely, Floridi's ontological pluralism, which serves as a general and unified reply to all the forms of criticism levelled at Floridi's ontological approach to ethical issues.

In this perspective, we would like to start, nonetheless, from Floridi's important reply to the accusation that naturalistic fallacy is implied in the ontological equality principle. For the reason mentioned above, we make reference to the ontological equality principle, which has a founding role in IE, even if the same accusation has often been directed at Floridi's ethical ontocentrism as such. We turn to Floridi's reply (Floridi 2008b, 202) to Hongladarom (2008), which seems to us of great importance:

> As Hongladarom remarks, an ontocentric approach is often threatened with the naturalistic fallacy. This presupposes a value-empty or value-neutral reality, from which then not a single drop of morality could be squeezed, on pain of contradiction. The 'no ought from is' principle, with its Humean roots, is perfectly fine. If Being (or reality or nature or indeed the infosphere) is interpreted as being entirely and absolutely devoid of any moral value [...], then any moral value, any goodness, and the corresponding ethical orientation that we long for, must come from elsewhere. A drained and dry container cannot fill itself. But if the ontic source, from which we seek to draw some moral guidance, is not empty, if, following Plato and Spinoza for example, we acknowledge that Being and Goodness are intrinsically intertwined well before any metaphysical or ethical discourse attempts to rescind them, then trying to extract values and the corresponding moral lessons from Being becomes a very natural process. One may try to find guidance and inspiration in the life of the universe without committing any logical fallacy.

Floridi's reply is very clear in its main tenet: Being and Goodness are intertwined and hence any moral value does not come from elsewhere. Moral value or Goodness is intertwined with Being as an intrinsic or first-order property. This sort of intertwinement is, in our view, the first part of a larger and more comprehensive reply. In fact, a full reply has to include an interpretation of Being and Goodness. Floridi provides us with such an interpretation by frequently emphasizing that Being and Goodness are to be interpreted, in his theory, in informational terms (recall that this is not a proposition on some *noumenal* nature of Being, which is beyond scope; infosphere is more simply Being considered informationally, i.e., an informational interpretation of Being). If we lose sight of this fact, we end up projecting onto Floridi's ethics and philosophy of information the shadows of other accounts of Being and Goodness (and of their possible intertwinement). As Floridi clearly formulates it (2008b, 201): "'Esse est information', where here information is not a semantic but an ontological concept (imagine a structural pattern)".

In this perspective (i.e., from the informational standpoint), we would like to point out a crucial point that concerns the question of ontological pluralism conceived in informational terms. More explicitly: the philosophical problem is not just, as many seem to believe, whether or not Being is in itself justified, i.e., whether Being possesses an intrinsic value as a result of the equation between Being and Good. Rather, the problem is whether or not IE endorses a *pluralistic* conception of Being and Good. It appears quite clear to us, although surprising, that many scholars overlook or underestimate Floridi's theoretical and ethical choice for pluralism or even treat such a choice as a separate chapter of his reflection that provides no theoretical or ethical basis or explanation for his treatment of the ontological equality principle.

In fact, criticism of the ontological equality principle always contains an implicit premise that is never fully brought to light and discussed. Scholars treat and understand the nature of Being (of the Infosphere) as if the variety of informational objects (i.e., the richness of the Infosphere or the pluralism of Being) and the proliferation of reality in different objects and levels of abstractions were only a second-order property: that is to say, an added quality that supervenes at a later time, as if from the outside, to give a further qualification of Being or of the Infosphere. This is in our view the crucial point of Floridi's conception of the ontological equality principle as well as of scholars' criticism of the principle: namely, the way the variety of informational objects, the multiplicity of the informational reality, is treated.

We do think – as we will try hereafter to demonstrate– that Floridi believes that the variety of informational objects, i.e., the multiplicity of the informational reality, is not a degradation of (the unity of) Being (as for a longstanding tradition that goes back at least to Plotinus), but on the contrary represents its full expression and exaltation. The expression 'Being is' translates in Floridi's terms into the expression 'the Infosphere is rich', where richness is not a system or a sum of variables of the Infosphere, but its primary property. This does not prevent, obviously, the Infosphere from being *more or less* rich, in the same sense in which Floridi notices, in line with Cartesio, that something, be it more or less extended, is still a *res extensa*. The richness of the infosphere is not a matter of degree, but the proper ontological definition of the informational environment.

We believe that many critics have not adequately grasped the question of pluralism because they have overlooked the intrinsic value of information and the nature of the informational objects qua *informational* objects. Many scholars have mainly concerned themselves with the question of the intrinsic value of informational objects considered merely as entities (hence criticism of the ontological equality principle) and have lost sight of the fact that intrinsic value, however it may be defined, should concern an intrinsic quality of information and of all entities viewed as *informational* objects. This is the origin of many misunderstandings concerning Floridi's information ethics.

6.4 Information and Informativeness

In order to grasp Floridi's line of reasoning, we should not approach information ethics as a fragmentary theory made of several self-contained propositions. In fact, Floridi's theoretical construction always seeks to be rigorous and systematic. To be rigorous, Floridi endorses an analytical approach that requires him to precisely define all the theoretical tools he deploys (i.e., ideas, concepts, argumentations, premises), in order to construct his own speculative system. We can disagree, of course, with Floridi's main theoretical tenets and ideas, but it is difficult to claim not to understand them. As already stated, the problem with Floridi's information ethics is not so much a question of possible misunderstandings. Rather, it is more often a problem of either overestimation or underestimation as to his main standpoints. To be systematic, Floridi knows he needs to endorse a strong *philosophical premise* that could provide a rational basis for his theory and its own developments. We believe this basis resides in the notion of information, as conceived in its philosophical nature and in its correlated attitude to inform, that is, in its informativeness (i.e. the value itself of information). For this reason, we have to concentrate our attention on a philosophical aspect of the concept of information that appears to us of a critical importance: this is the conceptual statute of the *data* that necessarily makes up information. Let us start by citing Floridi (2010, 22):

> The fact is that a genuine, complete erasure of all data can be achieved only by the elimination of all possible differences. This clarifies why a datum is ultimately reducible to a *lack of uniformity*. Donald MacCrimmon MacKay highlighted this important point when he wrote that 'information is a distinction that makes a difference'. He was followed by Gregory Bateson, whose slogan is better known, although less accurate: 'In fact, what we mean by information - the elementary unit of information - is a difference which makes a difference'. More formally, according to the *diaphoric interpretation* (*diaphora* is the Greek word for 'difference'), the general definition of a datum is:
>
> Dd) datum $=_{\text{def.}}$ *x* being distinct from *y*, where *x* and *y* are two uninterpreted variables and the relation of 'being distinct', as well as the domain, are left open to further interpretation.

This is an extremely crucial point. According to Floridi (2010, 22–23), this *lack of uniformity* that characterizes and defines data can be applied in three main ways: (1) in the real word; (2) between (the perception of) at least two physical states of a system or signals; (3) between two symbols. Floridi (2010, 23) clarifies that the data in (1) "may be either identical with, or what makes possible *signals* in (2), and signals in (2) are what make possible coding of *symbols* in (3)". Many other clarifications should and could be introduced here to fully understand the relation between the occurrence of syntactically well-formed data and the coding of symbols, or to grasp the distinction between data and environmental information, but this is not the most important point in the present context. What we would like to remark and reflect upon is the philosophical vocabulary that is used to account for the meaning of information intended as a set of data. This vocabulary rotates around three terms: *lack*, *difference* and *relation*. We have to focus our attention on those terms, since their interplay is meant to trace the conceptual perimeter of a pluralistic conception of information.

6.5 Lack, Difference and Relation

6.5.1 Lack

First of all, the crucial idea of a lack of uniformity does not imply any connotation of lack as a negative term, that is, as a degradation of being, like a vacuum or incompleteness. This lack is neither the lack of an entity (the *ontic lack* that is manifested by the destruction or the mere absence of an entity: e.g., when we look for something we have lost or we dig and we find nothing: no entity) nor the lack of being (the *ontological lack* that is manifested, in Heideggerian terms (Heidegger 1996), by the concealing of truth: the fact that such concealment that does not let an entity *be* what it is). The lack of uniformity is not a lack of entity, since data need not necessarily have a material nature ("Although there can be no information without data, data might not require a material implementation", Floridi 2010, 61); nor it is a lack of being, in the above-mentioned sense, since the lack of uniformity (the "fractures in the continuum", Floridi 2010, 61) lets data *be* what they are, that is, it lets data be *informative*. However paradoxical it may appear, this lack of uniformity enriches the world instead of impoverishing it: "The universe is fundamentally composed of data, understood as *dedomena*, patterns or fields of *difference*, instead of matter or energy, with material objects as a complex secondary manifestation" (Floridi 2010, 62). This brings us back to the second term of interest, that is, difference.

6.5.2 Difference

It is impossible to recall here all of the philosophical interpretations and implications of the concept of difference from modern to post-modern philosophy. Nonetheless, it bears noting the crucial role played by the concept of difference in contemporary philosophy in paving the way toward any pluralistic ethical or epistemological theory today. That is why the concept of difference makes its own appearance here: it is a first-order property of data (ontological lack of uniformity) that might be endorsed by material objects (ontic lack of uniformity), which rests a complex secondary manifestation. In other words, contrary to the view taken by many scholars who conceive difference as the secondary manifestation of the variety of material objects (and therefore by analogy, although mistaken, of informational objects), difference primarily concerns the ontological lack of uniformity, namely, the reason why data are what they are. This can only mean that data are informative, because they are patterns or fields of differences. In this perspective, difference is viewed as the way the richness of being expresses itself in informational terms. Data are informative because they are patterns or fields of differences. From another standpoint, this amounts to saying that they are informative since they enrich the world with something different or, in other words, they add something different to the world, i.e., something *new*. This newness is not necessarily an ontic newness: that is, patterns or fields of differences do not necessarily always entail the creation or the implementation of new material objects. This newness is relational: it is brought about by the formation of new relations of distinctness between variables. This leads us to consider the third concept, that of relation.

6.5.3 Relation

Information always requires data and, therefore, new relations of distinctness between variables. When destroying information (or more precisely, informational objects), we are not just destroying an object in its informational status. We are depriving the universe of relations between variables, which are implemented in informational objects. The informational environment is also made of the web and threads of those relations, whose entanglement constitutes much of the richness of being in its pluralistic dimension. Pluralism grows out of an increasing number of differences (i.e., different informational objects, different points of view or levels of abstraction, as Floridi words it) as well as of new relations between variables. This brings about a fundamental consequence from a practical (i.e. moral, political and legal) standpoint. When destroying informational objects, not only are we erasing differences, but we are also tearing the threads of those relations, and this results in stratified impoverishment of the infosphere as a whole and of pluralism. In fact, pluralism is not only concerned with the elimination of the secondary manifestations of the variety of informational objects (which are implemented in material objects), but it is more crucially embedded in the ontological roots of the infosphere.

6.5.4 The Value of Information

Within this perspective, the ontological equality principle is not to be regarded as a mere, indiscriminate protection of everything that exists, or a sort of blind levelling out that equalizes every instance of life and the world. It should rather be understood as an affirmation of a form of ontological pluralism that conceives the informational universe of objects as a sum of differences and relations. This interpretation is backed by the idea itself of informativeness, which expresses the value of information and is based on the above-mentioned concept of *newness*. Before turning our attention to the notion of ontological pluralism, something should be said with regard to this idea of informativeness. We will not make direct reference here to Floridi's treatment of the idea (Floridi 2010, 47–49), but to an insightful comment by Jannis Kallinikos (2006, 53–54) that may help illustrate this point:

> In order to be informative, information must be able to add a distinction and confer something new on what is already known. In this respect, the value of information, what may be called its informativeness, is indeed a function of the kind of 'news' it is capable of conveying, and 'news' differs substantially with respect to what it adds to that which is already known. As a rule, the value of 'news' is traceable to its unique (contingency) and novel (time) character.

We would like to adapt Kallinikos' epistemological assertion and put it in ontological terms, which we believe do not alter the overall meaning of his statement: "information add a distinction (you may read as well, 'concrete and relational points of lack of uniformity', in Floridi's terms, 2010, 63) and confers something new on *what is already*. In this respect, the value of information, what may be called its informativeness, is indeed a function of the kind of 'news' it is capable of conveying, and 'news' differs substantially with respect to what it adds to *that which is already*. As a rule, the value of 'news' is traceable to its unique (contingency) and novel (time) character".

Kallinikos stresses, thus, that information not only involves a distinction but also an addition that confers something new on what is already (known). What is already (known) grows out of a multiplicity of information. The value of information, its informativeness, is for that reason inconsistent with the representation of the infosphere as an environment where everything should be protected and conserved, on the basis of the ontological equality principle, *as it is*. According to our interpretation, everything deserves a minimal level of respect and protection in the infosphere, for the very simple reason that it is what it is in informational terms, that is to say, since it brings about a distinction that confers something new on what is already (known). This does not amount to providing a further, additional reason, in order to acknowledge a minimal level of respect towards informational objects, since this reason is already ontologically rooted in what structural entities are as informational objects, that is, as "cohering clusters of data, understood as concrete, relational points of lack of uniformity". Does the value of information, i.e., a distinction that confers something new, always deserve a minimal level of respect and protection? It is exactly in the terms laid down by such an interrogative that we can understand why Floridi's ontological equality principle must therefore be interpreted as a form of ontological pluralism.

6.6 Ontological Pluralism

Floridi (2008a) has always stressed that the impoverishment of the infosphere depends on the destruction of informational objects and not of information as such. This statement has to be correctly understood: it means that the impoverishment of the infosphere is tragically real and does not leave the world as it finds it. However, it does not conceive the destruction of informational objects as with any other ontic destruction: indeed, it considers such destruction from an ontological point of view as the destruction of objects *qua* informational objects, namely, in what way they are informational. It is precisely the value of information that is destructed, that is to say, the relational points of lack of uniformity: a sum of differences.

Thanks to the differences that each informational object is meant to introduce into the infosphere, Being is not, in Floridi's view, a catalogue of objects that strive to protect and conserve themselves (an indiscriminate and conservative attitude towards the *status quo*). On the contrary, Being grows out of the flourishing of differences that allow informational objects to be what they are, namely, to be recognized for their own identity, that is to say, to be distinguished from each other. What many scholars fail to acknowledge is that Floridi's ontology, which IE is based on, is not only *hospitable* (namely, it attempts to widen the class of entities that deserve a minimal level of respect) but it is, first and foremost, *pluralistic* (namely, it is aimed to broaden the set of differences that develop and enrich the infosphere from both an epistemological and an ecological standpoint).

This form of pluralism is ontological, because it does not concern the differences that cause entities to vary according to (the multiple set of) second-order qualities that are mere qualifications of the same entity (the same 'seat' can be white or black, cheap or expensive, etc.). It concerns the differences that make entities be what they are and to differ from a set of related objects: there is no ontological pluralism, i.e., the richness of Being, without a *principium individuationis*, which is conceived, here, in informational terms. According to the IE, the multiplicity of ontological pluralism (the Spinozian multitude) is made up of a sum of differences *and* a sum of relations ("relational points of lack of uniformity"). The proliferation of LoAs is ultimately based in those sets of differences and relations that enable the same entities to be distinguished among different relations (of cohering clusters of data). This point is important, since it shows us that the multiplicity of informational objects and, correspondingly, of LoAs is not entrenched in any form of relativism. On the contrary, it is the wealth of the informational status of the object (a sum of differences and a sum of relations) that governs the multiplicity of representations of the object itself.

Floridi's endorsement of a pluralistic approach (both to epistemology and ethics) is not a matter of a subjective preference (for pluralism), but is deeply rooted in his ontological equality principle, that is, in the correlation between the proliferation of points of view (i.e., of LoAs or systems of observables) and the proliferation of reality (i.e., of informational objects). This correlation – and this point is crucial – is made, *simultaneously*, of a sum of differences (points of lack of uniformity) and of a sum of relations (relational, cohering clusters of data). It is not an added, supervening property, but an intrinsic quality of the infosphere, that is, of conceiving and treating the cosmos as an informational environment. Thanks to this correlation, Floridi's endorsement of pluralism is neither simply theoretical (namely, there are many irreducible and incomparable points of view or explanations, but their multiplicity is never understandable as a property of the infosphere) nor simply naturalistic (namely, there are many irreducible and incomparable objects, but their multiplicity is never understandable as a quality of the informational environment).

Floridi's endorsement of pluralism is ontological, since it based on the correlation between theoretical and naturalistic pluralism, which in turn is deeply rooted in the informativeness of each informational object. In other words, this correlation is based on an intrinsic property that belongs both to the theoretical and the naturalistic conception of the informational environment: this first-order property is the informativeness, the value of the ecological information, its intrinsic capability of conferring something new or different to the world, by generating a multiplicity of relations. Informationally interpreted, Being is not at all something monolithic and full of uniformity. On the contrary, it grows out of a sum of differences that make differences, to employ Bateson's terms. The informational viewpoint is important for a different, pluralistic conception of Being. As we have pointed out, 'Being is' means informationally 'Being is rich'. This last statement means that Being develops and grows out of a sum of differences and of relations. Being possesses its own history, which, however, is not to be necessarily viewed as a form of *becoming*, that is, a constant passage from being to non-being. The history of Being is the history of ontological enrichment. Being, interpreted informationally, is made of its own richness. This implies a different conception of history itself.

In the Western modern tradition, we are acquainted with a conception of history conceived in terms of a true record of memory (namely, a transcription or conservation of the past events) more than in terms of a progressive enrichment of Being, as in some other traditions. However, history should mainly be conceived as *magistra vitae*, namely, as a set of teachings that come from the richness of experience. This form of richness – a difference that makes difference: Bateson's definition of information seems to us a perfect description of the essence of history – is made possible precisely by the ontological pluralism of information. There would be no pluralistic evidence and account of what has been in the past (*res gestae*), without strong, informational protection of all differences that make difference, that is, of all cohering clusters of data, understood as concrete, relational points of lack of uniformity. This brings us back to our main point: the protection of what exists is just the necessary starting point for an ethical approach. Ethics is never concerned with the mere, indiscriminate protection of the *status quo*, but with our care and responsibility towards all that is and may be, or in informational terms, towards what is rich, because it is different and new.

For all of these reasons, the ontological equality principle needs to be interpreted, on the basis of a correct interpretation of informativeness, i.e., of the value of information, as a firm, patent defence of an ontological pluralism, according to which Being must not be represented as a static and self-referential reality. Being is instead synonymous with an informationally interpreted reality that possesses its own dynamic and pluralistic history. It is precisely the informational richness of Being that allows history to be *magistra vitae*. We would therefore like to devote the last section of this chapter to an historical example that tells us more than it originally intended and thus may serve as a response to criticism of Floridi's principle of ontological equality.

6.7 Conclusions: The 'Nazi Example'

To sum up the issues dealt with in the present chapter, one particular episode mentioned by Floridi seems particularly apt: "I still recall one conference in the nineties when a famous computer ethicist compared me to a sort of Nazi, who wished to reduce humans to numbers, pointing out that the Nazis used to tattoo six-digit identity tags on the left arms of the prisoners in their Lager" Floridi (2008b, 191). We do not wish to discuss here the content of the accusation that Floridi had been charged with; he has already replied to it. What catches our attention is that so many people refer to Nazi atrocities when they want to make a morally loaded, strong and irrefutable accusation. We call this the *Nazi example*, meaning an example that is both shocking and irrefutable. And the reason that it is so striking and so often cited lies in the monstrous and horrifying nature of the evil it refers to and that nobody wants to be associated with. Yet what is it that makes it such a self-evident example of evil, that can neither be rebutted nor called into question? In other words, what makes it not just to be a prime example of evil but, first and foremost, an *indisputable* example of evil? It is not that the Nazi atrocities were so blatantly evil (that would be recursive). The reason is actually much more subtle than that and derives from the fact that the simple act of *negating the blatant evil of* the Nazi atrocities (the so-called *Negationist thesis*) has in itself become blatantly evil. This view is clearly justified, of course, but we wonder how an historical event comes to be considered blatantly evil not just for what took place, but also insofar as it is denied by the historiography.

We believe that this happens when everybody (or at least a large number of people) endorses the idea that nobody should remove, cancel or conceal whatever historical trace is left of the Nazi period and evil scheme, since the mere fact of *negating* these traces, i.e., of having these traces erased, is in itself judged to be unashamedly evil. In other words, this happens if and when anybody recognizes that the traces of the most ominous and monstrous evil (such as the Nazi atrocities) must not be negated or erased in their informational status, since they bear crucial witness to such tremendous evil. The indelible mark, the six-digit inmate identification numbers tattooed on the skin of Jewish prisoners (information about reality that becomes information as reality, to employ Floridi's information taxonomy to be discussed in the last chapter of the book), is part of that evil; as such, it needs to be morally condemned as a trace of that evil, in being a "new name", a "gratuitous violence" and "pure offence" (Levi 1989, 119).

Nevertheless, it has to be preserved because of its informational status, which makes it immoral to deny it or having it erased. In the same sense, Floridi's information ethics is not concerned with reducing human beings to mere numbers or information, but with preserving the informational status of even that "indelible mark upon the body which uniformly signified difference" (Gilman 1991, 219), of that tragic indelible mark that bears witness of such *difference*, as long as prisoners and historians preserved it from erasure (from entropy, to employ Floridi's terms). Therefore, that indelible mark of evil also proves to have a moral value and significance as an *informational object* (and only as such). We believe that preserving an informational object does not mean protecting an object *per se*, which could be in addition described in informational terms. On the contrary – as the Nazi example demonstrates so well – it means preserving the informational status of an object, i.e. that which constitutes a difference, a lack of uniformity. Here, that difference is what makes the truthfulness of the historical tale possible, relevant and instructive: the historical tale refers to *a difference that makes a difference*, which can no longer be neglected, negated and erased. Evil cannot stand differences and loves uniformity.

It would therefore be blatantly evil to negate the informational status of what has been blatantly evil. It is thanks to an informational attitude if we want to preserve even the trace of what leads us to the memory of evil. Since we attach a moral value to that informational attitude, it is extremely important to us that no informational objects be erased. Thanks to the ontological pluralism (the protection of differences) endorsed by the ontological equality principle of information ethics, an informational object, even one that is an "indelible mark" of evil, plays a crucial role in making us recognize why that instance of evil is an irrefutable example of blatant evil. This is what Floridi's IE signifies, and what Primo Levi best acknowledged, *avant la lettre*, in his inspired words recalling how much this informational attitude is a matter of personal responsibility:

> At a distance of forty years, my tattoo has become a part of my body. I don't glory in it, but I am not ashamed of it either; I do not display and do not hide it. I show it unwillingly to those who ask out of pure curiosity; readily and with anger to those who say they are

incredulous. Often young people ask me why I do not have it erased, and this surprises me: why should I? There are not many of us in the world to bear this witness (Levi 1989, 119–120).

To erase such a tattoo? That would unquestionably be evil, as evil as the force that impressed it on his arm.

References

Benkler, Y. (2006). *The wealth of networks: How social production transforms markets and freedom*. New Haven: Yale University Press.

Castells, M. 1996. *The Rise of the Network Society, The Information Age: Economy, Society and Culture*. Vol. I. Cambridge, MA/Oxford: Blackwell.

———. 1997. *The Power of Identity, The Information Age: Economy, Society and Culture*. Vol. II. Cambridge, MA/Oxford: Blackwell.

———. 1998. *End of Millennium, The Information Age: Economy, Society and Culture*. Vol. III. Cambridge, MA/Oxford: Blackwell.

Durante, M. 2009. Re-designing the Role of Law in the Information Society: Mediating between the Real and the Virtual. In *Law and Technology: Looking into the Future*, ed. M. Fernandez-Barrera, N. Gomes de Andrade, P. de Filippi, M. Viola de Azevedo Cunha, G. Sartor, and P. Casanovas, 31–50. Florence: European Press Academic Publishing.

Floridi, L. 1999. Information Ethics: On the Philosophical Foundation of Computer Ethics. *Ethics and Information Technology* 1: 37–56.

———. 2003. On the Intrinsic Value of Information Objects and the Infosphere. *Ethics and Information Technology* 4 (4): 287–304.

———. 2006. Information Technology and the Tragedy of the Good Will. *Ethics and Information Technology* 8 (4): 253–262.

———. 2008a. Information Ethics, Its Nature and Scope. In *Moral Philosophy and Information Technology*, ed. J. van den Hoven and J. Weckert, 40–65. Cambridge: Cambridge University Press.

———. 2008b. The Method of Levels of Abstraction. *Minds and Machines* 18 (3): 303–329.

———. 2010. *Information. A Very Short Introduction*. Oxford: Oxford University Press.

———. 2013. *Information Ethics*. Oxford: Oxford University Press.

Gilman, S. 1991. *The Jew's Body*. New York: Routledge.

Heidegger, M. 1996. *Being and Time* [1927]. Trans. J. Stambaugh. New York: SUNY.

Hongladarom, S. 2008. Floridi and Spinoza on Global Information Ethics. In Ess, C. (ed.). Luciano Floridi's Philosophy of Information and Information Ethics: Critical Reflections and the State of the Art. *Ethics and Information Technology*, 10(2–3), 175–187.

Kallinikos, J. 2006. *The Consequences of Information*. In *Institutional Implications of Technological Change*. Cheltenham/Northampton, MA: Edward Elgar.

Levi, P. 1989. *The Drowned and the Saved* [1986]. Trans. R. Rosenthal. New York: Vintage Books.

Moore, G.E. 2004. *Principia Ethica [1903]*. Cambridge: Cambridge University Press.

The Ontological Interpretation of Informational Privacy

7

Abstract

In the present chapter, Luciano Floridi's innovative and insightful approach to privacy is examined with regard to the central role played by privacy in defining personal identity in the information age. Today's notion of privacy relates not only to protection of our intimate personal space from unwanted or unauthorized intrusion or interference, but also – and above all – it has to do with the construction of identity. Floridi's approach proceeds from the radical claim that we are our information. If this is so, then it follows that every instance of the use of or the reliance on such information is implicated in (and is to be evaluated and judged in relation to) the creation of our personal identity. It is from this stance that Floridi conducts a detailed and thought-provoking inquiry into a notion of privacy construed in informational terms, congruent with the progressive digitization of personal identity in the information society. His reflections help us better understand how personal data can be accessed, inferred and aggregated, and thereby manipulated, disposed of and put at risk. They also alert us to the importance of maintaining an ontological balance between the protection of privacy and the benefits we stand to gain from compiling and sharing informational resources.

7.1 Introduction

This chapter follows on directly from the last one, which presented an information-based interpretation of the concept of personal identity. We saw that personal identity is no longer conceived strictly in terms of methodological individualism, according to which each individual is "an atom" of society that remains separate from the others and from the surrounding environment. Instead, personal identity is now defined and constituted in relation to others and to the environment of interaction, thereby revisiting and expanding Heidegger's notion of *Mit-Dasein* (for an

M. Durante, *Ethics, Law and the Politics of Information*, The International Library of Ethics, Law and Technology 18, DOI 10.1007/978-94-024-1150-8_7

updated definition of *being-with-and-within*, see Chap. 5, first part). Relatedness is thus seen as an ontological attribute of being in the world. In this perspective, it is no longer possible to account for one's relationship with others without also accounting for one's relationship with the environment. The multiplicity of interactions that individuals engage in with others and with the environment are also co-constitutive of each other, in the sense that the relationships individuals have with others affect the relationships they have with the environment, and vice versa. This remark will be particularly salient in the course of this chapter, in which the informational approach to privacy will show precisely how the design of the environment in terms of conditions that favor or hinder the flow of information is likely to affect our relationships with others and to contribute to the construction of our personal identity.

In fact, if we grant that personal identity today is defined and constituted in informational terms (i.e., as the sum of the information that concerns us), then anything that can influence the design of the environment and our relational life from an informational standpoint can also affect, either positively or negatively (and therefore in morally qualifiable terms), the constitution of our personal identity (Floridi 2013, 228–258). Awareness of the role of information in the construction of identity is pertinent not only to philosophy (from a theoretical or moral point of view), but also to law and, more specifically, to the fabric of legally relevant intersubjective relationships. Law scholars are required to rethink a number of traditional legal notions, such as privacy, and to update them in informational terms. On the one hand, this is anything but new, since the law evolves along with society, or rather, in this case, the law evolves along with the power of technology to shape conditions that impair or undermine the ability of norms to protect the rights of individuals. In this perspective, which offers a substantially continuous representation of society and law, the law is adapted to the evolution of society (and is already part of its evolution) by modifying the variety and intensity of legal responses to the growing number of challenges raised by the technological evolution. On the other hand, however, it represents a significant novelty, since the evolution of the law depends on a renewed understanding of society or, more precisely, on a renewed and deeper understanding of how the technological evolution involves qualitative changes that affect the nature of intersubjective relationships and, thus, the nature itself of the rights that the law is intended to ensure and protect. In other words, Floridi's informational approach raises an extremely important point (and a challenge) for any legal analysis that intends to be in accordance with its own times. The re-ontologization of the world brought about by ICT is not limited to situations and tools that hinder or prevent legal norms from protecting the rights of individuals, thereby replacing legal normativity with technological normativity; it rather changes the nature of the protected legal interests. It is in this direction that the analysis must move. It is not so much a question of what new answers the law has to envisage in response to the challenges raised by the incessant evolution of technology. More importantly, it is a question of how these developments change the nature of the legally relevant interests that the law intends to continue to secure and protect, ranging from issues of personal identity, privacy and autonomy to the right to tell one's own story and the self-determination of personal data and personal memory. In other words, it is a question of how these developments impact on the sphere of subjective situations variously attributed to the notion of privacy.

Given these circumstances, we can also understand why privacy has assumed such a central role in our information society. There are three main reasons for the centrality of privacy, each of which has to do with the basic assumptions of any information society.

First, information societies are characterized by access to information. Privacy is viewed as the dialectical counterpart of the (new) surveillance society, or, to put it more mildly, as the countermeasure that tempers the rigidity of the allegedly widespread ethic of absolute transparency. In the information society, where the ability to access information is so pervasive and where free and full access to data is seen as a priority, the right to privacy is a bulwark that is meant to safeguard that area of opacity, secrecy and confidentiality on which some basic rights and personal freedoms are based. This first reason for the centrality of privacy is rooted in a rather traditional view that sees privacy as a garrison for shielding the individual's sphere of action. The second reason is that the information society is characterized by the sharing of information. Privacy is thus of crucial importance because, through the right to privacy, we articulate the artificial (i.e., constructed) distinction between what is public and what is private, by delimiting, on the one hand, the sphere of sharing and, on the other, the sphere of life over which we have exclusive control. The ethics of sharing, powered by the pervasiveness of ICTs, has gradually eroded our ability to maintain exclusive control over our personal data and information. Within this context, the protection of privacy aims to ensure that distinctions can be drawn between what is sharable and what should be prevented from being shared. Privacy thus has not only a defensive (as in non-intrusion) or a protective stance (as in non-interference), but also a proactive stance, meaning that we can control our personal data or exclude others from the sphere of our own lives. The third reason for the centrality of privacy is that the information society is characterized by the diffusion of information. This point is endorsed by the principle of information ethics that emphasizes that wealth of information constitutes the well-being of the infosphere. If we accept this to be true, then the creation of informational objects contributes to the well-being of the infosphere and should be encouraged (as stated in Floridi's fourth law of the infosphere). However, the ethics of information is fully aware that the value of information, like any other good, increases with its scarcity. From this, it also follows that the scarcer the information, the more it deserves to be protected. Paucity of information is not merely a quantitative but – first and foremost – a qualitative matter. This point is emphasized in the principles of information ethics, as already noted when we stated that the re-ontologization of reality is mostly qualitative (even before quantitative). Hence, privacy provides a means of protecting our personal information, which is considered scarce (and thus qualitatively valuable), since it forms our personal identity. Within an informational perspective, privacy is central not only for its protective or proactive attitude (because it allows us to defend ourselves from intrusion or interference, or because it allows us to possess or have control over the information) but also and above all for its ethical and axiological dimension, because, through it, individuals are called upon to select the information that is most relevant and valuable to the very integrity of their person (the information that makes a difference), and it is exactly this meaningful selection (Durante 2011b) that contributes to the construction of their personality. Let us now take a closer look at what constitutes the ontological interpretation of informational privacy.

7.2 Informational Privacy and Ontological Friction

Floridi's treatment of the concept of privacy[1] is based on some preliminary methodological remarks and assumptions. Firstly, Floridi recognizes that there are different concepts of privacy and that it is not possible to deal exhaustively with each of them. He therefore identifies four main concepts of privacy (Floridi 2013, 229–230): (1) physical privacy, referring to the freedom of individuals from sensory interference or intrusion, achieved thanks to the restriction on others' ability to have bodily interactions with them; (2) mental privacy, referring to the freedom of individuals from psychological interference or intrusion, achieved thanks to the restriction on others' ability to have access to their cognitive sphere and to manipulate their mental states; (3) decisional privacy, referring to the freedom of individuals from procedural interference or intrusion, achieved thanks to exclusion of others from their sphere of decision; and (4) informational privacy, referring to the freedom of individuals from epistemic interference or intrusion, achieved thanks to a restriction on facts about their sphere of life that must remain unknown or unknowable.

Floridi is primarily interested in the concept of informational privacy, but it is important to note how the concept of privacy has progressively expanded its scope, covering a plurality of spheres of interest of individuals that not only includes their ability to make decisions and to act, but extends to factors affecting those capacities, such as the ability to represent the world and to select information that is relevant to the individuals' life. In addition, by placing the emphasis on the individual's freedom and capacity right from the start, Floridi makes it clear that he opts for a conception of privacy no longer conceived of as purely protective or reactive, but as active and constructive. This means that the rhetoric of the death of privacy mainly refers to a fairly traditional conception of privacy, understood as a protective or reactive stance concerning the *status quo* of a person, as opposed to a more modern conception of privacy, understood as the ability to participate actively in the development and construction of our own identity. This second conception, absolutely central to the notion of informational privacy, takes into account not only what a person *is* (in a given place and time), but, first and foremost, what this person *seeks to be*, in a constitutive tension between present and future, here and elsewhere, the real and the virtual, us and others. The meaning and the importance of informational privacy reside entirely in the fact that the progressive formation of the person is an

[1] For analysis and remarks on Floridi's conception of privacy see Tavani 2008; Burk 2008. On the related issue of informational privacy see also Martin 2012; Pagallo 2008; Matheson 2007; Tavani 2007.

expression of this plurality of constitutive tensions, so if there is anything that privacy still intends to protect and secure, it is precisely that certain degree of homeostasis (that is, exchange and balance) between the poles in tension.

Secondly, Floridi warns us, as mentioned in the previous paragraph, against focusing our analysis of privacy on the most visible but, at the same time, most indirect and secondary aspects of the quantitative dimension of data. While the increase in the capacity and speed in the processing and sharing of data has clearly exacerbated privacy-related issues, this should not blind us to the deeper implications of the changes taking place that concern, as mentioned, the conformation of reality and the nature of the legal interests protected. It is only by paying attention to these consequences that one can understand why so many people (notably young digital natives) consistently (and sometimes naively) say in a single breath that they are *not particularly attentive to privacy but very interested in the representation of their own person, for example, through social networks.* It should be understood, now, that a trusting attitude, thanks to which we expose our information to the interpretation of others (which implies the risk of decontextualization, manipulation, recombination or aggregation of data) is, nowadays, part of the conceptual area of privacy (Durante 2011c).

Thirdly, Floridi observes that the evolution of ICT does not necessarily imply a negative impact on informational privacy, but may also result in its reinforcement. This can be seen in many areas, such as the ability to be anonymous, information security policy, encryption techniques, the ability to manage information remotely, and the inherent volatility, caducity and revocability of much digital data. From this we realize that the process of adaptation to the informational environment in which we increasingly interact with one another is complex but open, and that the reasons for understanding its characteristics and structure are not only theoretical but eminently practical. On the basis of these preliminary remarks and methodological premises, we can now focus on the ontological approach to informational privacy.

Floridi moves from the simple observation that, given a certain amount of available information, the greater the informational gap between two agents (i.e., the less information one has about the other), the more private are their lives. This generates a series of consequences easily deducible from this premise. In the first place, it is possible to state that "the informational gap is a function of the degree of *accessibility* of personal data" (Floridi 2013, 231.) This degree of accessibility is "an epistemic factor that depends on the ontological features of the infosphere (Floridi 2013, 231). This means that the degree of accessibility is conditioned in three different ways: (1) in *subjective* terms, with regards to the nature of agents (e.g., the degree of propensity of a person to talk about herself), (2) in *objective* terms, with reference to the nature of the environment in which agents are found to interact (e.g., the thickness of the walls in a house), and 3) in *procedural* terms, with reference to the typology of interactions implementable through the communicative channels adopted by agents in the informational environment (e.g., the use of a particular social network).The ontological features of the infosphere (*subjective, objective and procedural*) determine a specific level of "*ontological friction,* which in turn determines the flow of information within a system" (Floridi 2013, 232).

Ontological friction thus refers to "the forces that oppose the information flow within (a region of) the infosphere, and hence (as a coefficient) to the amount of work and effort required for some kind of agent to obtain, filter and/or block information (also, but not only) about other agents in a given environment, e.g. by establishing and maintaining channels of communication and by overcoming obstacles in the flow of information such as distance, noise, lack of resources (especially time, memory space and processing capacities), amount and complexity of the data to be processed, and so forth" (Floridi 2013, 232). This logical chain culminates in the formulation of a sort of equation that expresses the complex relationship between ICTs and informational privacy in the following terms:

> Given some amount of personal information available in (a region of) the infosphere *I*, the lower the ontological friction in *I*, the higher the accessibility of personal information about the agents embedded in *I*, the smaller the informational gap among them, and the lower the level of informational privacy implementable about each of them. Put simply, *informational privacy is a function of the ontological friction in the infosphere.* (Floridi 2013, 232).

Informational privacy is therefore a function of all the ontological features of the infosphere that determine the degree of ontological friction within a system. This approach has the advantage of displaying both a *quantitative* (with regards to the amount of information available, the amount of personal information accessible and, accordingly, the amount of existing informational privacy) and a *qualitative* assessment of the informational privacy (with regards to the specific nature of agents, environment and interactions in the environment). In this perspective, Floridi's main tenet becomes apparent: we are in the midst of an evolution of ICTs, namely, a transition from old to new ICTs that alters the impact of ICTs over the informational environment and, therefore, over the production of the ontological friction in the infosphere. Such a change necessarily affects informational privacy and, therefore, it requires us to examine more closely what constitutes the difference between old and new ICTs.

7.3 The Transition from Old to New ICTs

Like their modern counterparts, traditional ICTs (from simple alphabets to complex writing systems, from photography to printing and so forth) reduced the informational privacy of agents. In this sense, over the course of the twentieth century, the evolution of the concept of privacy has reflected the development of ICTs or, more precisely, the advancement of how such technologies entailed new ways of violating informational privacy, thus signaling a delay in the pace of the law with respect to technological change. This delay has forced the law to respond more and more forcefully and to adapt its response to changing technological scenarios and social customs. When technological scenarios and/or social customs change, the lawyer is called upon to consider whether the existing body of law has (at least potentially) foreseen this evolution; if so, the existing law can be interpreted extensively, thus maintaining some sort of continuity with the past, and adapted to present issues. In these cases, the development of technology (and society) also follows a certain line of continuity with the past. For example, this happens when a new technology simply enhances a previous technology without involving a real qualitative change in the circumstances to which it is applicable. However, when a technological evolution involves a fracture (or more simply, a qualitative difference) with the previous technology, the law is hard-pressed to adapt its existing categories to the changed technological reality. This requires us to start to rethink the changed reality from the point of view of its technological and social development. This sums up precisely the difference between old and new ICTs in terms of their impact on informational privacy.

According to Floridi, old ICTs have always tended to reduce the ontological friction in the infosphere and hence the informational privacy of the agents, precisely because they have progressively *improved* or *enhanced* the ability of agents to access someone else's information in the infosphere (Floridi 2013, 233). Against this backdrop, old ICTs have been consistently interpreted on the basis of a fairly traditional conception of technology in the course of modernity (from Bacon onwards), which sees it as primarily a means of progressive empowerment (virtually unlimited or, at least, destined to grow incessantly) of the agent's capacities. Floridi rightly focuses attention on this point, by remarking that:

> old ICTs have always shared the fundamental features of facilitating the informational flow in the infosphere by increasingly empowering the agents embedded in it. This 'agent-oriented' trend in the old, pre-digital ICTs is well represented by dystopian views of informationally omnipotent agents, able to overcome any ontological friction, to control every aspect of the information flow, to acquire any personal data, and hence to implement the ultimate surveillance system, thus destroying all informational privacy, 'the dearest of our possessions' (Floridi 2013, 233–234).

According to Floridi, it would be a mistake to view new digital ICTs on a continuum with old ICTs, considering them simply as new and improved tools for accessing other agents' information in the infosphere. It would be wrong for two main reasons. Firstly, the new ICTs do not only reduce ontological friction in the infosphere by expanding the flow of information; they also increase it, thereby ensuring greater protection to informational privacy. This happens, as already pointed out, because the technology can incorporate and implement technological norms (such as cryptographic systems or privacy by design) intended to design the environment and the interactions that take place in it in a manner consistent with the expectations of greater protection of informational privacy rights. Secondly, new ICTs have a far-reaching impact on the infosphere, including all of its ontological elements: the environment, the agents and their interactions. This impact results in a re-ontologization of reality, which is likely to modify the very nature of the protected legal interests. It is thus crucial to pay attention to the direction that this process of re-ontologization of reality is taking in the context of informational privacy. Analysis of the process needs to be broken down into three elements: a) the agents; b) the environment; c) the interactions.

7.3.1 Agents

The reality re-ontologized by digital ICTs is chiefly characterized by the agents' awareness of the centrality of the information life cycle. One of the main results of the information revolution (Floridi 2010a, b, c) consists in the agents' understanding that the entire information life-cycle (which is split up into generation, access, distribution, sharing, recording, use, storage or deletion of information) contributes in a direct and decisive way to the construction of the reality in which we make decisions, act and live. Information has a threefold relationship with reality (Floridi, 2004; also see Chap. 10 here). There is information *as* reality (which is constitutive of reality itself); information *about* reality (which represents reality and allows us to be informed about it); and information *for* reality (which is a set of instructions that we need in order to interact with reality and to change it). The information life cycle is thus likely to affect each aspect of reality (ontological, epistemological and practical). As a result, each informational agent has stronger awareness and, correspondingly, greater power relative not only in its ability to access, collect and process personal data (which implies a decrease of ontological friction), but also in its ability to manage, control and protect such data (which implies an increase of ontological friction). This remark is essential to understanding what constitutes the broad notion of politics in information societies (as explained in Chap. 4), from both an individual and a collective standpoint. The informational approach allows us to treat the individual and the collective dimension of politics in a unified way. On the individual level, politics is no longer viewed solely as an expression of consent, access to opportunities, protection of rights and participation in democratic life. On the collective level, politics is no longer understood as a form of control over a territory and a mechanism for collective decisions. In both cases, politics can be understood and described as a form of access to and control over the whole information life-cycle. The new political challenge of mature information societies will consist exactly in understanding how and to what extent individuals will be really involved in the formation of the *public mind* (Castells 2009). This challenge is already inherent to the protection of the right to informational privacy, which requires us to combine and balance the individual and the collective dimension of the information life-cycle, as clearly emerges from Floridi's observation (2013, 236):

> If privacy is the right of individuals (being these single persons, groups, or institutions) to control the life-cycle (especially the generation, access, recording and usage) of their information and determine for themselves when, how, and to what extent their information is processed by others, then one must agree that the digital ICTs may enhance as well as hinder the possibility of enforcing such a right.

This remark is particularly important, because it helps us to understand two major aspects of the approach to informational privacy. Firstly, the concept of the information life-cycle allows us to combine the idea of informational privacy with that of informational self-determination, as elaborated by the German Constitutional Court, and to connect it both with the idea of personal autonomy (Glorioso 2012, 389–390) and with the cornerstone of democratic life, which consists in the production of dissent (Durante 2013b). In this perspective, it is significant to recall in this context the explicit and prescient formulation by the German Constitutional Court (*Bundesverfassungsgericht*, decisions volume 65 l ff, 1983):

> A social order – and the legal order that supports it – in which citizens are no longer able to determine who knows what about them, when, and by what means, would be incompatible with the right to *informational self-determination.* Anyone who suspects that his or her dissenting behavior can be recorded at any time and permanently stored in the form of information, will try not to attract attention through such behavior. This would preclude not only opportunities for individuals' personal development but also for public good, as self-determination is a pre-requisite for a free political order based on the ability of political action and cooperation of its citizens.

This formulation introduces us to the second major aspect of the approach to informational privacy. It is undoubtedly true that the new ICTs have granted individual agents wider powers over the control and management of their personal data in both the legal and the technological dimensions and *privacy-enhancing technologies*, or PETs can be seen as counterbalancing *privacy intruding technologies*, or PITs. However, the fact remains that people today have to deal with real power differentials, as observed by Victor Mayer-Schonberger (2009),[2] arising from the ability of certain supra-individual agents, such as search engines or companies, to gather and aggregate large masses of data. Any discussion of symmetries or asymmetries of information in the collection, aggregation and distribution of information, whether it concerns informational privacy or any other aspect of information policy, must take into account the existence of such power differentials, which could potentially call into question the exercise of individual rights and, more broadly, the participation of individuals in information policy making. Information policy as well as informational privacy may result in balanced and fair solutions only where it is possible to combine the reduction of information asymmetries with the reduction of power differentials. To paraphrase the renowned Kantian formula (on the current importance of which see McDowell 1996), reductions of information asymmetries without corresponding reductions in power differentials are empty; reductions of power differentials without parallel reductions in information asymmetries are blind (Durante 2015).[3]

---

[2] According to Victor Mayer-Schonberger (2009, 108), this is the case, for instance, for digital remembering: "So far, we have looked at how digital remembering alters the balance of information power in a dyadic relationship, and how this causes transactions to take place and under what conditions. Consumers, for example, may pay more for goods and services because of the information differential a well-informed seller utilizing digital memory possesses. Think of a database of worldwide automobile accidents; those renting a car could be charged differently based on their past driving history, which through digital could be made instantly accessible to rental companies. [...] A shift in information power therefore doesn't have consequences just for a particular transaction, whether and under what conditions it takes place, it also has the potential to influence how humans behave".

[3] See Durante (2015): "Information asymmetries occur when, in the relationship between two (or more) parties, one holds more (relevant) information than the other. Such party enjoys an informationally privileged situation that may (or may not) be turned into a concrete advantage over the

7.3.2 Environment

The new ICTs have profoundly changed the environment in which we live, make decisions and interact (see Chap. 2). Until recently, the environment was viewed as a passive agent, registering traces of our passage that we could return to, collect and revisit. However, this conception of the environment has since undergone a tripartite change that not only puts at potential risk our informational privacy, but also gives it new shape and meaning. This change entails a gradual shift in the ability of the environment to collect and process information on our behalf and extends to very the way in which society relates to forms of temporality.

The first aspect of this change regards the widespread use of tools and devices, ranging from cameras to cash registers and so on, that record our passage, making these records available, in whole or in part, to qualified third parties. While these records are often made quite passively and with no ulterior purpose in mind, the pervasiveness of such an immense body of potential data has given rise to a surveillance society, or rather, to a *new* surveillance society.[4] Nevertheless, this form of data collection, however pervasive it may be, confronts us with a traditional conception of ICT and, all things considered, of surveillance, according to which a society focuses on the past (i.e., on the traces of the past), in order to know (and have a control over) the present. In this context, surveillance continues to be based on the past, that is, on archives, recorded memories, databases, and so forth. As a corollary, we continue to speak of this type of data collection and processing in terms of the principles of necessity and proportionality, as well as of the right to be forgotten. We are still therefore operating within a *society of the memory*, where knowledge of the present is heavily based on reconstruction of the past.

A second dimension of change is that the environment has been designed as a smart place that can communicate and exchange information with the agents involved. The result is a world that is not inanimate: it is populated with objects that collect data on our behalf (personal data, preferences, desires, etc.) and then process and share it through interactions with us and with each other. This shift in conception from a passive to a more or less active environment emphasizes communication between things and agents. Through this form of communication, data is collected and processed, so to speak, in real time. In this sense, surveillance is not focused exclusively on traces of the past. It also concerns communication that is taking place in the present. In a certain sense, it is as though society possesses a capacity for

---

other party. A power differential occurs when, in the relationship between two (or more) parties, one party has greater powers than the other. This situation of advantage may (or not) depend on previous information asymmetries". A fair and balanced solution is possible only when the reduction of information asymmetries is combined with the reduction of power differentials.

[4] The new surveillance differs from traditional surveillance: namely, traditional surveillance was used to collect data, the content of which was known by their holders; new forms of surveillance are able to collect data, the content of which may be unknown even to the holders of such data. On the transition from surveillance to the new surveillance, see Lyon 2007 and, more recently, Lyon and Bauman 2013; for the consequences on privacy and the balance between security and civil rights, see Pagallo 2013; Hildebrandt 2013.

self-control, a type of self-regulatory dimension. It is within this context that we speak of an intelligent or smart environment (along with a new paradigm for law known as ambient law),[5] the Internet of things, smart cities, robotic agents, and so forth, which can interact with each other and with us, collecting and processing data in real time. This is no longer a society of memory based on surveillance of the past, but an intelligent or *smart society*, where surveillance is conceived as a self-regulating capacity of a multi-agent system, and knowledge of the present is based on the collection and communication of data in real-time rather than on the reconstruction of the traces of the past. The lapse of time with which data are collected and processed is no longer that of the (historical or judicial) critical reworking of the memory, characteristic of a society of the memory; it is that of a multi-agent system that adapts to the constantly changing environment, characteristic of an intelligent or smart society founded on the present.

Finally, there is a third aspect of the environment that is changing. Like the second, it is still under construction. As we have seen, the environment (meaning the overall context being forged by the new ICTs) is conceived as a place for gathering and recording data (the society of the memory) as well as a space where things come into communication with each other and with agents (the intelligent or smart society). In addition – and perhaps above all, the environment is seen as a place where the collection and aggregation of large amounts of data *(big data)* allows us to draw inferences relating to the preferences and future behaviors of the agents. Informational privacy is thus no longer thought of in reference to the agents' past or present, but with reference to their future. Data collection and processing allows reconstruction of the past and interaction in the present, but even more significantly, it allows inferences to be made about the future, including hypotheses, predictions, trends and guidelines This forward-looking vision may have a strong impact on morality as well as on the law, since the present is compared with the future and is, therefore, examined and evaluated on the basis of models constructed from those inferences. Surveillance is no longer seen in terms of retrospective control or present self-control, but in terms of a prospective basis, as part of society's ability to conform to models and expectations. The attention is focused here on the future or, rather, on foreseeing the future. Although not a new paradigm, data-intensive science[6] lends a particular gravity to this trend. Against this backdrop, it is possible to speak of a true *society of inference*, where knowledge and assessment of the present are influenced by anticipatory considerations about the future.

These three possible forms of the social environment (manifested in the society of memory, the intelligent or smart society, and the society of inference) are not mutually exclusive, nor do they represent a progression in which one stage replaces another; for the moment at least, they co-exist within the information society. The informational approach thus allows us to appreciate the scope of the re-ontologization of reality being brought about by new digital ICTs and the complexity of the issues underlying the protection of informational privacy, since the latter takes on the

[5] On this point Hildebrandt and Koops 2010.

[6] See on this point Hey T., Tansley S., Tolle K. 2007; Nielsen, 2011.

inside of the dialectical tension between different social forms that reshape the concepts of environment and surveillance, with emphasis on the different forms of temporality (i.e., past, present or future).

In this sense, it is clear that "the information society has revised the threshold of ontological friction and therefore provides a different sense in which its citizens appreciate their informational privacy" (Floridi 2013, 238). In the interconnected and global environment of the infosphere, the spatial metaphor of "inside/outside" that still dominates much of the interpretation of privacy tends to disappear in favor of the complex conceptualization of time represented by the three forms of social environment described above. Privacy is seen less in topological terms (here, there), and more in temporal ones (before, after). In today's information societies, the re-ontologization of reality not only changes the tools put at our disposition by law and technology to protect our informational privacy but, first and foremost, it changes the legal interest to be protected. That interest is our identity, which is socially constructed in the dialectical tension between a past to be reconstructed (the society of the memory), a present in which to interact (the intelligent and smart society), and a future to foresee (the society of inference).

7.3.3 Interactions

Regarding the interactions among agents in the re-ontologized reality of the infosphere, Floridi distinguishes between two conceptions of privacy with which to compare the ontological approach to informational privacy. Floridi analyzes two renowned conceptions of privacy and distinguishes between (1) the reductionist interpretation of privacy, and (2) an interpretation of privacy based on property:

> The reductionist interpretation argues that the value of informational privacy rests on a variety of undesirable consequences that may be caused by its breach, either personally (e.g. distress) or socially (e.g. unfairness).Informational privacy is a utility, also in the sense of providing an essential condition of possibility of good human interactions, e.g. by preserving human dignity or by providing political checks and balances (Floridi 2013, 240–241).
>
> The ownership-based interpretation argues that informational privacy needs to be respected because of each person's right to bodily security and property, where 'property of *x*' is classically understood as the right to exclusive use of *x*. A person is said to *own* his or her information (information about him- or herself), (...), and therefore to be entitled to control its whole life-cycle, from generation to erasure through usage (Floridi 2013, 241).

These conceptions of privacy have the merit of putting the emphasis both on the relationship that the person entitled with the right to informational privacy has with other agents (as a condition of possibility of positive human interactions or as a limit to the use of someone else's data) and the decisive importance of control over the life-cycle of information in the person's interaction with other agents. However, these conceptions appear both insufficiently radical in their theoretical approach and not always able to give an account of the transformations engendered by the information revolution. From a theoretical point of view, both are tied up with a rather traditional interpretation of privacy, for which informational privacy is something new (that is, an instrumental or proprietary good) that nonetheless occurs in an environment that has remained essentially unchanged, and not in the re-ontologized reality of the infosphere, as remarked by Floridi:

> Unsurprisingly, they both compare privacy breach to trespass or unauthorized invasion of, or intrusion in, a space or sphere of personal information, whose accessibility and usage ought to be fully controlled by its owner and hence kept private (Floridi 2013, 241).

In addition, both approaches have specific limits. The first approach – reductionist or utilitarian – is extremely reasonable in paying attention to the consequences that may result from a breach of informational privacy, but, in so doing, it tends to conceive privacy only as an instrumental good, aimed at ensuring the protection of other final goods (e.g., dignity, freedom and security), with which it ends up being confused. This approach fails to provide informational privacy with an autonomous theoretical foundation and does not explain why we should continue to protect privacy in contexts like our own, to a large extent, where the data market may turn out to generate higher utility in terms of social welfare. The second approach – based on property – is extremely reasonable in paying attention to the right to privacy from the point of view of property owners in a context which is, as just remarked, dominated by the constant quest for marketing data. However, even this approach fails to provide an autonomous theoretical foundation for informational privacy with, according to which information (or informational objects) have autonomous values extending beyond their mere market value. Furthermore, the property-based approach cannot account for some specific situations raised by the evolution of new digital ICTs. As suggested by Floridi, this approach is not able to treat situations in which the amount of information that a person owns:

(1) is enriched by external contributions that may be undesirable from the standpoint of passive privacy informational (think of the case of unsolicited e-mail or information regarding us that has been involuntarily acquired from external sources);
(2) has been gained in public contexts or spaces, which are structurally and implicitly governed by rules that permit some data collection and processing: in this case, is consent to data collection and processing implicit, or should such consent be obtained in some explicit form?);
(3) is not really diminished by the fact that others have access to it (for this purpose, one should also distinguish between *rival goods* [which are consumed by their use: *e.g.* a sandwich]; *exclusive goods* [which prevent someone else's use but are not consumed by the use: *e.g.* the panoramic view enjoyed through a pair of binoculars]; *positive goods* [which are increased by their use: *e.g.* a civic tradition]; and *common goods* [which can be shared by different users: *e.g.* knowledge]).

7.3.4 The Value of the Ontological Interpretation of Informational Privacy

The three aspects examined above (relating to the nature of agents, environment and interactions) that characterize the re-ontologized reality of the infosphere allow us a better appreciation of what constitutes the theoretical foundation of the re-interpretation of privacy in ontological terms. Let us make reference to Floridi:

> Such re-interpretation is achieved by considering each person as constituted by his or her information (...) and hence by understanding a breach of one's informational privacy as a form of aggression towards one's personal identity. Such ontological interpretation of informational privacy is consistent with the fact that ICTs can both erode and reinforce informational privacy, and hence that a positive effort needs to be made in order to support not only PET but also 'poietic' (i.e. constructive) applications, which may allow users to design, apply and maintain their identities as informational agents (Floridi 2013, 243).

These remarks reveal the value of re-interpreting informational privacy in ontological terms. This value lies primarily in the idea that information does not constitute an external good that is added to the wealth possessed by an individual. On the contrary, information is already inherent and, so to speak, constitutive of the wealth or, rather, characteristics that make up the identity of the agent. Information does not accrue to the person but is constitutive of the person and, more particularly, of the person as an agent that interacts with the environment and with other agents. Let us consider the case in which a person very dear to us gave us a keepsake while lying on their deathbed. The object itself could be a letter, an old watch, a necklace or so forth, and is devoid of any great economic value. Should we ever lose the object, what would be lost is not the object's exchange value, but the symbolic value (i.e., the shared information) that we attributed to it that is, our being part of a network of significant relationships that exist in space and time. Information (as seen in Chap. 6) constitutes us, in this sense, as part of an overall plot or network of significant relationships that occur within space and time. The significance of information cannot be entirely separated from the exchange value of the data (from which the information is formed), but is in general not reducible to this value alone. Therefore, any merely utilitarian, consequentialist or economic interpretation of privacy is unable to fully account for the notion of informational privacy, or to make its protection the default rule (which can be negotiated, balanced or limited, but always with regards to the preeminent value of the person):

> The advantage of the ontological interpretation over the reductionist one is then that consequentialist concerns may override respect for informational privacy, whereas the ontological interpretation, by equating its protection to the protection of personal identity, considers it a fundamental and inalienable right, so that, by default, the presumption should always be in favor of its respect.(...) This is not to say that informational privacy is not negotiable in any degree (Floridi 2013, 243).

Beyond the legal classification (for which other conceptions of privacy would be prepared to recognize that privacy is a fundamental and inalienable right), what matters in this context is the importance attributed to privacy as a defense of the person's immunity (which we have previously interpreted as the integrity of the narrative or network of significant relationships of an individual) from both an active and a passive standpoint, as pointed out by Floridi:

> Looking at the nature of a person as being constituted by that person's information enables one to understand the right to information privacy as a right to personal immunity from unknown, undesired or unintentional changes in one's own identity as an informational entity both *actively* and *passively*. Actively, because collecting, storing, reproducing, manipulating etc. one's information amounts now to stages in stealing, cloning or breeding someone else's personal identity. Passively, because breaching one's informational privacy may now consist in forcing someone to acquire unwanted data, thus altering his or her nature as an informational entity without consent (Floridi 2013, 243–244).

Taken together, these observations allow us to understand why the ontological approach can cope with some theoretical difficulties that characterize the interpretation of informational privacy based on property. Indeed, from the ontological standpoint, breaches of privacy and, more generally, the use of someone else's information, concern the person as such, and not just the person's possessions (Floridi 2013, 244–245). Once we grasp that the sphere of personal information and that of personal identity are "two sides of the same coin" (Floridi 2013, 244) we can begin to understand another important consequence in this context. As explained in Chap. 5, personal identity is a diachronic concept, since the individual's personality is formed over time. This affects the notion of informational privacy, for it can no longer be understood within a context of space alone, but must first and foremost be understood within a context of time. This aspect brings into play a diachronic conception of informational privacy, which occupies a central role in the ontological interpretation of informational privacy:

> The ontological interpretation stresses that informational privacy is also a matter of construction of one's own informational identity. The right to be let alone is also the right to be allowed to experiment with one's own life, to start again, without having records that mummify one's personal identity forever, taking away from the individual the power to mould it. Every day, a person may wish to build a different, possibly better, 'I'. We never stop becoming ourselves, so protecting a person's informational privacy also means allowing the person the freedom to construct and change herself, ontologically (Floridi 2013, 246).

The essential philosophical aspect that characterizes informational privacy represents a radical shift stemming from the evolution of new digital ICTs and concerning our relationship with 'the negative', or 'what is not'. In the traditional view of informational privacy (whatever is its specific declination), the negative is conceived as a set of data that the individual wishes to keep inaccessible to others. In this context, the negative today seems to be accompanied by a sense of guilt. It is not, in fact, unusual to hear people say they have nothing to hide; in a similar sense, the principle of absolute transparency holds that there is nothing to make it inaccessible. Hence, one implicitly claims that everything is of interest to everyone, or, in other words, that it would be worth concealing only what is generally devoid of interest (a State or some companies, for example, would have an interest, for different reasons, in collecting and aggregating data that would otherwise be [that is, when considered individually] of no interest). On the basis of the ontological approach, the relationship to the negative has changed and no longer concerns the data to be kept hidden. It concerns primarily what the person *is not yet*, but which is already part of her ability to build and transform her personal identity. The negative content of informational privacy is the positive content of the process of self-construction. Protecting the process of self-construction implies making it possible for individuals to give a unitary and identifiable meaning to the network of significant relationships in which they are engaged at the individual or supra-individual level.[7] This also explains why, at least in this sense, informational privacy seems to describe something broader and more complex than the protection of personal data alone (although the protection of informational privacy requires the protection of personal data as structures that can be filled with meaning). In other words, one can state that informational privacy consists of two essential components: a) the protection of personal data; and b) the protection of our ability to turn data into information relevant to us (i.e., to provide this data with a unitary and identifiable meaning).

7.4 Challenges to the Theory of Informational Privacy

Floridi is aware of the fact that a mature theory of informational privacy must deal with a number of challenges that can call into question some of the underlying assumptions on which the theories of privacy are traditionally built. Throughout this section we will focus not only on the challenges highlighted by Floridi, but also on some issues specifically relating to the ontological approach in philosophy and the ethics of information. We have already made reference to some of these assumptions, but they are worth examining now more extensively in the order they are discussed in Floridi (2013, 249–257). These assumptions are all concerned, for different reasons, with the context in which the concept of privacy is developed and the right to privacy is applied.

[7] This is a specific problem that Floridi accounts for by remarking that (2013, 246): "The union of the agents forms a single unity, a supra-agent, or a new multiagent individual. Precisely because entering into a new supra-agent is a delicate and risky operation, care should be exercised before 'melding' oneself with other individuals by sharing personal information or its source, i.e. common experience. Confidentiality is a bond that is hard and slow to forge properly, yet resilient to many *external* forces when finally in place, as the supra-agent is stronger than the constitutive agents themselves. Relatives, friends, classmates, fellows, colleagues, comrades, companions, partners, team-mates, spouses and so forth may all have experienced the nature of such a bond, the stronger taste of a 'we'. But it is also a bond very brittle and difficult to restore when it comes to *internal* betrayal, since the disclosure, deliberate or unintentional, of some personal information in violation of confidence can entirely and irrecoverably destroy the privacy of the new, supra-agent born out of the joining agents, by painfully tearing them apart".

7.4.1 Cultural and Linguistic Context

The first challenge concerns cultural and linguistic context. The emphasis on the process of globalization and the worldwide spread of the Internet often fails to mention that the overcoming of national boundaries, notably from the legal or economic standpoint, does not necessarily and automatically imply the overcoming of cultural and linguistic boundaries (Durante 2013a). The circulation of data is, as has often been pointed out, different from the flow of information, the semantic content of which requires the users to share not only data but also a common symbolic universe. In this sense, many theories of informational privacy have been elaborated within the western culture on the implicit, but in fact widely debatable, assumption of its universality. Of course, this assumption carries with it the risk of cultural colonization, whereby one ends up believing that the limits of our world are the limits of the world, as if it were possible to interpret all of reality in the light of our symbolic universe. At the same time, rejection of this assumption in its entirety (relative to the degree of universalization of our categories) exposes us to the equal and opposite risk of radical relativism, according to which the symbolic universes ('cultures') constitute cultural and linguistic contexts that can never be transcended, thus defeating any claim to dialogue or intercultural communication. Can the ontological approach to informational privacy accommodate these opposing poles? Can it provide answers or at least some useful methodological suggestions for meeting this challenge? Floridi provides two observations in this regard, and we would add a third. First, while recognizing the impossibility of adopting a point of view that is totally free from every prejudice and assumption ("an impossible view from nowhere", Floridi 2013, 250), the ontological approach seeks to minimize its ontological commitment by adopting as neutral and universalizable a point of view as possible, consisting in conceiving any agent as an entity modeled in informational terms. This allows one to adjust different conceptions of privacy to all those agents that can be defined as entities modeled in informational terms, thus relieving the researcher from having to adopt the point of view characteristic of (and thus limited to) a given culture. Second, the informational ontology underlying the interpretation of informational privacy already sees agents as part of the re-ontologized reality of the infosphere. This joint membership, while not expected to lead to a "universal language or culture", is likely to generate "the shared *koiné* among future netizens" (Floridi 2013, 251). Third, we must not forget that the informational approach allows us to interpret the notion of context, from outside of a strict spatial representation, as a set of informational elements that characterize a specific situation (Dey 2001), thereby allowing the charitable interpreter (Davidson 1984) to process this information ('the context') and to give it an intelligible and sharable meaning.

7.4.2 The Axiological Context

The second challenge a mature theory of informational privacy must deal with concerns the context of values. Traditional conceptions of privacy are elaborated within the framework of an underlying value choice in the direction of methodological individualism that has typified Western culture over the course of modernity. In this sense, privacy is conceived exclusively in terms of the sphere of action and interests of an individual, where that individual agent is thought of as the only possible owner of the right to privacy. This happens because modern (moral, legal or religious) anthropology tends to base the idea of personal responsibility on the single figure of the individual, in order to identify, with absolute certainty, a single and unitary locus for the allocation of rights and duties:

> Where there is personal responsibility also there is an individual capable of shouldering it, but then there is some conception of a single human being, different from society, capable of desiring some form of privacy for his or her own life (Floridi 2013, 252).

However, this methodological approach is not able to account fully for some of the current changes engendered by the development of new digital ICTs. First, the person is perceived, not as a separate entity from the rest of the world on the basis of a purely atomistic conception of the individual, but as a relational entity (see Chaps. 5 and 6), namely, as part of a network of significant relationships, which fill the individual's life with meaningful content. Second, there are, notably online, spheres of action and interests, such as social networks, which are conceived and constructed from the start as group phenomena and integrated contexts rather than as the mere addition of single actions and interests. Third, it is no longer possible to assume equivalence between agents and human beings or between agents and individuals; on the contrary, we are constantly interacting with artificial agents or with supra-agents made up of a plurality of (human or artificial) agents. This makes it harder to establish theories of privacy based on a rigid conception of methodological individualism in strictly anthropological terms; in fact, it requires, that the conception of agent be expanded. Against this backdrop, Floridi observes that:

> The ontological theory of informational privacy can help in this process in that it does not presuppose either a personalist or a substantialist conception of the agents involved in moral actions.[...] Agents need not be persons, they can be organizations, for example, or artificial constructs, or hybrid systems. And they do not need to consist of some sort of self-like entities, as they may be constituted by bundles of properties and processes [...].Once again, this 'lite' ontology can be adapted to further interpretations and cultural needs. It helps to frame the discussion in a minimalist way that does not exclude *a priori* some interlocutors (Floridi 2013, 253).

7.4.3 The Context of Application of the Notion of Informational Privacy

The third challenge concerns the scope of the notion of informational privacy, that is, the limits that define its context of application. Recognition of the importance of information in contemporary societies and, in the present context, of informational privacy, must not result in the converse risk of absolute and hence excessive protection of the sphere of information that a person owns or controls, as if every access to someone else's information were a potential violation of privacy. In this regard, Floridi observes that any "theory of informational privacy needs a criterion of discrimination to be able to explain why some information processes do *not* count as violations of informational privacy" (2013, 254). As pointed out in the previous section, the fact that societies can behave as societies of inference makes it harder to distinguish what counts as a violation of informational privacy on the basis of ownership or data control. Although these concepts are more sympathetic to the logic of the market and more appropriate to the current process of marketing data, they cannot take full account of the systematic process typical in societies of inference of deducing data from other data. It is difficult, today, to argue that the owner or controller of a data-set with the right to informational privacy over it can stake an equal claim to the right to informational privacy over data extrapolated from it by someone else; after all, the resulting data is the exclusive product of someone else's capacity of extrapolating data from data. From this point of view, however, it is useful to remember that, according to the ontological approach to informational privacy, "agents do not own information but are constituted by it" (Floridi 2013, 256). This means that the emphasis placed by this approach on the development of the person (i.e., the relationship to the negative that characterizes the formation of personality) allows us to imagine and expect, at least from a theoretical standpoint, that protection should also extend to the data inferred (as being potentially constitutive of our personal identity).

7.4.4 The Context of Publicness

The fourth challenge concerns the context of publicness (i.e., of what is public), within which one must nevertheless be able to enjoy the right to informational privacy. Theories of informational privacy must first of all be able to provide a definition of the notion of context for the application of a law and, in particular, to distinguish with certainty between the private and public contexts (there is, in fact, nothing that would be ontologically private or public [Mathieu 2004; Durante 2011a]). In addition, they are also called upon to account for and even protect "public informational privacy" (Floridi 2013, 256, who refers to Nissenbaum 1998, 273, and 2010; Margulis 2003, 267), that is, the privacy enjoyed, to some extent, in public contexts. Hence, holders of the right to informational privacy retain their legitimate claim to protection within the public context; the only change is in the degree of reasonable expectation of protection commensurate with the nature of the social context (Floridi 2013, 256). The degree of reasonable expectation must be, at present, also commensurate with the greater or lesser transparency in information derived from the computerized processes of retrieval, collection and processing of data entering the network. Thus, this reasonable expectation of protection should be implemented, according to Floridi, with reference to a notion of informational privacy understood both in passive and in active terms. With respect to passive informational privacy, Floridi suggests that the notion of public should be understood in a broader sense to include what the individual is involuntarily but often violently exposed to:

> On the one hand, each of us has a fundamental right not to know: this is why violent scenes, disturbing news, pornography, advertising, reports or unwanted spoilers [...] and, I may add, mere idiocy, of which there is an overabundance throughout all media, may be suffered as contamination of one's own self, as breaches of one's own informational privacy, brain washing of the worst kind.[...] On the other hand, each of us has a fundamental duty to ignore (or pretend not to know): in human societies privacy is also fostered through tacit agreements. TMI, as the younger generation says: *too much information*, more than one wants to have (Floridi 2013, 257).

Deliberately provocative and forthright in his wording, Floridi hones in on an important aspect of the information society: given that we live in informational contexts often impaired by exposure to an overabundance of (violent, repulsive, etc.) information, passive informational privacy must be recognized and protected and not conflated with the conception of informational privacy as a question of personal choice and selection of information. At the same time, Floridi emphasizes the importance of active informational privacy, which is the natural complement to or development of passive informational privacy:

> By 'active informational privacy' in the public sphere I mean to refer to those practices that facilitate and foster the development of individuals, by guaranteeing relevant conditions of informational privacy construction. What the latter may be varies from culture to culture and through time, it seems quite clear that the right to informational privacy is not merely a negative right not to be *x*-ed, but also a positive right to *x*-ing (Floridi 2013, 257).

7.4.5 The Context of Information Ethics

The final challenge to be added to those suggested and expounded by Floridi is concerned with the very notion of information ethics. The ontological approach to informational privacy might, in fact, be called into question on the basis of the tenets of information ethics itself, which sees in the generation, circulation and dissemination of informational objects the means for achieving the well-being of the infosphere (or of its regions). From this perspective, the informational foundation of the ontological interpretation of privacy should stand against any form of ontological friction obstructing or reducing the flow of information. However, what may seem obvious at first sight is based on a simplistic interpretation of information ethics. This happens for two reasons. First, information ethics insists that the informational well-being of the infosphere (or of its regions) is the result of an overall assessment that takes into account the existence of unavoidable *trade-offs* between vying informational objects. Therefore, the destruction or limitation of certain informational objects is justified and compensated for by the promotion or protection of other informational objects.[8] From this point of view, the ethics of informa-

[8] In this perspective, see what Jane Yakovits says with regard to the importance of research data and the risk of the tragedy of the data commons (Yakovits, 2011). Notably, people should undergo the risk of disclosing some of their data (which are nonetheless, according to Yakovits, protected to a large extent through anonymization), to enjoy "the fruits of the data commons" (Yakovits, 2011, 5). "The data commons is the tax we pay to our public information reserves" (Yakovits 2011, 66).

tion as a resource (Floridi 2013) acknowledges the fact that the agents' moral behavior can in some cases be achieved through appropriate limitation of information (as in the case of the "veil of ignorance" by John Rawls [1971]). Secondly (although this remark is actually just a specification of the first point), we must not overlook that our rights to (active or passive) informational privacy (as well as all other rights) are themselves informational objects worthy of protection and development.

7.5 Conclusions

This chapter has tried to show that technological developments (in this case, the evolution of new digital ICTs) call not only for reinterpretation of traditional legal categories and their adaptation to changing social needs, but also for reexamination of the underlying reality that is captured and represented within the framework of the law, which intends to recognize and ensure the protection of legal interests considered essential for society. Recognizing and protecting informational privacy in today's information societies requires us to reconsider the nature of the agents, the environment and their interactions from an informational standpoint. In doing so, one understands why – despite outcries of it being dead – privacy is the topic of such frequent and vehement debate, and has become one of the chief interpretive elements of our time and of our personal identity:

> Privacy does not play a significant role in macroethics because it is the property of a class of entities as patients, not of actions. It becomes a central issue only within a culture that begins to recognize that entities are clusters of information, and that privacy is a fundamental concept referring to the integrity and well-being of an informational entity as a patient. Privacy is not only an individual's problem, but may be a group's problem, a company's or corporation's problem, or a whole nation's problem, since all these entities have their natures fully determined and constituted by the information they are (Floridi 2013, 258).

Informational privacy cannot be conceived, then, in relation to isolated individuals understood as atomic entities that remain separate from the others and from the environment, and who deal with information, like with any other object, as things entering and exiting their sphere of control. Perhaps the enduring popularity of this view derives from the reassuring sense it gives that the world of information is potentially entirely available to us, meaning we can potentially control, manipulate and trade it as we like. However, this conception is fallacious, because individuals are not isolated, atomic entities, but parts making up a whole, the infosphere, which comprises all of the informational objects and the constitutive interactions among and between these objects and the environment. When individuals manipulate, alter or exchange information relevant to this web of interactions, it affects both their constitution as informational objects and the meaning they attach to their lives through the web of interactions:

> Within the infosphere, entities form a web of dependencies and symbiotic relations. The data output by data collection and analysis processes can easily become the input of other, or even the same, information processes (no hierarchy is implied). Complex relations among data-producers, data-collectors, data-processors and data-consumers constitute an ecosystem in which data may be recycled, collated, matched, restructured and hence used to make strategic decisions about individuals. [...] Accessing information is not like accessing physical objects. Physical objects may not be affected by their manipulation, but any cognitive manipulation of information is also performative: it modifies the nature of information by automatically cloning it (Floridi 2013, 258–260).

Manipulating information that is constitutive of our identity, or having it altered, is not like physically misplacing items that, with any luck, we may find later at the lost and found counter.[9]

Manipulating information alters the personal integrity of the individual: namely, tearing the fabric of significant relations of which the person is a part and which form her own world. One must understand, therefore, that privacy is an informational tool for protecting intersubjective relationships, thought of not so much as relationships occurring between already constituted subjectivities, but rather as constitutive of the individual's subjectivity itself:

> We are our information and when an informational entity is a human being at the receiving end of an action, we can speak of a me-hood. [...] Intrusion in the me-hood is therefore equivalent to a process of personal alienation: the piece of information that was meant to be and remain private and unique is multiplied and becomes public, it is transformed into a dead piece of myself that has been given to the world, acquires an independent status, and is no longer under my control. Privacy is nothing else than the defence of the personal integrity of a packet of information, the individual, and the invasion of an individual's information privacy, the unauthorised access, dispersion, and misuse of her information is an infringement of her me-hood and a disruption of the information environment that it constitutes (Floridi 2013, 260).

Since personal identity is not constituted once and for all in a single time frame but is a dynamic and continuous (*life-consuming*) process, one must understand that informational privacy can no longer be conceived exclusively or mainly within a context of space, but that it can and should be seen all together within a context of time. This means that the personal integrity of a packet of information is not understood as the integrity or consistency of a static description, but as the integrity and consistency of an informational microenvironment that evolves through time (we are "equivalent to an information microenvironment, a constantly elastic and permeable entity with centers and peripheries but with boundaries that are neither

---

[9] "The suggestion is finally advanced that a person has a right to both exclusive ownership and unique control/use of her private information and that she must be treated differently from a mere packet of information. According to IE, however, this view is at least partly mistaken and fails to explain the problem in full. Instead of trying to stop agents treating human beings as informational entities, we should rather ask them to realize that, when they deal with personal and private information, they are dealing with human beings themselves, and should therefore exercise the same care and show the same ethical respect they would exercise and show when dealing with other people, living bodies or environmental elements" (Floridi 2013, 259).

sharply drawn nor rigidly fixed in time", Floridi 2013, 259). In this regard, we have outlined the different temporal forms that today's information society can take in relation to the issue of informational privacy and surveillance: i.e., the *society of memory* (founded on the acquisition of traces of the past), the *intelligent or smart society* (founded on communication and interaction in the present), the *inference society* (based on the capability of anticipating the future). Understanding the notions of personal identity and informational privacy within a context of time therefore requires us to reconstruct and examine the complex dialectic between these modes of temporality and, correspondingly, between the types of information societies built on them. Against this backdrop, the individual is understood as a packet of information that forms part of a web of meaningful relations, built on the trails of the past, defined in the present by the information exchanged with agents and the environment and, increasingly, measured against the expectations built on inferences drawn from large amounts of aggregated data.

In conclusion, the analysis expounded in this chapter wants to reinforce the idea of the agent as informational *homo poieticus* (see Chap. 3) who is called on not only to defend informational privacy but to build it. Accordingly, privacy should no longer be predicated upon the individual's short- or long-term desire or ability to withdraw from the tempests of the world into a cloistered area without interference and intrusion, but rather upon the individual's desire and ability to construct a world within the world, a network of significant relationships within the vast fabric of the information society:

> The violation [of privacy] is not a violation of ownership, of personal rights, of instrumental values, or consequentialist rules, but a violation of the informational self, an offence against the integrity of the me-hood, and the efforts made by the individual to construct it as a whole, accurate, autonomous entity independent from, and yet present within, the world. The intrusion is disruptive not just because it breaks the atmosphere of the environment, but because our information is an integral part of ourselves, and whoever owns it possesses a piece of ourselves, and thus undermines our uniqueness and our autonomy from the world (Floridi 2013, 260).

References

Burk, D.-L. 2008. Information Ethics and the Law of Data Representations. *Ethics and Information Technology* 10: 135–147.

Castells, M. 2009. *Communication Power*. Oxford: Oxford University Press.

Davidson, D. 1984. *Inquiries into Truth and Interpretation [1974]*. Oxford: Clarendon Press.

Dey, A.-K. 2001. Understanding and Using Context. *Personal and Ubiquitous Computing Journal*, 5(1): 4–7. Available at: http://www.cc.gatech.edu/fcc/pubs/PeTe5-1.pdf.

Durante, M. 2011a. Normativity, Constructionism, and Constraining Affordances. *Etica & Politica/Ethics & Politics*, Symposium on Luciano Floridi's Philosophy of Information, XIII(2): 180–200.

———. 2011b. Rethinking Human Identity in the Age of Autonomic Computing: The Philosophical Idea of the Trace. In *Law, Human Agency and Autonomic Computing. The Philosophy of Law*

Meets the Philosophy of Technology, ed. M. Hildebrandt and A. Rouvroy, 85–103. London: Routledge.

———. 2011c. The online construction of personal identity through trust and privacy. *Information*, 2(4), 594–620.

———. 2013a. How to Cross Boundaries in the Information Society: Vulnerability, Responsiveness, and Accountability. *Acm Sigcas Computers and Society* 43 (1): 9–21.

———. 2013b. Informazione e regolazione. Internet come problema democratico. *Teoria politica* 3: 39–65.

Floridi, L. 2004. On the Morality of Artificial Agents. *Minds and Machines* 14 (3): 349–379.

———. 2010a. *Information. A Very Short Introduction*. Oxford: Oxford University Press.

———. 2010b. The Philosophy of Information as a Conceptual Framework. In Demir, H. (ed.). Luciano Floridi's Philosophy of Technology: Critical Reflections. *Knowledge, Technology & Policy*, 23.

———. 2010c. Information Ethics. In *The Cambridge Handbook of Information and Computer Ethics*, ed. L. Floridi, 77–99. Cambridge: Cambridge University Press.

———. 2013. *Information Ethics*. Oxford: Oxford University Press.

Glorioso, A. 2012. Un nuovo concetto di 'autodeterminazione informazionale' come bussola concettuale per navigare il nuovo mondo digitale. In Durante, M., and U. Pagallo (ed.). 2013. Manuale di informatica giuridica e diritto delle nuove tecnologie, 383–394. Torino: UTET.

Hildebrandt, M. 2013. Balance or Trade-Off? Online Security Technologies and Fundamental Rights. *Philosophy and Technology* 26 (4): 357–379.

Hildebrandt, M., and B.-J. Koops. 2010. The Challenges of Ambient Law and Legal Protection in the Profiling Era. *The Modern Law Review* 73 (3): 428–460.

Lyon, D. 2007. *Surveillance Studies: An Overview*. New York: Polity.

Lyon, D., and Z. Bauman. 2013. *Liquid Surveillance: A Conversation*. New York: Polity.

Margulis, S.-T. 2003. Privacy as a Social Issue and Behavioral Concept. *Journal of Social Issues* 59 (2): 243–261.

Martin, K. 2012. Information Technology and Privacy: Conceptual Muddles or Privacy Vacuums? *Ethics and Information Technology* 14 (4): 267–284.

Matheson, D. 2007. Unknowableness and Informational Privacy. *Journal of Philosophical Research* 32: 251–267.

Mathieu, V. 2004. *Privacy e dignità dell'uomo. Una teoria della persona*. Torino: Giappichelli Editore.

Mayer-Schonberger, V. 2009. *Delete: The Virtue of Forgetting in the Digital Age*. Princeton: Princeton University Press.

Nielsen, M. 2011. *Reinventing Discovery: The New Era of Networked Science*. Princeton: Princeton University Press.

Nissenbaum, H. 1998. Protecting Privacy in an Information Age: The Problem of Privacy in Public. *Law and Philosophy* 17 (5–6): 559–596.

———. 2010. *Privacy in Context: Technology, Policy, and the Integrity of the Social Life*. Stanford: Stanford Law Books.

Pagallo, U. 2008. *La tutela della privacy negli Stati Uniti d'America e in Europa. Modelli giuridici a confronto*. Milano: Giuffré.

———. 2013. Online Security and the Protection of Civil Rights: A Legal Overview. *Philosophy and Technology* 26 (4): 381–395.

Ralws, J. 1971. *A Theory of Justice*. Cambridge, MA: Belknap Press of Harvard University Press.

Tavani, H.-T. 2007. Philosophical Theories of Privacy: Implications for an Adequate Online Privacy Policy. *Metaphilosophy* 38 (1): 1–22.

———. 2008. Floridi's Ontological Theory of Informational Privacy: Some Implications and Challenges. *Ethics and Information Technology* 10 (2–3): 155–166.

Yakovits, J. 2011. The Tragedy of the Data Commons. *Harvard Journal of Law and Technology* 25 (1 Fall): 1–67.

8 Ontic Trust and the Foundation of the Information Society

Abstract

Throughout the history of political modernity, the process of legitimation of Western society has been portrayed through the lens of human conflict. This, however, is not the only possible way of telling the story. The hypothesis set forth here is that reframing the narrative is possible and, at present, even necessary, as the impact of computing and the spread of information and communication technologies invite us to reconsider the foundations of the information society. We are being called on to revisit the nature of modern conflict and the statute of their participants, breaking away from a traditional anthropocentric view of society to embrace a new perspective that challenges human narcissism. From this perspective, we are forced to envisage a new social or natural contract for the globalized, networked information society, one that acknowledges a relevant 'third' perspective: namely, that of nature (Serres) or the infosphere (Floridi).

8.1 Introduction

The purpose of the present chapter is to consider the social impact of ICTs from outside an anthropocentric perspective and to sketch out, accordingly, the outlines of a new social contract for today's globalized and networked information society. To this end, we discuss the meaning of the social impact of ICTs and explore the extent to which conflicts play, or do not play, a crucial role in the structuring of society in the Modern and Contemporary Ages. Against this backdrop, we shall argue that it is precisely because of the conceptual limits of the notion of conflict that the social impact of ICTs cannot be persuasively explained in terms of straightforward technological determinism, but in terms of affordances requiring norms of coordination. We then proceed to examine the challenges posed by the evolution and spread of ICTs to the theoretical premises of the model of political and social conflict (i.e. contractualism), upon which much of Modernity has been based. This,

M. Durante, *Ethics, Law and the Politics of Information*, The International Library of Ethics, Law and Technology 18, DOI 10.1007/978-94-024-1150-8_8

then, is the main theoretical consequence of the social impact of ICTs: we are required to abandon a limited anthropocentric perspective in order to reconstruct the political foundations of society. (This provides the necessary conceptual background for our reflections on an informational approach to politics presented in Chap. 4). To achieve this conceptual shift, we need to revise the long-standing notion of political and legal subjects as well as the theoretical premises that have shaped this notion over the course of modernity. In the final section of this chapter, we draw some conclusions from the previous analysis and explain how the philosophers Michel Serres, in the field of the philosophy of science, and Luciano Floridi, in the field of the philosophy of information, come to proposing the idea of a new natural (Serres) or social (Floridi) contract for the information society, paving the way towards a new environmentalist perspective.

8.2 The Social Impact of ICTs

The social impact of ICTs is a central, complex and unavoidable theme of reflection and discussion in our age of the information society (Castells 1999; Benkler 2006; Floridi 2010a). Framing the issue in terms of its impact is problematical, since it leaves open whether this impact is either governed by human will and decisions or is deterministically brought about by the ongoing technological evolution. However, in both cases, the notion of impact relies on the same epistemological and political foundation of modernity: the dichotomy between the subject and the object (Serres 2009). For instance, law is still mainly understood in light of this dichotomy and is structured in terms of subjective or objective law. How are subjects and objects represented in modernity? We will deal with this issue throughout the entire chapter, but a few comments are in order here. Across Modernity, subjects have been considered as the only entities (free, rational and autonomous human beings) vested to govern reality: they are vested with rights and obligations because they are the only animated beings that can take initiatives towards the world and towards themselves. Objects have been thought of as 'non-subjects', that is, as a predetermined?, bare and raw reality, i.e. the world at large, which is subject to the control and governance of subjects, and which cannot take any initiative towards those subjects. In this perspective, objects have no rights and no obligations (no legal or moral standing). In fact, to convey that a subject has been stripped of all dignity, we say that it has been objectified; in other words, it has been reduced to the status of an object. Let us briefly explore how the meaning of this dichotomy (whose epistemological status is beyond the scope of the present text) has been construed across political modernity.

In the modern political tradition of contractualism, representation of the subject is rooted in anthropological premises, which although usually portrayed in terms of their negative attributes, nevertheless are endowed with positive aspects that allow them to overcome their negative dimension. For instance, according to Thomas Hobbes, the father of modern politics, human beings are sufficiently irrational and heteronomous to be driven by their passions (the desire to possess everything as well as the fear of being dispossessed or killed), but are at the same time sufficiently free, rational and autonomous to opt out of the State of Nature and to stipulate a social contract, thanks to which they become citizens ([1651] 2008). Thus portrayed, the modern subject has three characteristics. The subject is (1) a human being; (2) subject to conflict; (3) a citizen (the only entity vested with rights and obligations). This depiction has accompanied us throughout the entire Modern Age up to now because of the persistence of the dichotomous subject/object model.

Here we argue that all three characteristics of the modern subject are being transformed by the impact of ICTs. We must therefore consider not just the first and third characteristics, but also the second. For even if the current information society still seems to be politically and legally legitimized on the basis of underlying conflict, one may argue that, just as the nature of the conflict and of the actors involved is undergoing profound change, so too is the very paradigm that sees conflict as the basis of society.

Let us take as an example the long-taught adage in political philosophy courses that, for modernity, *the State makes war and war makes the State.* This adage simply no longer holds true. In the globalised, networked information society, however counterintuitive it may seem, there is a crisis of (military) power (Serres 2009). Although war will never disappear altogether, it will mainly be waged in the form of cyber wars rather than relying primarily on conventional (kinetic) weapons. In other words, armed conflict is no longer uniquely capable of governing the networked space of the information society. Whether we consider this to be a shift from hard power to soft power (Nye 2008) or from State power to media power (Castells 2009), we are witnessing a radical transformation of reality from both an epistemological and a political standpoint, one that is fostered by the current informational turn (Floridi 2010a). This also implies a larger crisis of the political lexicon of modernity based on notions such as sovereignty, citizenship, force, violence and national borders, just to name a few.

The other side of the coin is the most controversial and debated aspect of the information society: the fact that its globalized, networked space has been depicted time and time again as an unregulated, anomic space. In other words, it is generally perceived as a non-democratic space devoid of rules and norms, and thus requires a new form of legitimation, i.e. a new social contract. Yet can we even still speak in terms of a social contract? And if so, who are the parties of the agreement and what is its content? In the present chapter, we defend three main claims: (1) the relations between the actors of the globalized, networked information society cannot be explained in terms of conflict alone; (2) the beneficiaries of the contract (of interests and rights thereof) are not limited to human beings; (3) a different political and legal sensibility should arise in order to culturally account for the decentralization of human beings from their role as exclusive beneficiaries of the social contract.

8.3 Beyond Socio-technological Determinism

This chapter relies on the premise that the impact of ICTs does not obey, nor can it be explained in terms of strict technological determinism. According to the informational representation of reality as constituted by the infosphere, the globalized, networked information society consists of a plurality of (human and artificial) agents and "patients", whose complex relations are not subject to deterministic laws alone (Taylor 2001). Rather, a key to understanding the social impact of technological evolution is to interpret it *both* through the conflicts and the norms of coordination that it is able to generate. It is essential to note that, on the one hand, we need norms of coordination even when conflict is not involved (Floridi 2014a), and on the other, that conflict need not always have a negative connotation. In a sense, as suggested by Paul Valery (1998), the concepts of peace and war are both overdetermined by that of conflict: peace is a form of conflict between human beings that is aimed at creation, whereas war is a form of conflict between human beings that is directed towards destruction. Conflict is inherent to the social nature of agents, but it is not inevitably negative. On the contrary, they can release energy and produce innovation (Benasayag – Del Rey 2007). How does this concern technology and undermine socio-technological determinism? Let us make reference, here, to some ideas presented in full elsewhere (Durante 2007).

People very often display either a utopian or a dystopian attitude towards technology, as noted by Don Ihde (2003). A utopian attitude towards technology assumes that the nature of technology is merely instrumental, and that the considerable power and means of technology is directed towards ends set through fully-aware human deliberations and plans. A dystopian attitude towards technology assumes, on the contrary, that technology sets itself, intrinsically, beyond human control and therefore has the power to shape social reality according to unrestrained and unpredicted effects. Both of these attitudes err in their radicalism. Technology is never merely instrumental, nor is it merely and directly capable of overdetermining a social reality. Let us review some of the methodological points covered in Chap. 1.

8.3.1 Non-instrumentalism

As already noted, there are two main reasons for which a purely instrumental conception of technology is at present inadequate. First, the relation between means and ends is not bound up entirely with the structure of the instrument used, but also with the act through which a means is concretely oriented towards an end. This means that every instrument is designed for an end. In contrast, the actual use through which this instrument is destined towards a particular end can always differ from the use for which it was designed. A screwdriver can be used to kill someone. On this basis, we cannot speak of the mere instrumentality of technology (and this includes any claim about the shaping of society by means of a specific technology), given that it is impossible to define a priori the overall class of ends that an instrument can be destined for in reality. Secondly, every instrument is constructed and designed to meet a given class of needs. However, it is difficult, if not impossible, to identify from the start the importance and weight a particular instrument will have, or in other words, whether or not the instrument will be able to meet a wider class of needs than that for which it was designed. The case of a computer is paradigmatic in that the computer today is expected to meet a practically unlimited class of needs. In this case, too, one cannot speak of the mere instrumentality of technology, since it is impossible to identify in advance the whole class of needs the computer will be able to meet. Such arguments (namely, the possibility for an instrument to be destined to an unintended class of ends; and the possibility for an instrument to meet an unexpected class of needs) prevent us from conceiving technology as being strictly characterized by a stable and predictable instrumental relation between means and ends. On the contrary, such arguments seem to better support the idea of a "multistability" of technologies (Ihde 2002). It goes beyond the purposes of this text to examine this idea in detail. However, it may be useful to recall the feature of "potentiality" (Durante 2007) of technology (namely, its ability to engender new possibilities that people may turn into power), since this feature is likely to have a strong impact in the political and legal fields, as will be discussed here and in the next two chapters. Let us recall what has already been said in this regard in Chap. 1.

8.3.2 Potentiality

Technology often creates and endows people with new possibilities. These possibilities can hence be understood as affordances (Wellman et al. 2003; Kallinikos 2011). Against this backdrop, Benkler (2006) suggests that technology makes it either easier or more difficult to perform some actions and human interactions. *Ceteris paribus*, Benkler says, the easiest things to do are more likely to be done, whereas the most difficult ones are less likely to be done. However, the other variables never remain constant. This is why strict technological determinism – according to which, if provided with a technology *t*, we can expect the emergence of the social relation or structure *s* – is false (Benkler 2006). This has an important consequence that is also relevant to the fields of politics and law.

Even if the possibilities provided by a particular technology are not all implemented or durably embedded in society, many of them are adopted and become a part of our daily lives. When this happens, the possibilities may be transformed into real powers that people take advantage of; in other words, it can be said that people are empowered by the technology.[1] In this sense, the crucial social impact of technology (which may, therefore, significantly affect both politics and law) is that its implementation is capable of altering the pre-existing distribution of powers in a society, which often takes place as a redistribution of, rather than as an expansion of, powers) As already noted, this is why the political, legal or moral discourse in favor or against a given technology is, in truth, often much more concerned with and troubled by the potential redistribution of power made possible by the technology

[1] See on this, for instance, Ziccardi 2012; Amichai-Hamburger, McKenna, Tal 2008.

than with the technology itself (Durante 2007). Thus, discussion about the implementation, development and social acceptance of a technology is not only or principally guided by the representation of determined ends to pursue or needs to meet. Rather, it is first and foremost explained and guided by the need to coordinate negative conflicts or positive competition between interests and values that permeate and affect the information society. The implemented technology is able, in its turn, to spur new conflict or competition as a result of the repositioning of powers it has made possible. This *circularity* based on conflicts and competition challenges the direct and fixed correlation between technology and society postulated by socio-technological determinism. It also forces us to think about the social impact of ICTs on the information society by revising the traditional notion that social and political conflict form the basis of society. In this perspective, we need to understand what has led to the crisis in the modern political tradition of social contractualism. To this end, it is important to understand how the evolution of ICTs has changed the political space in which the political actors of modernity used to interact, meaning that we must also recall how this space was constructed. In this chapter we will touch briefly on this theme as it relates to the notion of a social contract posited at the foundation of society. A more detailed examination will be made in the next chapter, where we look at how the foundation of politics across modernity has been construed.

8.4 The Crisis of the Modern Tradition of Contractualism

Let us call to mind the premises of contractualism upon which modernity is based. Since the Treaty of Westphalia of 1648, the European space of international relations has been definied through the establishment of national sovereign boundaries, according to the paradigm of sovereignty (Pagallo 2006). Each nation state was thus conceived as an *absolute subject* of history that regulates its own space on the basis of the principle of *superiorem non recognoscentes* (that no State recognizes another State as superior within its territorial borders). Geography became the main subject of politics, and politics was conceived as a form of control over a territory. The production of law has been understood, primarily, as a context-dependent process: the creation and interpretation of legal norms regulating the interaction and communication between human beings (by granting rights and obligations) have been contingent upon a given bounded context. Although human rights are acknowledged in theory as inherent to all human beings, in the period of modernity up to now people have been concretely vested with rights and obligations insofar as they are *citizens*. Hence, their citizenship not only conveys their being empirically (linguistically and culturally) embedded in a national, bordered space (identity) but, notably, their being institutionally rooted in a legal system, i.e., in a secured, guaranteed space (sovereignty) protected by enduring and stable political and legal conventions. The modern political and legal space is a space in which life is secured because, in that space, beliefs, pacts and behaviors are stable. If on thinks, for instance of the Hobbesian foundation of political modernity, *stability* is really the first and main virtue of a system in equilibrium. This notion still permeates our culture, for the challenges posed to it by the evolution of ICTs often go unnoticed. According to Yannis Kallinikos, today's general and widespread use of ICTs calls into question our traditional tendency to think about the world and about our identities in terms of stable and enduring structures constituted, understood and experienced within well-established and bounded contexts. The networked process of globalization enables us to interact with other people on a larger scale, by crossing national borders and affecting the world. Moreover, the process of digitalization and de-contextualization of data has an important impact on the construction and perception of reality, and this has "far-reaching implications in the sense of recapturing a growing proportion of the physical and cognitive landscape of contemporary life into the medium of permutable and recombinable information" (Kallinikos 2006).

The informational turn driven by the evolution of ICTs calls into question the very model upon which modernity has been based. We must therefore take stock of the implications of this shift in philosophical terms. Recent and profound reflections by the philosopher Michel Serres provide a useful starting point. For Serres, the history[2] of the relation between human beings (the subjects) and the world (the objects) can be divided into three ages (Serres 2009): *antiquity*, in which prudent and wise human beings recognized what depended on them and what did not, concerning themselves only with the former and not worrying about ruling over the latter; *modernity*, in which human beings began to regard themselves as the centers of the universe and the masters of the world, believing that everything could be dependent upon their decisions and plans; and *the contemporary age*, in which human beings depend ultimately on those things (notably ICTs, as we will see in the next chapter), which in turn depend on us in many regards (e.g., implementation, development, regulation). This reveals a certain circularity, according to which people depend on a number of things, which are, to a large extent, dependent upon us (Serres 2009) as responsible *demiurges* (Floridi 2011, 23).

This leads Serres to affirm that our vision of ourselves over the course of modernity has been as *finite* beings confronted with a supposed *infinite* nature or world. Accordingly, our understanding of conflict (and the ensuing social contract structuring the conflict) is that it is unique to human beings who, as subjects (the only political and moral agents vested with rights and obligations), are engaged in a constant battle with one another to control and exploit the world, i.e., the inanimate object. However, this view is no longer tenable. It is we who are the *infinite* beings (as to our extended capacities of reason, research, desire, will, power, processing and exploitation [Serres 2009]) and it is nature or the world that is *finite*. This realization should lead us as responsible subjects to revise our current understanding of the nature of conflict and reconsider our own role as coordinators within the world, thereby entering into a new version of the social contract. To do so, we need to understand how human conflict has been construed from modernity until now.

[2] As will be seen in the next chapter, Floridi's critical examination of political modernity is also based on historical reflections divided into three parts. The convergence between the two philosophers is interesting and noteworthy, since they come from different philosophical backgrounds.

Fig. 8.1 Francisco Goya "Fight with Cudgels" (1820–1823) (Source: Wikipedia)

Serres observes that conflict has always been regarded in the modern and contemporary political traditions as a game between two players [in Serres' words, "un jeux à deux"]: "[...] the Master and the Servant, the Left against the Right, the Republicans against the Democrats, an ideology against another one, the green against the blue [...]" (Serres 2009). Furthermore, it has always been seen as human player against human player, locked in a struggle for control over the world. A third player, representing nature or the world, has never been envisaged. Serres likens this portrayal of the world to Goya's great painting, "Fight with Cudgels" (Fig. 8.1), which shows two men bludgeoning each other desperately while mired to their knees in quicksand. The more violent the blows, the deeper the men sink into the quagmire. Serres considers this losing battle that neither man can win as an apt representation of the self-destructive nature of the two-player game, which fails to take into account the *third* instance or viewpoint lying outside human conflict.

Paradoxically, it is the modern political tradition of contractualism itself that gave rise to the potential for a third instance or figure of authority stemming from the contract established between human beings (Hobbes [1651] 2008; from the social perspective: Simmel 1964). However, this paradox can easily be explained, for in the political tradition of contractualism, the third party is always a projection of human interests (i.e., the legitimation of the sovereign or of civil society). According to Serres, the thirdness of the third must therefore be reconsidered in relation to a new, concrete third, i.e., the world, which can be interpreted from outside of any anthropological standpoint, either in *ecological terms* (as, in the case of Serres, by coupling his ecological stance with an epistemological, legal and political dimension) or in *informationally environmental terms* (as, in the case of Floridi, by coupling the idea of infosphere [2003] with that of a new environmentalism [2010a]). In both cases, this entails the creation of a new and revised contract that challenges "human narcissism" (Serres 2009) and the political lexicon of modernity, so firmly rooted in the notion of citizenship. Theories about the form this contract should take have been proposed by Serres (1995, 2009) and Floridi (2007a, b) and were outlined in the previous section. Our present aim is to understand the basic requirements of the conceptual shift necessary to account for the transformation of our conventional and durable beliefs, practices and institutions that can no longer govern the infosphere in the same way they have governed the (analogical) political space of modernity.

8.5 New Political and Legal Subjects

Our hypothesis is that we need to develop a political and legal responsiveness and sensitivity (more on this in the following chapters) capable of challenging the philosophical premises of the modern notions of political and legal subjects. These notions have traditionally been grounded upon the following three main assumptions:

(1) political and legal subjectivity is the exclusive prerogative of human beings;
(2) human beings are the only legitimate sources of the politically and legally relevant information for the recognition and granting of rights and obligations;
(3) political and legal subjectivity is mostly based on the strict symmetry between rights and obligations.

All of these assumptions need to be re-evaluated and revised. The theoretical grounds for this discussion and revision may be found, to our understanding, in a theory of information, for the simple reasons that: (a) we are undeniably part of a globalized, networked information society (see Chaps. 2 and 3); and (b) we behave as human agents and patients that relentlessly transmit, exchange and share information (i.e. messages) with artificial agents and patients (see Chap. 4) and with the things of the world (Serres 2009). Here lies a pivotal epistemological point (an authentic gestalt switch), which needs to be fully grasped and understood, since it enables us to eventually revise the epistemic dichotomy that has fashioned the whole of modernity, namely, the dichotomy between subject and object. This crucial point has been perceptively observed by Michel Serres, and we must closely follow his main line of reasoning through reference to Floridi's more articulated philosophy of information before making some more general remarks.

Against the backdrop of modernity's dichotomous division and opposition between a subject and an object pole, the subject has been anthropologically conceived as a thinking human being *determining* the way the objective reality is experienced and construed. In contrast, the object has been understood as what is *determined* and hence can, to a greater or lesser extent, be manipulated, exploited and disposed of. The object (*objectum*, *Gegenstand*, *objet*, *oggetto*) is, in its literal meaning, that which *stands before* the subject, without being able to take any initiative towards the subject, which, in contrast, can take any initiative towards the object. This is the theoretical core of the basic asymmetry characterizing the relation between subject and object. According to this asymmetry, the human subject is thought of and understood as the only legitimate producer of the relevant information on the basis of which people are meant to take decisions, behave and be (politically, legally and morally) measured. As a result, human beings are understood to be the only subjects vested with rights and obligations. For this reason, the respect we may owe to objects is always founded upon some form of human interest; it is, in fact, a mirror view of this interest and forms part of a theory of *reflected interests*. In this sense, the asymmetry that characterizes, in epistemic terms, the dichotomy between subject and object is indeed reinforced in political, legal and moral terms, by the idea that an object cannot be understood or taken as what counts as a political, legal or moral subject (on behalf of which people would thus be able to claim respect).

According to Serres, this view may change to the extent that we recognize that both human beings and the things of the world (i.e. both subjects and objects) share the same informational nature, that is, they are both *information systems*, which are able to perform four universal informational operations: they can receive, generate, store and treat information. Serres makes this point very clear (2009):

> [...] the things of Land and of Life, codified like us, are capable of receiving, producing, storing and treating information. [...] This quadruple attitude does not design us as subjects nor designs them [i.e. the things of world] as objects. In the same way that we communicate, we understand and speak, we write and read, both non-living and living things produce and receive information, store and treat it. Asymmetric and parasitic, the old division subject-object no longer holds; every subject becomes object; every object becomes subject.

Serres notes that human beings deal relentlessly with information received from non-human beings. We are more interested, here in the main conceptual tenets of Serres' theory than in the finer points that could be made from the standpoint of information theory. Let us assume that this idea is correct in relation to all those artificial agents able to perform the four universal informational operations. When it refers to inanimate objects, this view holds true, as granted by Luciano Floridi when he warns us against the risks implicit in some pancomputationalist views when we consider both inanimate things and the notion of information at the proper level of abstraction (Floridi 2011, 47-48):

> AI and cognitive science study agents as informational systems that receive, store, retrieve, transform, generate and transmit information. This is the *information processing view*. Before the development of connectionist and dynamic-system models of information processing, it was also known as the *computational view* (Floridi 2011, 35);
>
> Informational concepts are so powerful that, given the right *level of abstraction*, anything can be presented as an information system, from a building to a volcano, from a forest to a dinner, from a brain to a company. Likewise, any process can be simulated informationally: heating, flying, and knitting (Floridi 2011, 36).

However, in the present context, our aim is not that of defining the ontological status of information (see Floridi 2011, 42-45) or of determining the extent to which an information processing view might be accepted. Here we wish to highlight the profound role played by conceptual revision of modernism's subject/object dichotomy in redefining our understanding of the foundations of political and legal subjectivity and in stipulating a new social contract for the information society. From the standpoint of the most sophisticated information theory, it is enough to note that, according to Floridi's PI and EI, any entity is described and experienced as an informational object at the right level of abstraction (see Chaps. 1 and 3). At present, we are interested in examining the following three main theoretical consequences of the aforementioned conceptual revision.

8.5.1 From "Stand" to "Standing"

It is not that we have to naturalize human sciences or to humanize natural sciences, for that would merely reaffirm the existing dichotomy between subject and object. Instead, we have to recognize that what we used to defined in terms of opposed entities (subject/object) both belong to a global environment ultimately made up of information, or the infosphere (Floridi 2003). Both entities *cooperate* in the informational flourishing of reality.[3] This explains why the foundation of society is not necessarily and exclusively based on conflict, but also on positive competition (both of which require norms of coordination). Our epistemological attention is hence centered on the life-cycle of information, or how information is generated, shared, transmitted and accessed, rather than on the polarity between subject and object. This means that the object, either as a *source* of environmental data or as a semantic informational *resource* (Floridi 2011, 77), cooperates in the informational flourishing of reality, *in the same way and to the same degree as* other subjects, that is, of any informational object (Floridi 2003) or information system (Serres 2009). This is the theoretical premise according to which we may say that the object not only *stands before* the subject but has a (legal or moral) *standing* before it: (legal or moral) subjectivity can no longer be the exclusive prerogative of human beings.

8.5.2 From "Citizenship" to "Informationship"

In the modern age up to now human beings have been conceived as the only legitimate sources of law, thus producing the politically and legally relevant information for the well being of society and the world at large. They have been conceived as citizens producing and sharing politically and legally relevant information with other citizens, particularly in bounded contexts (the national sovereign states). It is citizenship – more than humanity – that provides humans with a set of rights and obligations. Citizenship expresses the political and legal embeddedness of the subject within a given territory and politics is thus understood as a form of control over this territory. The spread of ICTs, the emergence of a global informational

[3] In this sense, it does not matter whether they contribute in terms of semantic or environmental information (on this point see Chap. 10). For a model of trust for networked cooperation you may see Durante, 2008.

environment and the informational rendition of reality (Kallinikos 2006), the understanding of both human beings and things of of world as informational objects (Floridi 2003) or information systems (Serres 2009) – all of these developments lead us to deem that politics and law can no longer be understood (whether exclusively or primarily) as forms of control over a territory or a society in accordance with the political and legal formations of modernity. As we will describe more clearly in the next chapter, the contemporary and, notably, the impending political and legal frameworks will be increasingly concerned with control over the life-cycle of information. In this perspective, it is unlikely that human beings will be understood as the only producers of politically and legally relevant information: artificial agents, biological organisms, and any other informational objects or information systems, including the environment, produce data and informational resources that structure the global informational environment. There are two converging reasons for which informational objects (Floridi 1999) or systems (Serres 2009) may count as political, legal or moral subjects: (a) since, qua informational objects, they *enrich* the infosphere of relations and differences (Floridi 2003), by giving rise to an ontological idea of pluralism (Durante 2010); (b) since, qua informational systems, they do *exchange* information, by extending the limits of human communication (Serres 2009). Therefore, humans will no longer be considered the only legitimate sources of the relevant information for the recognition and granting of rights and obligations. We progressively move from an antiquated view of citizenship to a new form of global participation within the infosphere, which we may define as *informationship*, which reveals our relational and interactive embeddedness in an informational construct of reality.

8.5.3 From an "Agent-Oriented" to a "Patient-Oriented" Model of Responsibility

From a philosophical standpoint, the golden rule has been based on the fundamental principle of reciprocity, which can be formulated as follows: "Do unto others as you would have them do unto you". There is no reason, in principle, to alter this symmetry and make one of the terms of the relation prevail over the other. For instance, the point of equilibrium of a liberal society is given (e.g. according to Kant), by the equal coordination of external freedoms (and responsibilities thereof). In this perspective, rights are coextensive with responsibilities; in other words, responsibility is coextensive with freedom. People whose rights are infringed can ask the other party to account for its behavior before a third institutionalized figure (for instance, a judge), who is called upon to repair the breached symmetry. According to this *agent-oriented* model based on symmetry, the only one vested to ask for restoration is a subject able to take an initiative, or in other words, a human being. Obviously, an object, no matter how violated, cannot take any initiative towards a subject. Even if one is inclined to recognize that a tree has a moral standing, the tree will never be able to ask for an accounting of others' actions. In this sense, an object is able to receive protection only to the extent to which this protection is the reflection of a human interest.

This view may change if one takes a different standpoint, that of the patient (Floridi 2004a, b). On the basis of an agent-oriented model, it is generally held that we are responsible to the extent to which we *are* free (or conscious or provided with intentional stances, etc.). However, we are concretely responsible to the extent to which we *delimit* our freedom.[4] It is this delimitation of freedom that measures the extent of our responsibility, and we are responsible for our behaviors only within the scope of this delimitation. These limits are historically and culturally variable and depend on the way we account for the meaning of the world and of the society we live in, for the meaning of our own behavior, and for the meaning itself we attach to our idea of freedom. When delimiting our freedom, we are already involved in the moral and legal process of accounting for others and being responsible to our comprehension of ourselves and of the world in which we live. Paradoxically, we are free to the extent to which we have responsibilities towards others, whether they be subjects or objects. It is from the point of view of the patient and the patient's vulnerability that we are called upon to revise and update, from time to time, the way we delimit our own freedom. A tree will never be able to ask us to account for our behavior. However, a different sensibility towards the informational nature of the world will emerge to the extent to which we recognize that, when called upon to delimit our freedom and to set the legal or moral standards of our responsibility, we do this already *in response* to the informational objects (Floridi 2011, 77) that constitute the infosphere and give meaning to reality, or to the information we receive from all the information systems of the world (Serres 2009).

8.6 A New Social or Natural Contract

These philosophical considerations can provide us with the theoretical basis for a different understanding of the relation between politics, law and information, since human beings are no longer conceived, in the informational perspective examined, as the exclusive sources of the relevant political and legal information. As shown in the present chapter, the premise on which modernity is based - that a sharp division between subject and object, which makes the subject always prevail over the object both from an epistemological and a political, legal or moral standpoint - no longer holds. On the contrary, there is some form of interaction (Floridi 2010a) or of communication (Serres 2009)[5] between subjects and objects, according to which we

[4] For instance, we cannot be held responsible for the whole chain of consequences that stems from our action. There must be a point at which the chain of (moral or legal) responsibility is interrupted; otherwise, our ethical and legal commitments or responsibilities would be unbearably supererogatory. The point at which the chain of (moral or legal) responsibility is interrupted, i.e. delimited, is the result of our free, collective choice (which is not necessarily arbitrary, but often guided by reasons and/or values), through which we give a shared (moral or legal) meaning to both freedom and responsibility.

[5] We have also spoken, elsewhere, of a relation of mutual implication (Durante 2011).

depend on what depends on us, since we are codifying and codified things (Serres 2009) or, in Floridi's informational terms, structuring structures (Floridi 2010b).

On this basis, a new social (Floridi) or natural (Serres) contract has been envisaged and proposed, even if in different terms, by Luciano Floridi (2007b) and Michel Serres (1995, 2009). It is not possible, in the present context, to examine these proposals in full detail. What matters here is to stress the importance of two basic conditions necessary for the emergence of a new social or natural contract and which need to be added to the conceptual revision of the notion of political and legal subjectivity outlined in this chapter: (a) the *demiurgic* stewardship or responsibility of humanity (Floridi 2011); (b) the critical *tension* between knowledge and power (Serres 2009). We have already touched on these issues briefly in the chapter, but shall now look at them again in greater detail. Let us first consider Floridi's conception of a new social contract (Floridi 2007b), understood and constructed in terms of ontic trust between generations, outside of any strict anthropocentric perspective:

> Interpretations of the theory of the social contract tend to be highly (and often unknowingly) anthropocentric (the focus is only on human rational agents) and stress the coercive nature of the agreement. These two aspects are not characteristic of the concept of ontic trust, but the basic idea of a fundamental agreement between parties as a foundation of moral interactions is sensible. In the case of the ontic trust, it is transformed into a primeval, entirely hypothetical *pact*, logically predating the social contract, which all agents cannot but sign when they come into existence, and that is constantly renewed in successive generations (Floridi 2007b, 15).

Contrary to the modern political tradition, ontic trust is structured in such a way, according to which we may first observe that this agreement is no longer based on coercion, but on mutual interdependence as informational objects. Conflict is no longer held to be the only foundation of the society.[6] In contrast, mutual interdependence requires us to establish norms of coordination, which take the form of ontic trust:

[6] We will say more on this point in the following chapter. Contrary to a longstanding tradition throughout almost all of modernity, Floridi believes that norms of coordination are not only required in a conflicting society and that even a society of angels would need adopting norms, in order to coordinate their positive intentions and behaviours (Floridi 2014a, b). Almost in the same sense, Emmanuel Levinas proposed what has been defined by Miguel Abensour as an "extravagant hypothesis" (Abensour 2006), namely, the idea that the political and legal order of a society is not based on and deduced from the hypothesis of original violence (as, for instance, in Hobbes' political theory) but that it is based on and deduced from the hypothesis of original inclination towards justice, which humans beings attempt to translate into reality and realize (even if they can do this always only in part).Whilst the hypothesis of original violence turns out to be an implicit justification for the existing political and legal order (because the latter is by definition less violent than the former is supposed to be), the hypothesis of an original inclination towards justice requires the existing political and legal order to be more justified and to tend towards this normative dimension. For Levinas' extravagant hypothesis, see Levinas 1969 and 1990. For a commentary about this hypothesis and its political and legal implications, see Durante 2002.

> Generally speaking, a trust in the English legal system is an entity in which someone (the trustee) holds and manages the former assets of a person (the trustor, or donor) for the benefit of certain persons or entities (the beneficiaries). Strictly speaking, nobody owns the assets, since the trustor has donated them, the trustee has only legal ownership and the beneficiary has only equitable ownership. Now, the logical form of this sort of agreement can be used to model the ontic trust, in the following way:
>
> - the assets or 'corpus' is represented by the world, including all existing agents and patients;
> - the donors are all past and current *generations* of agents;
> - the trustees are all current *individual* agents;
> - the beneficiaries are all current and future *individual* agents and patients.
>
> By coming into being, an agent is made possible thanks to the existence of other entities. It *is* therefore bound to all that already is both *unwillingly* and *inescapably*. It *should be* so also *caringly*. [...] *Caringly* because participation in reality by any entity, including an agent – that is, the fact that any entity is an expression of what exists – provides a right to existence and an invitation (not a duty) to respect and take care of other entities. The pact then involves no coercion, but a mutual relation of appreciation, gratitude and care, which is fostered by the recognition of the dependence of all entities on each other (Floridi 2007b, 16).

However, Floridi explains that adopting a non-anthropocentric view in no way amounts to relieving human beings from the overall responsibilities that are incumbent upon them:

> [...] *demiourgos*, which literally means 'public worker', was originally used in Greek to refer to any artisan practicing his craft or trade for the use of public. So by *demiurge* I mean here an artisan whose extended, but not unlimited, ontic powers can be variously exercised (in terms of control, creation, modeling, design, shaping, etc.) over itself (e.g. ethically, genetically, physiologically, neurologically, narratively), over society (e.g. legally, culturally, politically, economically, religiously) and over natural or artificial environments (e.g. physically and informationally) for the use of humanity. This demiurge is like a gardener who builds her environment and takes care of it (Floridi 2011, 23).

On the contrary, a non-anthropocentric view extends the concept of what may count as a center of moral claim, that is, of the class of entities towards which we may be responsible (as we have seen more greater detail in Chap. 3):

> The EI brings to ultimate completion the process of enlargement of the concept of what may count as a centre of a (no matter how minimal) moral claim, which now includes every instance of *being* understood informationally, no matter whether physically implemented or not. IE holds that every entity, as an expression of *being*, has a dignity, constituted by its mode of existence and essence (the collection of all the elementary proprieties that constitute it for what it is), which deserve to be respected (at least in a minimal and overridable sense) and hence place moral claims on the interacting agent and ought to contribute to guiding and constraining his ethical decisions and behaviour whenever possible. The ontic trust (and the corresponding ontological equality principle among entities) means that any form of reality (any instance of information/*being*), simply by the fact of *being* what it is, enjoys a minimal, initial, overridable, equal right to exist and develop in a way which is appropriate to its nature" (Floridi 2007a, b, 17).

This last quotation of Floridi (which is commented on in detail in Chap. 3, and in Chap. 6, with regard to the basic ontological equality principle), shows us the potential asymmetry between those who are responsible for the ontic trust, i.e., the trustees and individual agents, and those who are the beneficiaries of their care and stewardship (i.e. the individual agents and patients, including all the informational objects). This asymmetry extends the sphere of political and legal responsibility and requires us to consider any instance of information/being as part of an overall reality (i.e., the infosphere), the protection of which may entail the protection of the interactions and relations we enjoy with each other and with our own environment. In this sense, the point is that, in that form of protection, we are not protecting passive objects (i.e. reflected interests) but spheres of interactions and relations (i.e. our co-constitutive interests). Our culture and society is largely dominated by a deep-seated sense of utilitarianism, according to which we should pay attention to and appreciate only that which is of concrete interest to us, namely, what is 'interesting'. However, we have hence lost sight of the profound meaning of the word 'interest', which comes from Latin (*inter-esse*) meaning 'to be among and in the midst of things', that is, to be in an enduring and interacting relation with all other things of the world that are constitutive of the environment we live in and we are confronted with (see on this point Chap. 5). This point is well made by Heidegger (1954, 5), who distinguishes the idea of interest from what is merely meant to be interesting:

> Interest, *interesse*, means to be among and in the midst of things, or to be at the centre of a thing and to stay with it. But today's interest accepts as valid only what is interesting. And interesting is the sort of thing that can freely be regarded as indifferent the next moment, and be displaced by something else, which then concerns us just as little as what went before. Many people today take the view that they are doing great honor to something by finding it interesting, The truth is that such an opinion has already relegated the interesting thing to the ranks of what is indifferent and soon boring.

Let us now turn our attention to Serres' conception of the social contract. Serres conceives the social contract as a natural contract (Serres 1995) that should be agreed upon for the benefit of human beings as well as for the benefit of the things of the world (life and earth). It can be argued, as remarked, that those things may have a moral standing (which is, nonetheless, very controversial) but that they cannot stand on their own to claim respect. Who should then be entrusted, nowadays, to take their word and speak on behalf of the things of the world?

According to Serres (2009), this role is to be undertaken by "the scientists". The French philosopher remarks that the community of scientists has often, if not always, entered into a strong tension with the existing powers that have structured modern societies, notably, the religious, political (military) and economic powers (Serres 2009). This tension consists in the fact that such powers have an interest in restricting access to information and to knowledge at large. The progressive universalization of access to information and to knowledge can be posited at the foundation of "a real democracy, whereas the entire previous hierarchy has been based on the exclusivity of information […]. On the contrary, democracy is at start the outcome of the revelation of mysteries; then, of the divulgation of secrets; and, in the end, of the universal vulgarization" (Serres 2009).

For this reason, scientists should be kept detached from the influence of those powers (*rectius*: those powers should be kept detached from the work of scientists in a democratic and secular information society) and, accordingly, the current and future epistemology should be more and more concerned with the "soft" sciences and powers of information (Serres 2009). The philosopher portrays, thus, in these terms the pivotal concept of "softness" (Serres 2009):

> Softness [...] defines also an ensemble of knowledge, technologies and practices – precisely, those of intervention and access – the importance of which rapidly overwhelms that of the *hard* technologies that we use, we celebrate, but that have been destroying our habitat since the industrial revolution, if not since the stone age. Soft changes, the three revolutions of writing, printing and computers have overturned history, practices, institutions and power in our societies, in a much more fundamental way than hard changes.

According to Serres (2009), the path towards a new understanding and foundation of the social or natural contract for the globalized and networked information society might not be just political, legal or ethical. It should be, first and foremost, informational and based on the theoretical commitment of the scientific community at large towards considering the role and the concept of the information systems. This concept becomes the cornerstone of a new first philosophy (*philosophia prima*), since it enables us to overcome the dichotomy subject/object and to be provided with a third viewpoint, i.e., that of information, which mediates the relation between us and the world and gives us a new sense of what is nature. This is the final and main point being made by the French philosopher of sciences, whose views can therefore be backed by the envisaged "regress" to a foundational philosophy of information (precisely in the terms of a *philosophia prima*), which has been clearly stated by Luciano Floridi (2011, 25):

> The scientific revolution made seventeenth century philosophers redirect their attention from the nature of the knowable object to the epistemic relation between it and the knowing subject, and hence from metaphysics to epistemology. The subsequent growth of the information society and the appearance of the infosphere, as the environment in which millions of people spend their time nowadays, have led contemporary philosophy to privilege critical reflection first on the domain represented by the memory and languages of organized knowledge, the instruments whereby the infosphere is managed – thus moving from epistemology to philosophy of language and logic – and then on the nature of its very fabric and essence, information itself. Information has thus arisen as a concept as fundamental and important as Being, knowledge, life, intelligence, meaning or good and evil – all pivotal concepts with which it is interdependent – and so equally worthy of autonomous investigation.

8.7 Conclusions

In line with Serres, Floridi notes the importance of reconciling *physis* (understood as nature or reality) and *techne* (understood as contemporary practical science and its application). And this is exactly what requires us to adopt an environmental approach that is conceived and formulated in informational terms, according to which any instance of being is understood, at the proper level of abstraction, in terms of informational object (Floridi) or information system (Serres). As Floridi (2010a, 119) has pointed out:

> This [environmental approach] should not privilege the natural or untouched, but treat as authentic and genuine all forms of existence and behaviour, even those based on artificial, synthetic, or engineered artefacts. This sort of holistic environmentalism requires a change in our metaphysical perspective about the relationship between *physis* (nature, reality) and *techne* (practical science and its application).

Floridi suggests that the reason for the "marriage of *physis* and *techne*" (Floridi 2010a, 119) lies in the relation of mutual dependence between information societies and ICTs, which is destined to affect our own lives not only in the short but also in the long run:

> It seems beyond doubt that a marriage between *physis* and *techne* is vital for our future and hence worth our sustained efforts. Information societies increasingly depend upon technology to thrive, but they equally need a healthy, natural environment to flourish. Try to imagine the world not tomorrow or next year, but next century, or next millennium: a divorce between *physis* and *techne* would be utterly disastrous both for our welfare and for the wellbeing of our habitat. (Floridi 2010a, 199–120).

The condition of possibility for this marriage to be successful resides, in the same line of Serres, both in changing the metaphysical (Floridi) or epistemological (Serres) perspective and in improving "the management of information" (Floridi 2010a, 120): "ICTs can help us in our fight against the destruction, impoverishment, vandalism, and waste of both natural and human resources, including historical and cultural ones" (Floridi 2010a, 121). This brings us back to the main tenet of the present chapter: we need to endorse an ethical intellectualism based on the correct management of the life-cycle of information. Only this can enable us to take part in the (political, legal and moral) game on non-absolutist and non-anthropocentric premises that will most likely diverge from "human narcissism" or "jeux-à-deux" (the game between two players), so heavily criticized by Michel Serres. Let us make final reference to Floridi's commitment to and interpretation of this renewed form of ethical intellectualism (Floridi 2010a, 121):

> So here is how we may reinterpret Socrates' ethical intellectualism […]: we do evil because we do not know better, in the sense that the better the information management is, the less moral evil is caused. With a proviso, though: some ethical theories seem to assume that the moral game, played by agents in their environments, may be won absolutely, i.e. not in terms of higher scores, but by scoring perhaps very little as long as no moral loss or error occurs […]. It seems that this absolute view has led parties to underestimate the importance of successful compromises. Imagine an environmentalist unable to accept any technology responsible for some level of carbon dioxide emission, no matter how it may counterbalance it. The more realistic and challenging view is that moral evil is unavoidable, so that the real effort lies in limiting it and counterbalancing it with more moral goodness.

References

Abensour, M. 2006. L'extravagante hypothèse, in Levinas, collectif aux éditions Bayard, Paris, 73–105.

Amichai-Hamburger, Y., K. McKenna, and S.A. Tal. 2008, September. E-empowerment: Empowerment by the Internet, Special Issue: *Internet Empowerment. Computers in Human Behaviour* 24 (5): 1776–1789.

Benasayag, M., and A. del Rey. 2007. *Eloge du conflit*. Paris: Editions La Découverte.

Benkler, Y. 2006. *The Wealth of Networks: How Social Production Transforms Markets and Freedom*. New Haven CT: Yale University Press.

Castells, M. 1999. *The Information Age: Economy, Society, and Culture*. Vol. 1–3. Malden, MA: Wiley-Blackwell.

———. 2009. *Communication Power*. Oxford: Oxford University Press.

Durante, M. 2002. *Comunità e alterità nell'opera di Emmanuel Levinas: il terzo, la legge, la giustizia*. Torino: Thélème.

———. 2007. Il futuro del web: etica, diritto, decentramento. Dalla sussidiarietà digitale all'economia dell'informazione in rete, Giappichelli, Torino.

———. 2010. The Value of Information as Ontological Pluralism. *Knowledge, Technology & Policy* 23 (1): 149–161.

———. 2011. Normativity, Constructionism, and Constraining Affordances. *Etica & Politica/ Ethics & Politics*, Symposium on Luciano Floridi's Philosophy of Information, XIII(2): 180–200.

Floridi, L. 1999. Information Ethics: On the Philosophical Foundation of Computer Ethics. *Ethics and Information Technology* 1: 37–56.

———. 2003. On the Intrinsic Value of Information Objects and the Infosphere. *Ethics and Information Technology* 4 (4): 287–304.

———. 2004a. On the Morality of Artificial Agents. *Minds and Machines* 14 (3): 349–379.

———. 2004b. Outline of a Theory of Strongly Semantic Information. *Minds and Machines* 14 (2): 197–222.

———. 2007a. A Look into the Future Impact of ICT on Our Lives. *The Information Society* 23 (1): 59–64.

———. 2007b. Global Information Ethics: The Importance of Being Environmentally Earnest. *International Journal of Technology and Human Interaction* 3 (3): 1–11.

———. 2010a. *Information. A Very Short Introduction*. Oxford: Oxford University Press.

———. 2010b. Information Ethics. In *The Cambridge Handbook of Information and Computer Ethics*, ed. L. Floridi, 77–99. Cambridge: Cambridge University Press.

———. 2011. *The Philosophy of Information*. Oxford: Oxford University Press.

———. 2014a. *The Fourth Revolution. On the Impact of Information and Communication Technologies on Our Lives*. Oxford: Oxford University Press.

———. (ed.). 2014b. *The Onlife Manifesto. Being Human in a Hyperconnected Era*, Dordrecht: Springer.

Heidegger, M. 2004. *What is called thinking?* [1954]. Trans. J. Glenn Gray. New York: Harper Perennial.

Hobbes, T. 2008. *Leviathan* [1651]. Oxford: Oxford University Press.

Ihde, D. 2002. *Bodies in Technology. Electronic Mediations*. Minneapolis: University of Minnesota Press.

———. 2003. Postphenomenology Again?, Working Paper n. 3, The Centre for STS Studies, Aarhus.

Kallinikos, J. 2006. *The Consequences of Information*. In *Institutional Implications of Technological Change*. Cheltenham/Northampton, MA: Edward Elgar.

———. 2011. *Governing Through Technology. Information Artefacts and Social Practice*. Houndmills, Basingstoke: Palgrave Macmillan.

Levinas, E. 1969. *Totality and Infinity: An Essay on Exteriority* [1961]. Trans. A. Lingis. Pittsburgh: Dusquene University Press.

———. 1990. Reflections on the Philosophy of Hitlerism [1934]. Trans. S. Hand. *Critical Inquiry*, 17: 63–71.

Nye, J. 2008. *The Powers to Lead: Soft, Hard, and Smart*. Oxford: Oxford University Press.

Pagallo, U. 2006. *Teoria giuridica della complessità*. Torino: Giappichelli.

Serres, M. 1995. *The Natural Contract*, Trans. E. MacArthur and W. Paulson. Ann Arbor: University of Michigan Press.

———. 2009. *Temps des crises*. Paris: Editions Le Pommier.

Simmel, G. 1964. *Conflict & The Web of Group Affiliations*. New York: Free Press.

Taylor, M. 2001. *The Moment of Complexity: Emerging Network Culture*. Chicago: Chicago University Press.

Valery, P. (1998). La crise de l'esprit. In *Varieté I et II*, Folio essais. Paris: Gallimard.

Wellman, B., et al. 2003. The Social Affordance of the Internet for Networked Individualism. *Journal of Computer-Mediated Communication* 8 (3.), available online.

Ziccardi, G. 2012. *Resistance, Liberation Technology and Human Rights in the Digital Age*. Dordrecht/Berlin: Springer.

An Informational Approach to Politics

9

Abstract

The information revolution engendered by the evolution of ICTs has a strong impact on our conception of politics, since it affects two fundamental notions on which politics has been constructed throughout modernity: regulation (notably, the relation between the rulers and the ruled) and space (notably, the idea of a territory controlled by a sovereign power). Politics is no longer merely understood, in descriptive terms, as a form of control over a territory and, in normative terms, as the art of making collective decisions. In the information age, politics is beginning to be understood as the efficient and effective management and control of the information life cycle, which almost always exceeds the spatial constraints of nation state territories. The main concern of politics is thus no longer that of the dichotomy or dialectics between the rulers and the ruled, as is typical with traditional notions of government. It is rather that of the dichotomy or dialectics between what is governable and what is ungovernable, characteristic of current notions of governance, understood as a measure of the degree of complexity of our information societies.

9.1 Introduction

This chapter examines the notion of politics as being redefined in the information age and thus serves as a bridge between the previous chapter on the foundation of the information society and the following one on the construal of law within an informational approach. Before turning to the issue of politics itself, a few remarks are in order concerning the notion of law, given that it is inextricably linked with both history and politics and, for some scholars (e.g. Gardner 2013), should even be considered part of politics. Without entering into this long-standing and complex debate, suffice it to say that the law is a largely historically determined phenomenon constructed within the margins of politics, particularly in the way that a society

M. Durante, *Ethics, Law and the Politics of Information*, The International Library of Ethics, Law and Technology 18, DOI 10.1007/978-94-024-1150-8_9

deals with certain issues pertaining to its own constitution. Howeverfascinating and theoretically permissible is to search for a perennial or supra-historical notion of the law (consider Cicero's beautiful formulation according to which the law is *hominis ad hominem proportio*, i.e., the measure of the relationship a person has with others), the law is essentially a product of its specific historical context. As already noted, the law is historically produced within a conception of politics that involves a number of key issues structuring the political and constitutional architecture of any society. During the modern age, these issues have included the genesis and legitimization of power, the founding of the modern state as a form of organization of human relations, the life of democracy, the relationship between law, morality, and politics. To fully grasp how the law is being reconceptualised in information societies, we must therefore understand how the information revolution might also be affecting our understanding of history and politics. This analysis necessarily requires a long-term investigation, inevitably introducing the risk of reducing their complexities or of trivializing – in terms that are homogeneous and settled – certain aspects that upon further examination would prove to be heterogeneous and controversial. We will nonetheless try to piece together a mosaic in the present chapter, drawing on Floridi's recent reflections on the topic. This portrayal, far from being exhaustive, intends only to give an account of the discontinuities or fractures that cross over modernity and separate it from our times and that, when examined from a theoretical viewpoint, allow us to highlight two basic *axial turns* that define, respectively, the conceptual background of politics in the modern and contemporary ages. Against this backdrop, let us start by considering Floridi's conception of history.

According to Floridi (2014a, b), the concept of history is dependent on the existence of ICTs. No historical narrative or historiography would exist if not for someone's ability to collect and record traces of the past and to imbue them with a meaning that survives over time and is communicated to others. This requires the existence of an ICT, no matter how rudimental or sophisticated. There would therefore be no history or historiography if we did not have an ICT capable of collecting, recording, interpreting and communicating records of the past. Human beings throughout history have lived in societies characterized by the ICT of the times. Floridi divides human life into three ages of development (Floridi 2014a): *prehistory, history* and *hyper-history*.

Since history coincides with the information age, prehistory refers to the period of time predating humanity's development of systems enabling it to collect, record, interpret and communicate traces of the past. History begins, as historiography, when humanity created tools allowing it to externalize memory, to deliver it to a support (however fleeting or fragile), allowing it to accumulate and rework traces of the past, transforming them into information relevant for others, i.e., in the wealth of experiences that make up the lessons of history (Floridi 2014a). The information and communication technologies used by humanity to structure and organize the historical narrative (e.g., from the oral to the written tradition, from direct to indirect testimony, up to history conceived in the modern sense as a narrative exclusively built on documents) have changed over time, and these changes have had enormous consequences on the level of meaning, human relations, power relations, the political and legal status of the different information societies. The fact remains, however, that all of these societies have been characterized by the availability of ICTs that contributed along with other factors (technological, political, economic, social, cultural, etc.) to the development of individual and social welfare.

According to Floridi, we have now entered a new and different age: hyperhistory. While throughout the historical development of humanity both individual and social welfare were *related to* the evolution of ICTs, in the hyper-historical age, they are mostly *dependent on* the evolution of ICTs and, accordingly, on our ability to efficiently and effectively manage the life cycle of information (Floridi 2014a). Floridi expresses this dependency succinctly as follows: "Prehistory and history work like adverbs: they tell us *how* people live, not *when* or *where* they live. From this perspective, human societies currently stretch across three ages, as ways of living" (Floridi 2014a). This means that the discontinuity between these different eras is not merely temporal, as if these ages or life forms were limited to a succession in time. In contrast, the discontinuity (between history and hyper-history) concerns this very relation of dependence, so it is quite possible that some information societies today (and perhaps a large majority) still live historically. In such societies, the role of ICTs has not yet supplanted, either in centrality or in importance, the role of other technologies, nor is it really possible to say that other factors of progress and development have been mostly or entirely rethought in informational terms. Nonetheless, a growing number of individuals are now living in informational societies, "where ICTs and their data processing capabilities are the necessary condition for the maintenance and development of any further development of societal welfare, personal well-being, and overall flourishing" (Floridi 2014a). These individuals already live hyper-historically: their conditions of life depend more on the life cycle of information than on any other factor. For this reason, we need to understand how deeply this change is affecting the way in which politics is conceived in our time.

Our hypothesis, which we intend to expound and test in the course of this chapter, is that we are experiencing an axial turn in politics. The conceptual basis upon which politics is built and predicated in modernity is changing, precisely because of the progressive unfolding of hyper-history, understood in the sense just explained as a relation of dependence on the life cycle of information. First, the centrality of the life cycle of information reduces the conceptual gap between descriptive and normative conceptions of politics. As traditionally understood, the descriptive view of politics concerns the ability to control a territory, whereas the normative view concerns the art of making collective decisions. The informational perspective links the descriptive and normative standpoints and allows us to consider them together, for the art of taking collective decisions depends less and less on the sword *(hard power)* and more and more on the public mind (*soft power),* i.e., on the ability to manage the life cycle of information efficiently and effectively. Thus, politics ceases to be conceived with regards to the *life of people* (politics is what makes people die or lets them live in the Hobbesian perspective of modern natural law; or, in contrast, what makes people live or lets them die in the post-modern perspective of Foucault's biopolitics[1]), to be conceived in relation to the *life cycle of information*. Another facet of this shift can also be seen, in our opinion, as the second axial turn in politics.

The first axial turn is that which characterizes modernity. It supports the notion that the political order of a society is an artificial construct of human design, and places at the center of the political discourse the relationship between the rulers and the ruled (or the governors and the governed). This view results from "disenchantment of the world" (Gauchet 1985) and emphasizes the legitimacy of power understood as the genesis of democratic life. It hence conceives of politics as a dialectic between the rulers and the ruled based on the quest for consent by the former and the request for participation by the latter.

The second axial turn is that which characterizes hyper-history. Like the first axial turn, it also accepts the notion that the political order of a society is an artificial construct of human design, but one that is viewed as an emergent property of a system intended to govern an increasingly complex structure of reality (depending on the life cycle of information) that focuses the political discourse on the relationship between (what is) governable and (what remains) ungovernable. This view results from the information revolution, and places the emphasis on *governance* as a dimension that qualifies democratic life and understands politics as (the ability to include political actors in) control over the life cycle of information against the backdrop of the growing complexity of information societies. To test our hypothesis, we must take a closer look at what might be the conception of politics stemming from Luciano Floridi's informational approach to the question under exam.

9.2 The Transition from the First to the Second Axial Turn in Politics

For the sake of brevity, we limit our analysis to the period of modernity starting from the Peace of Westphalia (1648), when international political order was constructed through affirmation of the role of sovereign States as the primary political actors who recognized no higher authority above themselves (according to the doctrine of *superiorem not recognoscentes).* In this perspective, the State is sovereign in a vertical relationship over its territory and has a legal monopoly on the use of force), while it stands in a horizontal relationship of equality with other sovereign States in the international arena. In Floridi's words:

> The new system that emerged in those years, the so-called Westphalian order, saw the coming of maturity of Sovereign States and the National States as we will know them today [...]. After the design of such a new order, the physical and the legal spaces overlap and they are both governed by sovereign powers, which exercise control through physical force to impose laws and ensure their respect within the national borders. [...] With the Westphalian order, modern history becomes the age of the State, and the State becomes [...] the information agent, which legislates on and controls (or at least tries to control), insofar as it is

[1] On this issue see Foucault 2010.

> possible, all technological means involved in the information life cycle education, including census, taxes, police records, written laws and rules, press, and intelligence (Floridi 2014a, 200–201).

In this historical and political context, the first axial turn of politics emerged in the modern age. The birth and growth of the modern State called into question "the absoluteness of religious schemes: the fact that there are individuals who hold power implies that the organization and the social laws are subject to human will, since they can now be modified by the rulers. At a conceptual level, we switch from a *received* order to an order always *wanted* more: it is the beginning of the logic that will lead to the autonomy of the political sphere [...].With the State, by the political authorities, the man decides on his own things, and is the author of the laws of the society in which he lives" (Comensoli Antonini 2013, 276). Within this context, the organization and political order of society are produced and built on the basis of earthly forces, by means of the interaction of intentional agents mediated by a common framework provided by the sovereign power of the State, which is also a construction, namely, a device that governs the operation of all other devices, i.e., a *machina machinarum.* People that hold power give rise to a political order, and the society is recognized as something that exists in and by itself, thanks to the construction of a distinct political order, the representation of which thus makes common membership in the civil society recognizable to all individuals. In this sense, civil society is founded and predicated on political power. This gives rise to a paradoxical outcome, in the sense that the social space is first occupied by the political space, since it is the political space that makes the social space recognizable as something that exists in and by itself. From this it also follows that political power and legitimacy are understood as a *representative* power, expressed through the fundamental division between the rulers and the ruled, and are entirely founded *on* and implemented *within* the society (without resort to any transcendent origin). The conception of temporality underlying the construction of political order changes: time is, thus, conceived as a social dimension in which it is possible to give rise to[2] something new. The present is no longer attributed to "a mythical origin dating back to a time different from mundane time" (Comensoli Antonini 2013, 276), but is understood as a link between past and future, in which one can give rise to something new that extends and persists through time, is updated from time to time, and that has a purpose (and an end) inscribed in its origin. Time (the political temporality) is hence conceived as a *start-end* relationship in which the genesis of the foundation and legitimation of power thus assumes fundamental importance (even more important than the life of politics which it gives rise to). In this perspective, the cyclical nature (the rise and decline of power, the crises of the modern State, the electoral cycle that governs contemporary democracies and, ultimately, the whole cycle of politics) is already included and understood within the start-end

[2] However, this origin need not be necessarily interpreted in chronological terms, but can be understood as a logical or transcendental assumption. In this sense, it is the human origin that gives a specific meaning to the forms of temporality, rather than receiving one from the chronological temporality of events. In this perspective, see Esposito (2013).

relationship that places the focus on the moment of the genesis (and, thereby, conquest) of power.

In the framework just outlined, the modern State is therefore placed as the beginning and end of political life. Whether positioned in a vertical or horizontal relationship, it always figures as a centralized political organization that filters and frames the political and economic forces and the plurality of social relations that intersect it, using for this purpose and from the start all of the resources made available by ICTs. The modern State has played (and still plays to some extent) a noteworthy aggregating function; however, this does not require us to interpret the State historically as a monolithic and atomistic reality always equal to itself and resulting from an entirely deliberate design. On the contrary, the State can be conceived as the unintentional result of both conflicting and cooperating relationships between intentional agents, such as the government, judiciary, social classes, centers of interest and economic lobbies This is the case, for example, within an evolutionary concept of the State (Barberis 2013). Speaking in terms of an aggregating function of the modern State is meant to refer instead to the attempt to unify political and social fragmentation and to act as a mediator and catalyst of requests from different agents. This attempt has proven to be (relatively) successful so long as the State has been the main overseer of the information life cycle, entirely within the start-end relationship of politics. However, it is becoming more difficult to obtain and process the increasing amount of information needed to coordinate the requests of different agents in a complex and globalized world, and the modern State is hard put to fulfill its function of filtering, aggregating and coordinating information. The crisis of the modern State is determined not only by the process of (e.g., economic and political) globalization that has eroded national boundaries, but also by the process of globalization of ICTs and of information societies. The State is no longer capable of being the sole entity in charge of processing, controlling and managing the entire life cycle of information, of which it has in fact become an integral part (which is why modern States do not disappear from politics but, in some respects, still play an important role in it), as Floridi remarks:

> ICTs, as one of the main forces that made the State possible and then predominant as a historical driving force in human politics, also contributed to make it less central, in the social, political and economic life across the world, putting pressure on centralised government in favor of distributed governance and international, global coordination. The State developed by becoming more and more an Information Society, thus progressively making itself less and less the main information agent (Floridi 2014a, 201).

In the post-Westphalian order – which coincides with the dependence of the agents on ICTs and therefore with hyper-history – the State is no longer the sole or even the main informational agent, for the reasons we have just seen related to the increasingly decisive role played by the information life cycle in politics. Floridi analyzes these reasons in greater detail by making reference to three basic concepts in modern politics (power, geography, and organization), highlighting the sense in which the modern State is no longer able to entirely or sufficiently fulfill its traditional functions. In the following analysis, we show that these three concepts share an underlying philosophical basis related to the shift in the notion of temporality (the start-end relationship) brought about by informational ontology and upon which the first axial turn of modern politics is constructed and which is based, as already noted, on two main pillars: the genesis of power and the division between the rulers and the ruled).

With reference to the first notion, power, Floridi implicitly supports the idea that technologies (notably, the enabling technologies) create new possibilities that, when properly implemented and exploited by the agents, result in new powers. The upshot is that technological development alters the distribution of powers in a given society and influences its redistribution (in the same perspective, see Durante 2007).[3] This is one of the most important aspects of the evolution and spread of digital ICTs as Floridi acutely observes:

> ICTs 'democratise' data and the processing/controlling power over them, in the sense that both now tend to reside and multiply in a multitude of repositories and sources, thus creating and empowering a potentially boundless number of non-state agents, from single individuals to associations and groups, from macro-agents, like multinationals, to international, intergovernmental as well as nongovernmental, organizations and supranational institutions. The State is no longer the only, and sometimes not even the main, agent in the political arena that can exercise informational power over other informational agents, in particular over (groups of) human inforgs (Floridi 2014a, 204–205).

With reference to the second notion, geography, one can clearly perceive the twofold phenomenon pointed out by Floridi: namely, ICTs first favor and then end up undermining the development of the modern State. Geography (in particular political geography) is, in fact, the basis for the construction of modern political science, because the representation of a territory is a form of knowledge, on which a political power understood as control over the territory is based. Since ICTs create a particular space (see chapter 2), they call into question the idea of physical space as the horizon of politics in modernity (as related to the fundamental notions of territory, borders, nation, homeland, sovereignty, coexistence, and so forth). Let us follow Floridi, when he remarks that:

> ICTs de-territorialise human experience. They have made regional borders porous or, in some cases, entirely irrelevant. They have also created, and are exponentially expanding, regions of the infosphere where an increasing number of agents (not only human [...]) operate and spend more and more time, the onlife experience. Such regions are intrinsically stateless. This is generating a new tension between geo-politics, which is global and non-territorial, and the Nation State, which still defines its identity and political legitimacy in terms of sovereign territorial unit, as a Country (Floridi 2014a, 205).

[3] The technology alters the existing distribution of power in a society and redistributes it in directions not entirely predictable nor always necessarily democratic (Durante 2007). There is a thorny and controversial debate about the possibly predictable and democratic impact of ICTs on society that cannot be addressed in this context. We postpone the point made in Benkler 2006 and 2011; Castells 2009 and 2012; Morozov 2011 and 2013.

With reference to the third notion, organization, Floridi puts the emphasis on a basic issue. The State is not so much an institution whose nature is to be understood, but rather a form of organization of relationships between agents of different types and natures. If the way in which such relationships are structured changes together with the meaning we give to them, then the way in which one can organize them also changes. The re-ontologization of space in informational terms has significantly changed the formation and the meaning of such relationships, and this is clearly expected to also have an impact on the form in which they are organized:

> ICTs fluidify the topology of politics. They do not merely enable but actually promote (through management and empowerment) the agile, temporary and timely aggregation, disaggregation and re-aggregation of distributed groups around shared interests, across old, rigid boundaries, represented by social classes, political parties, ethnicity, language barriers, physical barriers, and so forth. This is generating new tension between the Nation State, still understood as a major organizational institution, yet no longer monolithic but increasingly morphing into a MAS [Multi Agents System] itself [...], and a variety of equally powerful, indeed sometimes even more powerful and politically influential (with respect to the old Nation State) non-state organizations (Floridi 2014a, 206).

The impact of ICTs on the foundations of politics is therefore decisive, since it concerns its content (power), the horizon of its constitution (space), and the way it is structured (organization). However, in our opinion, the information revolution is having an even greater impact on the philosophical premises underlying politics in the modern age. The ontological approach of the philosophy of information can help us understand the reasons for the transition from a first to a second axial turn of politics in the age of hyper-history. As already pointed out (chapter 1 and 6), one of the basic pillars of Floridi's ontology of information is to consider being as subject to interaction, so that the relation between interacting entities (or we may say events) becomes a criterion for existence in the infosphere. Here, we limit our discussion to recalling this fundamental idea:

> Finally, the criterion for existence – what it means for something to exist – is no longer being actually immutable (the Greeks thought that only that which does not change can be said to exist fully), or being potentially subject to perception (modern philosophy insisted on something being perceivable empirically through the five senses in order to qualify as existing), but being potentially subject to interaction, even if intangible. To be is to be interactable, even if the interaction is only indirect (Floridi 2010a, 12).

What does the notion of relations imply with regard to politics? What does it mean, in other words, that the existing entities that constitute reality are not isolated, atomistic entities, but that they form part of a pattern of relations constituting the criterion and the manner of existence of the entities themselves? What, ultimately, does the notion of relations challenge? Being in relation calls into question the start-end principle conceived as the modern, privileged way of understanding reality. In a relational view, there is no ideal starting point that is entirely isolated from the network of relations of which an entity forms part. The *homo poieticus* (referred to in chap. 3), for instance, helps configure the environment where she lives as part of a whole and to which she is always responsible. Her creation is a *co-creation* that does not constitute the end of a process in which the creator is the isolated, immutable cause: each creation is merely the premise of a further creation. There is no privileged origin. That which is created forms the basis of creation. The idea of a world made up of a dense network of relations, which calls into question the start-end principle, brings with it significant implications for the understanding of politics.

Firstly, there is no real genesis of power (a mythical or earthly origin of power that would legitimize its exercise once and for all) rigidly separated from the exercise of that power, namely, from the concrete democratic life. The process of acquiring and legitimizing political power is already constructed in response to something else (usually, although not necessarily, a conflict), and not by virtue of an untainted origin, which would be, in this sense, the start (and, thereby, the end) of the political life.

Secondly, it follows that the emphasis in a relational perspective is placed on the sheer complexity of the real democratic life rather than on its genetic dimension. Governing is not just about making decisions (launching the start and end of something), but dealing with the complexity of the environment, which is made up of a multiplicity of agents interacting with one another. This explains why it is necessary, at present, to combine the idea of governance with the traditional idea of government. Governance encompasses the need to account for the complexity of the political reality as made global and interconnected through the interaction of a plurality of different political actors (giving rise to multi-agent systems).

Thirdly, the very idea of a plurality of different political actors interacting at various levels tends to call into question the centrality of the rigid division between the rulers and the ruled as the main axis around which modern politics is constructed. Clearly, this division does not cease to exist in the age of hyper-history. However, it is combined with new and prevailing dialectics between what is governable, thanks to the availability of information helping us reduce the complexity of the environment, and what is ungovernable for the very opposite reason (i.e., the lack of relevant information). Of course, the dialectics between what is governable and what is not can also be manipulated and used as a smokescreen behind which the rulers hide and shirk their responsibilities to the ruled (Durante 2010). For example, consider the emphasis placed on the economic and financial global crisis that States complain – perhaps to some extent rightly so – about not being able to govern as they please.

It is for these reasons that Floridi is led to consider the possibility of a new theoretical understanding of politics, one not merely offering up new ideas about a more or less minimal State or entrusting the solution of political issues to the logic of the market, but a new understanding focusing on the idea of a multi-agent system [MAS], viewed as the main information agent of the process of governance in hyper-history. The logic of a market that is increasingly characterized by the economy of information and the volatility of financial markets is also largely dependent on the information life cycle. Let us therefore turn our attention in the next section to the salient features of the information multi-agent system.

9.3 The MAS as the Main Information Agent

In light of the foregoing, Floridi suggests that the main political actor and informational agent of the hyper-historical age is no longer the modern state, but a MAS, which is better equipped to account for and efficiently and effectively manage the issues outlined above. As noted, these relate to power, space, organization and the amount of data to be processed in order to provide the information necessary for governing a globalized and complex reality:

> Because of the previous three reasons, the unique position of the historical State as the information agent is being undermined from below and overridden from above by the emergence of MASs that have the data, the power (and sometimes even the force, as in the very different cases of the UN, of groups' cyber threats, or of terrorist attacks), the space, and the organization flexibility to erode the modern State's political clout, appropriate (some of) its authority and, in the long run, make it redundant in contexts where it was once the only or the predominant informational agent (Floridi 2014a, 206–207).

In such a context, it is worth addressing directly one of the critical observations often raised when discussing the crisis of the modern State. Many scholars argue that the delegation or lessening of sovereignty (in favor of supranational agencies, non-governmental organizations, forms of direct democracy, and so forth) has not depleted the State of its centrality but only modified it according to changing needs, with the result that the modern state has hardly been displaced or ousted from its prerogatives, but actually continues to flourish. And this also applies to the Nation State, as evidenced by resurgent forms of nationalism. Floridi himself acknowledges as much, recognizing the persistence of the idea, the role and, in many cases, the primacy of the modern State in the exercise of its sovereign power (Floridi 2014a, 207–208). However, this consideration loses sight of an essential point on which there is often a basic misunderstanding. Like any other device, the modern State is no longer sufficient to fully implement its functions, not because it is no longer in force, but because it still is. The crisis of modern States does not derive from the fact that the States have been displaced and ousted from their prerogatives (because no longer in use), but because they still are. To use a simple but intuitive comparison, consider five chairs in a room that accommodate five people. When a new person enters the room, the chairs become insufficient to accommodate six people, not because they are not in use, but, on the contrary, because they are. Insufficiency is not inutility. In this narrower sense, the modern State proves to be insufficient to account for the complexity of politics in the digital democracies of hyper-history and gradually gives way to multi-agent systems, not as a replacement for the modern States (at least not in the short term), but rather to be incorporated in the governance process among the different agents. A MAS is thus conceived as a mechanism intended to coordinate the relationship between a plurality of agents of different types (public or private), importance and size (contrary to some purely idealistic visions of digital democracy, it is obvious that not all agents or politically relevant stakeholders have the same importance and size), which aggregate, disaggregate and re-aggregate political consent (and dissent) around shared interests in a more or less fluid manner, and which are certainly less tied to rigid criteria for membership than traditional political parties. This creates problems in the relationship between representative and direct democracy in digital democracies, in part also because ICTs can open up new democratic scenarios, by including a growing number of individuals in shaping public opinion, but, at the same time, by contributing to the populist drift of contemporary democracies [Durante 2012]):

> We thought of forms of direct democracy as complementary options for forms of representative democracy. The reality is that direct democracy has become a mass mediated democracy in the ICT sense of new social media. In such digital democracies, MASs (understood as distributed groups, temporary and timely, and aggregated around shared interests) have multiplied and become sources of influence external to the Nation State. Citizens vote for their representatives but influence them via opinion polls in real time. Consensus-building has become a constant concern based on synchronic information (Floridi 2014a, 206).

Let us now turn to the specific features that characterize a MAS as the main political actor and informational agent in the hyper-historical age. Methodologically, Floridi highlights a series of features that characterize a MAS as a political agent (by adopting a specific level of abstraction that draws on the category of autonomous artificial agents [see chap. 4]):

> The political MAS is a system constituted by other systems, which, as a single agent, is
>
> a) teleological: the MAS has a purpose, or goal, which it pursues through its actions;
> b) interactive: the MAS and its environment can act upon each other;
> c) autonomous: the MAS can change its configurations without direct response to interaction, by performing internal transition to change its states. This imbues the MAS with some degree of complexity and independence from its environment; and finally
> d) adaptable: the MAS interaction can change the rules by which the MAS changes its states. Adaptability ensures that the MAS learns its own mode of operation in a way that depend critically on its experience (Floridi 2014a, 209).

Floridi also points out that: "The political MAS becomes intelligent (in the sense of being smart [...]) when it implements features (a)-(d) efficiently and effectively, minimizing resources, wastefulness and errors, while maximizing the returns of its actions" (Floridi 2014a, 209). The configuration of a MAS as a main political actor and informational agent is obviously not devoid of some specific problems that the MAS must be able to cope with if it is to be established as a multi-agent intelligent system. What follows is a summary of these problems.

9.3.1 Identity and Cohesion

As already pointed out, and in contrast to some simplistic representations, the modern State cannot be represented as a monolithic and atomistic entity, whose internal unity is always assured. Instead, the essence of politics since its very inception has always had to deal with a "divided city", to borrow the vivid expression with which Nicole Loraux (1997) depicts Athens and, with it, the natural tendency of the political community to be plagued by internal divisions that politics seeks to hold together, if not to reconcile. The modern State therefore had to constantly face the problem of its identity and internal cohesion, which it tried to solve through the equation of State, nation and citizenship, reinforced by the twofold rhetoric of the narrative based on the unity of space (territory: mother earth, etc.) and time (history: the founding fathers, tradition, etc.).

Floridi rightly points out that political MAS cannot make use of the same strategy (Floridi, 2014a, 210). For MAS, the political concepts of identity and cohesion are more fluid, less stable and anchored to stable data provided by the ontology of things: a certain degree of identity and cohesion can only be achieved through the sharing of information, based on the ontology of interactions. As already mentioned several times, one of the main consequences of the information revolution and the impact of ICTs lies in the fact that reality – including political reality – is structured and organized in ways that are no longer built on the stability of worldly things, but on the mobility of interactions and the ability to de-contextualize the data of reality. In this perspective, the concepts of identity and cohesion are more mobile and perhaps more mature, since they are inevitably affected by, if not made up of, something radically different, changeable and unstable. Their heterogeneous durability is not that of powerful buildings, whose foundations and walls are reinforced to withstand sudden, external shocks; rather, their durability can be likened to that of more malleable constructions able to withstand the constant impact of strong, deep waves in the ground, which is their natural environment. Floridi rightly emphasizes how the new informational environment also requires that we rethink the meaning of the identity and cohesion of political MAS:

> The Land is virtualised into the region of the infosphere in which the MAS operates. So Memory (retrievable recordings) and Coherence (reliable updates) of the information flow enable a political MAS to claim some identity and some cohesion, and therefore offer a sense of belonging. But it is, above all, the fact that the boundaries between offline and online are disappearing, the appearance of the onlife experience, and hence the fact that the virtual infosphere can affect politically the physical space, that reinforces the sense of the political MAS as a real agent (Floridi 2014a, 210).

9.3.2 Consent

In the tradition of the modern State, based on the start-end relationship, consent is seen as something *original,* not necessarily in the chronological sense, but certainly in the sense of being an unavoidable prerequisite of the legitimate foundation of politics. Such consent shall not in fact necessarily have a specific, historically documented date; it may also only be presumed, as a logical (inferred *a posteriori* from that which gives life) or transcendental assumption (as a condition of possibility) of the founding of the modern State. Thus, the consent that individuals assign periodically to different policy proposals is a renewed consent on the basis of a primary commitment that binds them in society, and is usually based on fairly rigid criteria of political affiliation. This scenario changes in hyper-historical politics, where the composite reality and political dynamics of the MAS, based on the logic of interaction, is not premised upon a presumed consent *(opt-out),* given once and for all and periodically renewed, but upon the need for a commitment to promote and conquer *(opt-in)* over time, often in relation to specific objectives:

> Gathering consent around specific political issues becomes a continuous process of (re) engagement. It is not a question of political attention span [...] but of motivating interest. The problem is therefore to understand what may motivate or indeed force agents (again, not just individual human beings, but all kinds of agents) to give such consent and become engaged, and what happens when such agents, unengaged by default (note, not disengaged, for disengagement presupposes a previous state of engagement) prefer to stay away from the activities of the political MAS, inhabiting a social sphere of civil but apolitical privacy. [...] What is moribund is not politics tout court, but historical politics, that based on parties, classes, fixed social roles, and the Nation States, which sought political legitimacy only once and spent it until revoked (Floridi 2014a, 211–212).

9.3.3 Political Space vs. Social Space

The scenario described above has its roots in a further distinction (between political and social space) that the transition from historical to hyper-historical politics tends to call into question. As already seen, political and social space in the historical politics of the modern State tend to be coextensive, since it is the political dimension (e.g., the political decision to enter into a social contract that allows individuals to leave the state of nature and enter into civil society) that establishes the social dimension, providing the latter with the criterion of its differentiation and thus delineating social space from political space. This establishes "the primacy of the political over the social" (Floridi 2014a, 212). In this perspective, the political has an all-encompassing vocation and thus tends to occupy the entire social space, with historically heinous results when taken to the extreme and transformed into the hegemonic pretension of totalitarianism.[4]This dangerous proclivity defines the essence of politics in history as "a tendency to unify duality by means of the excluding inclusion of the other" (Esposito 2013, 6). This means, for example, that one part includes another part, just in order to exclude it, as in the emblematic case of foreigners, who constitute that "portion of citizenship allowed in the city, but deprived of political rights" (Esposito 2013, 6).This consideration – to which we will return later – is important because it helps us to realize that "the essence of politics lies neither in conflict nor in peace as such, *but in the link joining, in antonymic form, inclusion and exclusion*" (Esposito 2013, 6), or, to put it even more explicitly, that "*the meta-political essence of politics lies in the tendency of one party to occupy the whole space, functionalizing the other to its own domain*" (Esposito 2013, 7). Differently, "in hyper-history, the social space is the original, default space from

[4] It is important to note, however, that the claim of domination and assimilation concerns not only totalitarian regimes; it is also potentially inscribed in the modern Western conception of politics as the tendency to elevate a part to the whole, subjecting the other part to one's own domain, as Roberto Esposito has acutely observed (2013, 6–7).

which agents may move to (consent to) join the political space" (Floridi 2014a, b, 212). In the social space, each individual enjoys, according to Floridi (2014a, 212–213), a certain degree of freedom, understood in a robotic sense, as agency, i.e., as the sum of the capacities to act, supported by the necessary resources to engage in specific actions for specific purposes. The social space emerges as such when the agent enters into a relationship with other agents, forming a multi-agent system, which can in turn generate further possible interactions that are also provided with social character: "a social space is thus the totality of degrees of freedom of the inhabiting agents one wishes to take into consideration" (Floridi 2014a, 213). In hyper-history, the dividing line between inclusion and exclusion already crosses over into the social space, and the place where the line is drawn is the result of a choice, whether expressed or implied, with obviously political relevance:

> In hyper-history, where to draw the line to include, or indeed exclude, the relevant agents whose degrees of freedom constitute the social space has become increasingly a matter of at least implicit choice, when not of explicit decision. [...] In either case, history or prehistory, what counts as a social space may be a political move (Floridi 2014a, 213–214).

From this standpoint – that of the degree of freedom enjoyed by the agents – social and political space are not separate, but are conceptually distinguishable precisely in relation to the degree of complexity that characterizes the logic of the interactions in the hyper-historical social space:

> If we now turn to the political space in which the new MASs operate, it would be a mistake to consider it a separate space, over and above the social one: both are determined by the same totality of the agents' degrees of freedom. The political space emerges when the complexity of the social space – understood in terms of number and kinds of interactions and of agents involved, and of degree of dynamic reconfiguring of both agents and interactions – requires the prevention or resolution of potential divergence and the coordination or collaboration about potential convergences. Both are crucial. And in each case more information is required, in terms of representation and deliberation about a complex multitude of degrees of freedom. The result is that the social space becomes politicised through its informatization (Floridi 2014a, 214).

This means, as we shall see in greater detail below, that the essence of politics in hyper-history lies not, as stated, in conflict or in peace as such, but in the link between inclusion and exclusion. However, unlike historical politics, such a link does not necessarily translate into the tendency of one part "to occupy the whole space, functionalizing the other party to its own domain" (Esposito 2013, 7), since, in the logic of interaction between informational agents, the part is no longer such in itself but only as it relates to the other parts, with which it exchanges information necessarily and incessantly. It is, therefore, indeed still possible for politics in the hyper-historical view to continue to produce some degree of exclusion; however, in this perspective, if the part occupied the whole space, functionalizing the other party to its own domain, it would end up interrupting communication with the other parts and with the whole, thus irremediably altering the life cycle of information and curtailing the part's ability to avail itself of the quantity and quality of information necessary for governing the complexity of reality. The idea of politics as a *vital* link (in the sense of the information life cycle) that exceeds both conflict and peace as such is explored in the following section, which raises the issue of the legitimacy of political power in the hyper-historical age.

9.3.4 Legitimacy

Floridi points out that the social space acquires its political dimension, legitimizing political power, "when the agents in the social space agree to agree on how to deal with their divergences (conflicts) and convergences" (Floridi 2014a, 214). This course of legitimizing political power must not cause us to fall, according to Floridi, into two possible errors. First, we must avoid the "Hobbesian" error, according to which the essence of politics lies in the conflict that politics is required to resolve (according to a tradition that runs through the modern age and that found its most complete formulation in Carl Schmitt[5]): in this perspective, the established order is born from the need to neutralize the conflict that threatens internal unity and stability. Furthermore, the political and legal order must be maintained through the ability to reject the destructive force of that conflict from which the established order emanates. Otherwise, the political and legal order could fall once again into the abyss from which it came. According to this view, the essence of the political lies exclusively in a form of exclusion. However, this view appears to be limited, because it does not admit the possibility for any form of inclusion, not even the assumption that politics might also be based on peace or goodness or that politics would be necessary, as remarked by Floridi, even in a hypothetical society of angels, to ensure harmony and coordination of actions:

> This is not the case, because even a complex society of angels (*hbmo homini agnus*) would still require politics in order to further its harmony. Convergence, too, needs politics. Out of metaphor, politics is not just about conflicts due to agents' exercises of their degree of freedom when pursuing their goals. It is also, or at least it should be, above all, the furthering of coordination and collaboration of degrees of freedom by means other than coercion and violence (Floridi 2014a, 214).

This means that the essence of politics demands (and thus transcends) both conflict and peace, and therefore manifests itself more as a link that is called upon to join exclusion and inclusion. This leads us to consider the second possible error Floridi warns us against, which is inherent to the very idea of regulation, and that Floridi attributes to a tradition of thought that can be traced back to Rousseau. This error consists in considering that "the political space is then just that part of the social space organized by the law" (Floridi 2014a, 214). Political space can be thought of as a space primarily governed by rules, to which, however, it is never entirely reducible (if not endorsing a purely procedural conception of politics and

[5] See Schmitt 2007. For an analysis of this issue against a background of the genealogy of political modernity see Galli 2010.

democracy). The rules are not in themselves constitutive of the totality of the political space, since for its formation and its operation that space requires further value choices, ideas and shared meanings that lie not at the level of syntax, but of semantics. In the next section, we will take up the connections made in Floridi's political thought between syntax and semantics, and this will also bring into play the distinction between ethics and infraethics.

9.4 Infraethics and Good Governance

In Floridi's conception of politics, the need to coordinate the complexity of the globalized reality produced by the new digital ICTs, is causing a shift from the traditional notion of government to the notion of governance. To understand what constitutes the ideas of governance and good governance in Floridi's terms, one must take into account, as noted jst above, the necessary link between syntax (rules, principles, procedures, etc.) and semantics (values, ideas, meanings, etc.), both of which are required for the proper functioning of democracy. According to Floridi, one cannot conceive democracy solely in terms of form (one-dimensional syntactical relations) or of substance (one-dimensional semantic relations). Good governance of democracy requires us to combine and coordinate the syntactical with the semantic. It must be said, to be accurate, that Floridi does not express himself in precisely these terms and he makes no explicit reference to any conception of democracy. Nevertheless, one can interpret his conceptual articulation of and distinction between ethics and infraethics as a reflection that may allow us to rethink democracy in the age of hyper-historical politics (and certainly to define the ideas of governance and good governance).

As we have made ample reference throughout this text to Floridi's conception of the ethics of information, the focus in this section will be on the concept of infraethics. Floridi correctly observes that contemporary society is placing ever greater emphasis on a number of concepts, including but not limited to: "trust, privacy, transparency, freedom of expression, openness, intellectual property right, loyalty, respect, reliability, reputation, and so forth" [Floridi 2014a, 225]). These concepts can be interpreted and work in practice as infrastructures that are meant to facilitate or make more difficult the agents' moral or immoral behaviors and their evaluation (Floridi 2013b, 225). These infrastructures are thus not provided with an intrinsic moral value, although they have moral relevance, since they may have a dual nature: they can be good or bad, because of the behaviors they facilitate or make more difficult. Infraethics differs from ethics in that ethics indicates, in the ontocentric perspective, what the moral value consists of and which state of affairs is hence morally preferable. While ethics governs the axiological evaluation of a state of affairs, infraethics is a set of conditions that facilitate or hinder the accomplishment of a morally qualified state of affairs. In more analytical terms, according to Floridi, infraethics is not an ethics of agents, actions or states, but a set of conditions that facilitate or hinder the agents and their choices, the actions and their consequences, the states of affairs and their developments, all of which are morally good or bad. For example, contrary to the common rhetoric, transparency is not necessarily an intrinsic moral value, but rather an infraethical condition that can either facilitate moral behavior – for example, when it leads to more efficient management of public resources – or can make it more difficult – for example, when elections take place publically in an authoritarian political regime).

In this perspective, infraethics plays an important, if not decisive, role because it in fact influences or guides the transition between states of affairs and helps guide agents' choices and behaviors. This means in practice that the resolution of divergences and the coordination of convergences in a society, can be applied as much through basic ethical choices as through infraethical choices, namely through the implementation of infrastructures that facilitate the making of ethical choices. For example, returning to the topic of transparency, corruption can be fought by enacting harsh punishments for acts of corruption (which entails detailed normative assessment concerning the seriousness of those acts and the adequacy of the response to penalties) or by enhancing the infrastructure of transparency (through higher standards and requirements for transparency), which is likely to reduce corruption.

No matter what their connection, the aspects of ethics and infraethics must be kept conceptually distinct, as confusing the two can have serious consequences. On the one hand, basic ethical choices risk not being made if they are not promoted and facilitated through implementation of the required infrastructures (notably, the conceptual ones), on which the debate is less sensitive and divisive (and therefore less ideologically biased) than on the basic ethical choices. On the other hand, infrastructures support some value choices but, since they are not endowed with intrinsic value, they do not justify them from a theoretical or moral standpoint. It is important not to confuse the ability to support with the ability to justify or provide a foundation: the infraethical choices identify a syntax, certainly vital for democracy, but they are not as such a semantics (Floridi 2014a, 227), i.e., a set of shared value choices, ideas and meanings. In other words, in no society does a technocracy of the just exist, since the rules do not lead by themselves to the just, which requires a preliminary comparison of values, ideas and meanings. It is also important to correctly distinguish between ethics and infraethics from a conceptual viewpoint, because they also differ in the nature of conflicts to which they give rise. Ethics concerns conflicts of priorities that a given society is called upon to single out and select; infraethics concerns conflicts relevant to the proper design of the infrastructures called upon to fulfill the basic ethical choices and to facilitate or make more difficult the agents' behavior. At the same time, we need to understand that ethics and infraethics are not even two completely distinct and separate domains, as often the actual decisions made within a society bring into play the ethical and infraethical aspects at the same time. For this reason, Floridi tends to depict ethics and infraethics on a Cartesian plane, with ethics along the vertical axis and infraethics along the horizontal one. This representation helps us understand more intuitively that both the ethical and the infraethical choices are, as a rule, a function of two coordinates. In other words, they are the expression of a combination (in varying proportions) of the ethical and infraethical, structural and infrastructural, substantive and formal aspects. It also lets us to place our current forms of democracy in a quadrant drawn from these coordinates, which can then be usefully interpreted as different combinations of the necessary ethical and infraethical aspects, rather than as contingent deviations from ideal-typical forms of democracy.

Floridi remarks on the importance of infraethics particularly in reference to the need to coordinate the complexity of the globalized world in which we live. For Floridi, complexity means the quantity and quality of interactions, degrees of mutual influence and dependency, and scope of their consequences within a network. Consequently, problems have become much more difficult to coordinate, because they require mobilization of the entire network (i.e. of the informational resources that constitute the whole network). In other words, the coordination of complex problems (which entails both the resolution of divergences and the arrangement of convergences) requires us to make choices that affect the semantic-ethical level and/or the syntactic-infraethical level. Therefore, it is in relation to the degree of complexity of a problem that one needs to decide where to place the answer: whether at the ethical or infraethical level or, most often, at a level combining the ethical and the infraethical dimensions. The answer to a political problem is political, but the content of the answer requires the mobilization of the informational resources available due to the complexity of the problem to be addressed, and this implies no longer understanding the sphere of collective decisions in the traditional terms of government, but in the more structured terms of governance and good governance. Hence, Floridi may distinguish the two notions according to the conceptual distinction between ethics and infraethics (Floridi 2014a, 189–93), and conceives governance as the design, management, and maintenance of the infraethical framework of a coordination-complex social system and good governance as efficient governance, namely, as the governance that facilitates the realization of the morally good states of the system to which it applies to.

This means that, according to Floridi, good governance has a twofold character: substantial (ethics) and procedural (infraethics). However, if we translate this reasoning into political terms, Floridi does not seem to think of minimal conditions of democracy understood in simply procedural terms, possibly supplemented or corrected by substantive considerations. Where he specifies the logical order between ethics and infraethics, he remarks that one first needs to accomplish the ethical work (the axiological work about the right states [what is morally good, or what is evil], and the normative work about the right processes leading to the realization of the right states) and, therefore, the infraethical work (the infraethical work about the facilitators and obstructers that can promote the implementation of the right processes leading to the right states [Floridi 2014a, 189–93]). In this perspective, the idea of good governance precedes governance in axiological terms and is meant to guide its orientation. This does not mean that good governance, understood as a prerequisite of political governance, chronologically precedes political governance, but rather that governance accomplishes in practice, to a greater or lesser degree, some level of good governance, which is, therefore, not only a term towards which governance tends teleologically, but also a term of comparison that allows us to appraise and judge the concrete process of governance. Against this backdrop, governance is not so much conceived with reference to the division between the rulers and the ruled, but rather in relation to the complexity that can be more or less coordinated, thus producing some level of good governance. What seems important to point out is that, in this perspective, the life of democracy is understood as a concrete response (assessed in terms of governance) to a specific question (assessed in terms of good governance). Once again, according to Floridi's methodological approach, we do not look for noumenal entities (*e.g.* the thing 'democracy') but for events or processes that exist in the coordination of questions and answers.

9.5 Conclusions

We are part of an epic shift. The age in which we live, interact and make decisions is increasingly dependent on the functions and properties of the new digital ICTs, thus marking the transition from the historical age to an age that Floridi defines as hyper-historical. We are not witnessing the "end of the history" (it is worth recalling, in this context, that this expression was coined in the context of political reflection on the Western democracies), but its reexamination, and this reexamination brings with it a rethinking of the issues underlying politics. As we have tried to make clear, if modernity was characterized by a first axial turn of politics (which has lasted to the contemporary age), we are now involved in a second axial turn that is challenging us to reconsider the essence of the political. Summarized below are the key features of the first and second axial turn of politics.

The first axial turn, upon which political modernity has been premised and developed, is characterized by three main ideas:

1. The political order is not derived from a higher-order, but is an artificial order built by human beings, which gives rise to the political community and, thereby, allows the society to be recognized as such, differing from its own political community. In this sense, the political that seems to emerge from the society in fact logically precedes and ensures its foundation. Political modernity is thus characterized by the start-end principle, where the start is not necessarily chronological but a premise that can be interpreted as a logical or transcendental assumption (a condition of possibility). As a result, the political order is not even justified by a higher order, from which it would be deduced, but must be justified on the basis of a decision that rests with human beings. This implies that the genesis of political power, the moment in which that power is created and legitimized, has a central role that establishes and directs democratic life. In this sense, true democratic life is degraded and conceived as a second and derivative order with respect to the genesis of politics, which, therefore, coincides with the seizure of power. This seizure of power is based on the conquest of consent, whose radicalization tends to transform politics into a kind of seduction of the audience. Politics, and with it democracy, becomes the prey of the circle of seduction when the slippery slope of seduction of the audience (which turns people into the popular [i.e., popular culture, popular discourse, popular examples, etc.], the popular into

popularity [which measures the degree of the capital of consent], and popularity into populism [which is the practical use of that capital]) makes it more difficult, if not impossible, to produce what could be called "the unpopular" (Durante 2013), which nonetheless is today a vital resource for the true political life of democracy.

2. Political power ceases to be conceived as a power embodied by means of (divine or hereditary) derivation, and becomes a representative power that is periodically re-created and entrusted, thus producing the divide between the rulers and the ruled that is the cornerstone of modern politics up to the contemporary age. Here lies a profound paradox of representative democracy from modernity to the present day. People (i.e. the ruled) exercise their political power through the expression of the sovereign will, which identifies and legitimizes the rulers' exercise of power on the basis of the consent provided by the ruled. However, to will means to bring closer to oneself something that is far away, in the same sense in which those who want to drink bring a cup of water closer to their lips. By expressing their will, the ruled turn away from themselves the sovereign power that should exist among them. In this sense, it has been remarked that, from the beginning of modernity, people no longer appear on the political scene in the first person. Hence individuals are excluded from that in which they are included: "If one goes back to the image depicted on the cover of *Leviathan,* made up of many little men welded into one gigantic body, one has the most perfect expression of this excluding incorporation. At the very moment in which individuals supply their rights to the Leviathan State, they are included therein in a form that excludes them from power. They authorize the great body that represents them to be the only actor of all actions that are beyond their control" (Esposito 2013, 8).
3. In political modernity (whose shadow, as we have seen, still falls over us today), the essence of politics seems to transcend the start-end principle that nonetheless characterizes it, since politics as such is neither due to its origin (conflict) nor due to its hoped for destiny (peace): "the essence of politics lies neither in conflict nor in peace as such, *but in the link joining, in antonymic form, inclusion and exclusion*" (Esposito 2013, 6), or, to put it in more explicit terms, that "*the meta-political essence of politics lies in the tendency of one party to occupy the whole space, functionalizing the other to its own domain*" (Esposito 2013, 7). In this perspective, one understands why the politics of modernity and of the contemporary age is pervaded by a strong tendency towards the theoretical foundation (and practice) of justice, peace and tolerance. However, this happens in the context of a concept of politics marked by the idea that "first and necessarily homogeneity and then – where necessary – the expulsion or cancellation of what is heterogeneous belongs to democracy" (Schmitt 1940, 97). This means that in the overall design of Western modernity there is a deep-seated tendency, already denounced by Emmanuel Levinas in the field of moral philosophy, to reduce the Other to the Same (Levinas 1969), or, to return to the political lexicon, to occupy the whole space, functionalizing the other part to its own domain. In this perspective, the part does not enter into communication with the other parts and

with the whole, if not in order to bring them back within its control, assimilating or excluding them.

The second axial turn emerging in the hyper-historical age is characterized by the following main ideas:

1. The political order of a society is an artificial construction, but this does not entail that it is, for that reason, the direct result of a deliberative process taking place according to determined plans. Political reality is not necessarily (and not even predominantly) the end product of a centralized and vertical resolution. In contrast, if we refer in particular to national politics, we must point out that the space of political decision-making has been drastically reduced. This has happened for several reasons: first, because an increasing number of relevant political decisions are being taken at different levels of government and often in a decentralized way; secondly, because the political reality is not always the result of deliberate actions but, in post-industrial societies, and still more in those of information, it is the result of the spontaneous actions of individuals; thirdly, because many choices are made as part of an operation of complex systems, which do not replace the state with the market, but introduce both the market and the state (along with other institutions) into the reticular pattern of connections and relations exchanged during the life cycle of information:

   The topological structure of the economic system, and thus the localization and distribution, in the multiplicity of relevant spaces, of agents and the organization of communication flows among innovative agents, the rules of communication and interaction, have a crucial role. The structures of connective networks and relationships between agents in the processes of defining endogenous preferences and technologies become the true structural parameters of the system, i.e. the real 'fundamentals', more than the famous original endowment of capital and labor (Antonelli 2005, xvi).

   In the hyper-historical age, the political order is constructed as an emergent property of a system called upon to govern an increasingly complex reality, which is no longer characterized by the principle of start-end, but by a relational logic based on interactions. In a relational logic there is never an ideal starting point that is completely isolated from the network of relationships of which it is part. In this perspective, there is no instantaneous genesis of power (a mythical or earthly origin legitimizing the exercise of power once and for all) rigidly separated from the exercise itself of that power, namely concrete democratic life. The process of acquisition and legitimation of political power is always accomplished in response to something, and not by virtue of a pure, untainted origin that would determine the beginning as well as the end of the political life. Hyper-historical politics challenges the myth of the origin.
2. The relational logic based on interactions focuses on the complexity of democratic life and not just on its genesis. Governing is not only about making decisions (giving the start and end of something), but dealing with the complexity of an environment made up of a multiplicity of mutually interacting agents.

This is why it is necessary, in the hyper-historical age, to associate the idea of governance to that of government. The idea of governance accounts for the complexity of the political reality, which is globalized through the interaction of a plurality of different political actors that create multi-agent systems of interdependence. The idea of a plurality of political actors that interact at different levels calls into question the centrality of the division between the rulers and the ruled as the main axis upon which contemporary politics is premised and developed. This division does not disappear in hyper-history, but is combined with a new and prominent articulation: that between what is governable, thanks to the availability of information that allow us to coordinate complexity, and what is ungovernable for the opposite reason. It is worth repeating that the state is not supplanted by the market (but is included in the political MAS) nor is the idea of government replaced by a more or less openly economic conception of governance (Floridi suggests that the notion of governance and of good governance are developed within the paradigm of complexity). This paradigm affects, in addition, both politics and economic policy:

> In terms of economic policy implications the effect of the paradigm of complexity is powerful because it emphasizes, first, the indeterminacy of the outcomes of the processes and, secondly, the fundamental importance of the systems of interdependence. The arrogant liberalism, confident that the free market interaction leads to a single optimal point of gravitation, and its historical antagonist, i.e. the dirigisme that, convinced of the inability of the market to produce positive effects, designs interventions in the economic systems asserting to fully predict all the effects, are replaced by a more cautious liberalism, which is more aware of the powerful effect of the processes of feedback of behaviors on structural data, both at the positive and the normative level. The subject itself of public intervention changes, so privileging relational systems, mechanisms of interdependence, the structure and composition of networks of connection between agents and the sequences of processes, rather than mechanisms of incentives and selection processes. The dynamic coordination becomes the privileged focus of economic policy: it is becoming increasingly necessary to ensure that the processes of interdependence are oriented and sometimes strengthened, in order to attain desirable dynamic results (Antonelli 2005 xvii–xviii).

3. The profound changes created by the information revolution that characterizes the hyper-historical age affects the concept of politics (regarding the content of politics from a normative and descriptive perspective) and of meta-politics (regarding the notion of politics) in relation to the centrality of the information life cycle in the informational environment in which the political MAS interact. The idea of the information life cycle, understood as the content of politics, reduces the conceptual space that exists between the descriptive and the normative conception of politics. Politics is traditionally conceived, from the normative point of view, as the art of making collective decisions, and, from the descriptive point of view, as the ability to control a territory. The informational perspective connects the normative and the descriptive points of view of politics, for the art of making collective decisions and of assuring them effective implementation depends less and less on the sword *(hard power)* and more and more on the public mind *(soft power)*, that is, on the ability to build forms of collective or distributed intelligence able to coordinate complex problems. Politics ceases to be

conceived, in this sense, as a form of control over the territory (i.e. on the lives of the members of the society), to be conceived as a form of effective and efficient management of the life cycle of information. Of course, it is also possible that this management will result in more or less authoritarian forms of control over the lives of associates as informational items made up by information. Regarding this ever-present risk, we have remarked that the effective and efficient management of the information life cycle concerns only the infrastructural level of governance and not that of good governance, which requires a comparison of the values, ideas and shared meanings that should guide democratic life. From the meta-political point of view, we have observed that, in the informational perspective, the concept of hyper-historical politics coincides neither with conflict nor peace as such, but lies in the complex relationship that connects inclusion and exclusion. However, unlike historical politics, this does not necessarily translate into the tendency of a part to occupy the whole space, functionalizing the other part to its own domain. This is not consistent with the logic of informational interaction between agents, which sees the part no longer conceived as an isolated and atomistic entity, but only in relation to other parts and to the whole, with which it necessarily and constantly exchanges information. In the hyper-historical view, it is certainly conceivable that politics will continue to produce some degree of (political, social, economic, etc.) exclusion. Nevertheless, in this perspective, if the part were identified with the whole, subjecting other parts to its domain or excluding them radically, this would likely cause that part to fail, because it would eventually prevent communication with the other parts and with the whole. This could irrevocably alter the information life cycle, with the result that the party may not have the quantity and quality of information required to manage the complexity of reality. It becomes clear that the three key ideas of the informational perspective (interaction as a criterion of ontological existence; the construction of personal identity as being-with-and-in the environment; the well-being of the infosphere as a significant network of relationships) constitute the conceptual lintels on which it is possible to develop a conception of politics and meta-politics that fits the theoretical and practical challenges of the hyper-historical age.

References

Antonelli, C. 2005. "Prefazione" a M. Antonelli, C. 2005. "Introduzione" to M. Taylor, Il momento della complessità.Taylor, Il momento della complessità. L'emergenza di una cultura a rete. transl. by it.di Benedetta Antonelli D'Oulx, Codice Editore, Torino, pp.B. Antonelli D'Oulx, Codice Editore, Torinoix-xx.

Barberis, M. 2013. La fine dello Stato e altri racconti. *Filosofia Politica* 2: 317–329.

Benkler, Y. 2006. *The Wealth of Networks: How Social Production Transforms Markets and Freedom*. New Haven CT: Yale University Press.

———. 2011. *The Penguin and the Leviathan: The Triumph of Cooperation Over Self-Interest*. New York: Crown Business.

Castells, M. 2009. *Communication Power*. Oxford: Oxford University Press.
———. 2012. *Networks of Outrage and Hope: Social Movements in the Internet Age*. New York: Polity Press.
Comensoli, Antonini L. 2013. Gauchet lettore di Kantorowicz. *Apporti alla teoria del disincanto, Filosofia Politica* 2: 271–294.
Durante, M. 2007. Il futuro del web: etica, diritto, decentramento. Dalla sussidiarietà digitale all'economia dell'informazione in rete, Giappichelli, Torino.
———. 2010. The Value of Information as Ontological Pluralism. *Knowledge, Technology & Policy* 23 (1): 149–161.
———. 2012. E-democracy as the Frame of Networked Public Discourse. Information, Consensus and Complexity, In ed. P. Mindus, A. Greppi, and M. Cuono. Legitimacy 2.0. E-Democracy and Public Opinion in the Digital Age, Paper Series – 25th IVR World Congress: Law, Science and Technology, Frankfurt am Main, Goethe University Press, 1–28.
———. 2013. Informazione e regolazione. Internet come problema democratico. *Teoria politica* 3: 39–65.
Esposito. 2013. Politica e metafisica. *Filosofia Politica* 3: 465–478.
Floridi, L. 2010a. *Information. A Very Short Introduction*. Oxford: Oxford University Press.
———. 2010b. The Philosophy of Information as a Conceptual Framework. In Demir, H. (ed.). Luciano Floridi's Philosophy of Technology: Critical Reflections. *Knowledge, Technology & Policy*, 23.
———. 2010c. Information Ethics. In *The Cambridge Handbook of Information and Computer Ethics*, ed. L. Floridi, 77–99. Cambridge: Cambridge University Press.
———. 2013. *Information Ethics*. Oxford: Oxford University Press.
———. 2014a. *The Fourth Revolution. On the Impact of Information and Communication Technologies on Our Lives*. Oxford: Oxford University Press.
———. (ed.). 2014b. *The Onlife Manifesto. Being Human in a Hyperconnected Era*, Dordrecht: Springer.
Foucault, M. 2010. *The Birth of Biopolitics: Lectures at the Collège de France, 1978–1979*. New York: Picador.
Galli, C. 2010. Genealogia della politica. Carl Schmitt e la crisi del pensiero politico moderno, il Mulino, Bologna.
Gardner, J. 2013. Putting Legal Philosophy at Its Place. *Rivista di filosofia del diritto* 2: 253–266.
Gauchet, M. 1999. *The Disenchantment of the World: A Political History of Religion* [1985], foreword by C. Taylor, Trans. O. Burge. Princeton: Princeton University Press.
Levinas, E. 1969. *Totality and Infinity: An Essay on Exteriority* [1961]. Trans. A. Lingis. Pittsburgh: Dusquene University Press.
Loraux, N. 1997. *La cité divisée. Oubli The dans la mémoire d'Athenes*. Paris: Payot & Rivages.
Morozov, E. 2011. *The Net Delusion: How Not to Liberate The World.* New York: Penguin.
———. 2013. *To Save Everything, Click Here: Technology, Solutionism, and the Urge to Fix Problems that Don't Exist*. London: Allen Lane.
Schmitt, C. Der Gegensatz von Parlamentarismus und moderner Massendemokratie (1926), in Positionen und Begriffe im Kampf mit Weimar-Genf-Versailles, 1923–1939, Hamburg, Dunker & Humblot, 1940; trad.Schmitt C. (1940), *Der Gegensatz von Parlamentarismus und moderner Massen demokratie* (1926), in *Positionen und Begriffe im Kampf mit Weimar-Genf-Versailles,* 1923–1939. Hamburg: Dunker & Humblot.
———. 2007. *Theory of the Partisan.* Trans. G.-L. Ulmen. New York: Telos Press.

An Informational Approach to the Law 10

Abstract

The evolution of ICTs is gradually transforming our postmodern habitat. We are witnessing the convergence of physical and virtual reality and the creation of a new environment, the so-called infosphere. It is likely that the evolution of ICTs will have a sweeping transformative impact on our conception of law: first, by multiplying the sources of norms (legal information); secondly, by introducing competition between different normative systems; thirdly, by changing the very reality that the law is intended to govern, through the re-ontologization of reality and changes in our notion of environment. Technological normativity is deeply embedded in our societies and democracies. We are thus not just moving from a State-based form of regulation towards multi-agent and multi-level forms of regulation that are technologically mediated. We are also experiencing a radical paradigm shift in our normative mind-set towards the representation of reality. Our normative beliefs are no longer rooted in and regulated solely according to a deep-seated, traditional representation of reality (i.e., the material objects of the world), but also according to its informational representation (i.e., virtual reality, informational entities, and streams of information).

10.1 Introduction

The purpose of the present chapter is to envisage how contemporary conceptions of law may change in response to the evolution of ICTs. Our basic premise is that the ongoing evolution of ICTs characteristic of the information revolution is not only raising specific legal issues the law has to cope with; but also, and above all, it is transforming the ontological statute of reality, which in turn imposes conditions and restrictions upon the law's ability to govern reality. Earlier in this book we saw that the technological evolution of ICTs is having a profound effect on the information revolution, forcing us to reevaluate our conception of the notions of space and

M. Durante, *Ethics, Law and the Politics of Information*, The International Library of Ethics, Law and Technology 18, DOI 10.1007/978-94-024-1150-8_10

environment and of how we represent reality (Chaps. 2 and 3). We also noted that technology is no longer understood in purely instrumental terms, with technology amounting to nothing more than tools designed for achieving specific ends (Chap. 8). Instead, by drawing on the framework of Floridi's informational interpretation of reality, we suggest that one of the main consequences of technology is that, in being intertwined with almost every aspect of our societies, it is reshaping the very world we inhabit. It is thus embedded both in our information societies and in our digital democracies (Chap. 9). Many approaches to technology fail to take this into account, as can be seen in the plethora of books and articles being published on the topics of Internet and Cyberspace regulation. It is also reflected in the spread of common catch phrases such as 'the law of the Internet' or 'the regulation of Cyberspace', as though the Internet and Cyberspace were merely *subject* to legal regulation rather than having regulatory properties of their own. Yet both the Internet and Cyberspace may have inherent topological dimensions (Pagallo 2006), for example, that bear normative values. Technology today is also to some – or even to a great – extent self-regulating, meaning that it may also constitute a normative system ("the code is the law", according to Lessig 2006). And the issue here is actually even more complex, for the information revolution brought about by the current evolution of ICTs is not just affecting legal or technological normativity.[1] It is profoundly re-shaping our notion of reality. In other words, we are faced with a new rendition of reality that is a "computational rendition of reality. (…) In this sense, the technological paradigm of computation pierces deep down to the invisible microscopic texture of things, which it reconstitutes as a large array of computational rules and procedures. In so doing, it exposes (or projects) a new, non-observable realm of reality" (Kallinikos 2006, 6). Therefore, a different ontology of reality (and therefore of society) may establish new conditions or restrictions upon the legal claims and force us to reconsider our understanding of the models of law. The methodological and epistemological point we would like to make here is that the reality of our information societies being fashioned by the current evolution of ICTs is comprised of many deeply-stratified and interwoven layers (physical, digital, networked, informational, and so forth), and that this view is well represented by the reality of the Internet, once properly examined and understood. As a result, our legal models, which are meant to govern reality, need to be re-assessed from the perspective of the current "proliferation of reality in different objects, levels and spheres of reality" (Ceruti 2009, 5). Contrary to simplistic interpretations, the informational representation of reality is not monolithic in its dimensions, but layered and multifaceted. Different aspects of reality may be subject to different and competing legal approaches.

There can be, in fact, different and competing legal approaches in relation to current dichotomies between State-regulation vs. self-regulation and centralized and vertical regulation vs. decentralized and horizontal regulation. In the next section, we examine the competition between State and self-regulation in the information society and single out, in Sect. 10.3, competition between centralized and

[1] On these different forms of normativity see Hildebrandt, 2008.

decentralized forms of regulation, by pointing out at least three different (and to some extent still overlapping) phases in the representation of the law as a normative system: (1) a bounded centralized model of law; (2) centralized vs. decentralized models of law; (3) distributed vs. decentralized models of law. Not only must we deal at present with different representations of law as a normative system, but with the law as it stands in increasing competition with other normative systems, as already pointed out by Enrico di Robilant in 1973, and recently noted, for instance, by Lawrence Lessig (2006). This is not a trivial consideration, for it underlines the fragmentation of today's regulation into different, competing normative systems (law, economy, design or architecture, social norms, and code), such that a complete depiction of the normative dimension (comprising both the regulating and the regulated reality) can only be achieved by taking into account how the different and competing normative systems interact (see also on this point Sartor 2015). There is much value in this approach, and law students as well as legal scholars should take it into serious account in order to understand that the claim of the law to govern reality is being increasingly challenged by all of the other normative systems, and thus makes up part of a wider normative phenomenon, which can no longer be accounted for in purely legal terms. However, what this approach seems to overlook is that reality itself, which all normative systems claim to govern, has also been ontologically altered as a result of the information revolution. In this sense, Floridi's informational approach (even if not addressed specifically to the law) allows us access to a more profound reflection of the overall normative phenomenon by suggesting that change is occurring not only in the way in which the normative claim is made, but, first and foremost, in the actual subject of regulation itself. In this perspective, much theoretical work still needs to be done. In the present chapter, we outline some possible directions for future research within an informational approach to law aimed at investigating how law can govern re-ontologized reality. This issue raises not only theoretical problems of how to reconceptualize our traditional legal categories, but also practical problems concerning the embeddedness of technology in our information societies and digital democracies.

10.2 Law as a Normative System and the Governance of Reality

As a normative system, law has always been concerned with governing reality. However, just how law governs reality has been the subject of endless theoretical disputes. It is a problem of jurisprudence involving no less than three basic elements: law, reality, and the normative relation that exists between them. This requires an accounting for and outlining of a conception of law, an ontology of reality and a theory of normativity. The evolution of ICTs is, in fact, likely to affect or even reshape all of these elements more radically than usually supposed. In this respect, let us take a step back and consider how Enrico di Robilant portrayed law in industrial society in 1973. Already based on the central importance of information, his analysis still serves to describe the competition between State and self-regulation and, to some extent, it applies to the information society as well.

Di Robilant conceives of law as a normative system, understood as a flow of informative inputs that circulate in the complex arrangement of systems (we would say in the multi-agent system today) that is constitutive of the industrial society (di Robilant 1973, 227–228). Legal norms are thought of as informative inputs guiding agents' behaviors, which are hence understood as informative outputs that serve as feedback for the self-regulation of the system (di Robilant 1973, 236–237). According to di Robilant, since agents' behaviors are guided by a plurality of informative inputs in the industrial society, thus playing the role of norms, there should be no reason to consider as norms a vast array of informative inputs that are not traditionally understood and portrayed as legal norms (di Robilant 1973, 250). This means that the industrial society is characterized by the emergence of a plurality of sources of informative inputs that add to the sources of law on which State-regulation is traditionally based:

> One of the elements that mainly characterize the industrial society and above all determine its complexity is given by the incessant flow of inputs stemming from a plurality of centers of emission and of outputs returning to these centers. In addition to the sources of State-regulation, understood in the widest possible meaning, economy, information and social organization are further centers of emission. The life of consociates is fashioned, in the industrial society, by this sum of inputs, and by the consociates' outputs given to them. (…) If we consider this sum of inputs as a whole characterizing the industrial society, and that these inputs are directed to guide the consociates' behaviours, thus amounting to norms, it seems clear that the traditional monistic schema of legal positivism that only contemplates State-regulation is inadequate to account for the normative phenomenon, and its outputs, in the industrial society (di Robilant 1973, 234–235).

Starting from this premise, the industrial society is understood as a general system of informative inputs and outputs, thereby based on the production, dissemination and exchange of information that can play the role of norms, and law is thought of as a dynamic, open and more comprehensive normative system, based both on the State and self-regulation, the function of which is to reduce the complexity of the environment, by selecting the relevant legal information that guides agents' conduct. In this perspective, "legal norms, as they are traditionally understood by legal positivism, are insufficient, in their informative capacity, in order to direct the great variety of guided behaviours in the industrial society, and to assure the organization of the system and of its constituting subsystems" (di Robilant 1973, 250). In contrast, "both the self-regulated and the organized informative capacity of the system are tightly linked to the flow of replies given to inputs. Without the feedback of outputs from receptors to the centers of emission, the system self-regulation, namely, its adaptation to the environment and to the interferences of other systems, would be impossible" (di Robilant 1973, 251). This means that the existence and the efficiency of the normative system is determined by several factors: (1) the plurality of centers of emission of informative inputs; (2) the wealth of information flow; (3) the feedback process enabling self-regulation of the system; (3) the dynamic and open structure of the system, i.e., its capacity to evolve, through information exchange with the environment; (4) the capacity to select the relevant legal information. In this sense, "information and information feedback, which constitute the two phases of the life-cycle of the normative system, are thus tightly linked to the availability of choices, i.e. of freedom, and to the availability of knowledge" (di Robilant 1973, 252). What is still remarkable in di Robilant's understanding of law in the industrial society (1973) is his informational representation of all the elements constituting the normative system and the environment: norms and their sources, agents' behaviors, the process of self-regulation and the complexity of environment are all understood and modeled in informational terms. Needless to say, some aspects of this analysis need to be refined and updated[2] but much of it is still of great value and may apply to the information society. Notably, in the information society, a normative system is still constructed and dependent on these factors: (1) norms are thought of as legal information guiding the agents' behavior; (2) the increasing plurality of sources of information is understood in terms of competing normative sources; (3) the normative system is intended as dynamic and open, that is, capable of evolving, through the exchange of information with the environment and by providing access to new information (and values: see Sect. 5.2 in the present chapter); (4) the normative system requires the well-being of the infosphere (namely, an increase in the flow of information inputs and outputs), but at the same time it needs to adopt filters of informational relevance and reliability[3] (namely, to select the legally relevant and reliable information).

A few points are nonetheless neglected in this scenario. Notably, we must: (1) address the dichotomy between centralized and decentered models of law, which is heightened and exacerbated in the information society through the multiplication and dissemination of centers of emission of informative inputs according to decentralized or distributed networked models of law (see the next section); (2) come to a clearer understanding of what might count as legal information, which requires us to take into account two of Floridi's key information taxonomies (see Sect. 5.4); (3) revise the main legal categories against the background of unfolding reontologisation of reality brought about by the evolution of digital ICTs (see Sect. 5.5). Let us start with the opposition between centralized and decentralized models of law.

---

[2] For instance, di Robilant's analysis of information systems is far too linked to the cybernetic model (even if see 1973, 238); his understanding of a multi-agent system is mostly based on agents' interactivity (1973, 251), overlooking their autonomy and adaptability (see on these notions Chap. 4); his concept of information sometimes tends to overlap with the notions of matter or energy (1973, 250).

[3] We cannot deal here with the question of how epistemic agents select relevant and reliable legal information (see on this Durante, 2010) in the information society, which is mainly jeopardized by informational overload.

10.3 Centralized and Decentralized Models of Law

In this section, we analyze the general understanding of the relation between law and reality in the information society, with regards to the opposition between centralized and decentralized models of law. The approach and treatment of this issue is often quite outmoded and draws on both legal and epistemological categories that are no longer fully capable of accounting for changes driven by the evolution of ICTs. We cannot examine, in the present context, the intricate issue of regulation and governance of the Internet. We limit ourselves to pointing out that the current stratification of models of law is related to the stratification of reality (and notably to the stratified reality of the Internet or, more generally, of cyberspace[4]).

Let us first recall how different models of law have grown increasingly intertwined. Initially, the legal debate was concerned with a bounded, centralized model of law (hierarchy); in the next phase, it concerned itself with the opposition between centralized versus decentralized models of law (networks); now it is concerned with the current dialectics between different forms of decentralized models of law, i.e., based on decentralized (with intermediaries) or distributed (without intermediaries) networks, (Durante 2007). These phases can be viewed diachronically, but to a large extent the different models of law still coexist and compete with each other today.[5] One must keep in mind that the reality of the Internet is stratified and therefore governed accordingly by traditional legal tools (hard and soft law, codes of conduct, customary rules, contracts) as well as by new social or technological forms of self-regulation (Murray 2007[6]). Since the reality of the Internet is composed of at least three layers (the physical, the logical and the layer of contents) (Benkler 2006), any discussion about Internet regulation requires us to identify the layer(s) of reality concerned.

[4] As pointed out in Cohen, 2007, 249–251.

[5] In this perspective, see Galloway & Thacker, 2007: 14: "We would like to situate it within a larger context by making reference to three diagrams for political conflict, each finding its own historical actualization: a politics of symmetry rooted in opposed power blocs, a politics of asymmetry in which power blocs struggle against insurgent networks, and a second model of symmetry in which networked powers struggle against other networked powers".

[6] Murray, 2007: 47: "To this we can now add a third complication, which applies equally in physical space and cyberspace – decentred or polycentred regulation. As has been alluded to earlier in this chapter, regulation rarely, if ever, emanates from a single source. The existence of polycentric regulation is the source of regulatory conflict, both between competing regulators and within a single regulatory body. Here I define polycentric regulation as the 'enterprise of subjecting human conduct to the governance of external controls whether State or non-State, intended or unintended'". On the topic of polycentric regulation, see also Pagallo, 2006: 21–23; 246–247. See also Galloway 2004.

10.3.1 The First Phase: A Bounded, Centralized Model of Law

This phase spans the entire age of legal modernity. It has its roots in the Treaty of Westphalia (1648), which established an organization of space and political-legal international relations based on the rigid principles of territorial and absolute sovereignty. Each State is sovereign over its territory and recognizes no State as superior to itself (*superiorem non recognoscentes*). This principle affirms a conception of law based on a legal system that is structured according to a bounded, central and vertical hierarchy. This model operates both between States and within single States. In the international space, it posits the problem of the lack of a third institutional power capable of mediating between conflicting States, whereas, in an individual State, the sovereign power is always the mediator between conflicting parties or individuals. The autonomy of law is based on the will of the national State, which is the principal (and often only) legal actor on the political scene (see Chap. 8). In each individual State, the law is produced by a central body of law (a government or a social body). In either case, the representation of the law is filtered by the notion of a sovereign power, which is centralized and vertical, both internally and in its external relation to other States. The reality governed by the law is based on a peculiar representation of space, philosophically re-elaborated by Kant (see Chap. 2). According to Kant, space is the horizon of politics as being the horizon of coexistence over time and thereby law is meant to assure the coexistence between external freedoms. This was the dominant model of law and politics up through the 20th century, and even now each national State tends to assert total sovereign power over its territory. Given that legal space, at both the national and international levels, is bound up less and less with territorial space, this model of law needs to be reconsidered. What we learn from this is that the spatial dimension and representation of reality (i.e., the reality that the law intends to govern) governs the conception and representation of law itself.

10.3.2 The Second Phase: Centralized vs. Decentralized Models of Law

The second phase concerns the contemporary age. It is based on the gradual affirmation of a network model, in contrast with the previous (yet still extant) model of the law, and is to some extent horizontal and decentralized.[7] National boundaries no

[7] The existence of networked models of law has been pointed out by Ost & van de Kerchove 2002. A horizontal and decentralized networked model of law is not necessarily and inherently more democratic than a vertical and centralized model of law. Galloway & Thacker, 2007, 13: "To have a network, one needs a multiplicity of 'nodes'. Yet the mere existence of this multiplicity of nodes in no way implies an inherently democratic, ecumenical, or egalitarian order. Quite the opposite". See also Gould 2004, 246: "Contrary to the optimistic views expressed by commentators such as James Rosenau to the effect that networks introduce horizontal modalities of interaction that contrast with older hierarchical modalities, we can observe that these networks themselves are often used in hierarchical and antidemocratic ways". Furthermore, networked models of law are not

longer define the limits within which the sovereign power governs reality: individuals and groups can produce legal (political, economic, social, etc.) effects that supersede the national space and call into question the affirmation of authority based on a bounded, centralized and vertical system. Individuals and groups progressively become the nodes of a supranational network capable of emanating its own regulation. The network model also concerns international relations. The autonomy of law is thus based both on the deliberate and spontaneous actions of individuals and groups, who are the principle actors in the new space of the network. The space of the network (the networked space created by the technological platform of the Internet and by ICTs at large) differs from the physical, Newtonian space on which Kant based his epistemological and political categories of modernity. The networked space is glocal, decentered, hybrid (physical and virtual), both expanded and contracted (Floridi 2007), geodesic (i.e., made up of nodes), computational and informational (see Chap. 2). Physical space no longer identifies the limits of the coexistence of its occupiers, since the occupiers are computational entities, whose main features result from their built-in "mobility, transferability and combinability" (Kallinikos 2006, 18). What we learn from this is that the governing of reality depends not only on the actors involved, but also – and primarily - on how space is re-configured, given that the reality meant to be governed by law is always construed within a specific conception of space. In this perspective, the status and role of nodes in a geodesic conception of space leads us to the current and more mature phase of development of the law.

10.3.3 The Third Phase: Distributed vs. Decentralized Models of Law

The networked space has often been presented as a pure, decentered space that is radically horizontal and almost anarchical. This (rather misleading) image stems from its diametric opposition to a centralized model of law and from underestimation of the topological characteristics of the networked space. Progressive analysis of the structures of networks and nodes has been fruitful in elucidating the model of law based on networks. Some distributed networks are radically horizontal and have nodes of equal importance, whereas others are decentered networks that are also horizontal, but whose nodes are not of equal importance and perform different functions. Nonetheless, the notion of centrality does not completely disappear in decentered networks: some nodes can play the role of intermediaries or even of filters for the production and dissemination of relevant information. However, decentered networks differ from centralized models in that the center of a centralized model

incompatible with (hierarchical forms of) sovereignty, as remarked by Galloway & Thacker, 2007, 20: "So networks and sovereignty are not incompatible. In fact, quite the opposite: networks create the condition of existence for a new mode of sovereignty. America is merely the contemporary figurehead of sovereignty-in-networks". See also on this point, Castells, 2009, 38–40, and Pagallo, 2003, 31.

necessarily precedes and governs user interaction, whereas the center of a decentered network is the by-product of user interaction. Again, the configuration of networked space, whether distributed or decentered, is a crucial element in defining the limits and conditions of governance. This phase represents both a present and a future trend to account for governance of reality in terms of the dialectics between different forms of networks, even if networks might be considered a manifestation of a deeper transformation of reality: "networks could be seen as a surface manifestation of a much more profound and comprehensive social and economic change. I connect some of these wider socioeconomic changes to the growing involvement of technological information in organizational and institutional life (Kallinikos 2006, 15). In fact, there is likely a major turn at stake, which is concerned with our normative mind-set towards the stability of the world: "Stability has been afforded and constructed through the relative insulation of organizational operations from environmental contingencies" (Kallinikos 2006, 8). In other words, the problem is how to face the contingency of a world made up of computational or informational entities, whose mobility, transferability and combinability cast some doubt on our claim for a stable set of beliefs and organizational relations. Our normative beliefs (i.e., what we believe to be stable) and organizational relations will no longer be based solely upon the common discernment of a material and bounded reality, but primarily on shared reliance upon a reality characterized by the dissolvability and disembeddedness (Kallinikos 2006, 15) of computational and informational entities.

10.3.4 The Stratified Reality of the Internet

Turning our attention to the stratified reality of the Internet, we can observe the above-mentioned models of law in action in the governance of the Internet. To the extent to which we move through the layer of protocols from the layer of the physical to that of contents, we also move from the first to the third phase of the governance of reality, depending on the physical or informational notion of space (see Chap. 2) on which these layers are mostly based. This has at least three main consequences:

1. the reality of the Internet is governed by different models of law, which can crisscross and overlap according to their technological architecture and as a result of the tangled layers of the reality of the Internet;
2. the first layer, the physical, is governed by the first and the second models of law, as has been discussed to some length in the debate initiated by Johnson and Post (1996).[8] Both the second and the third layers are mainly governed by the second and third models of law. In this case, the governance of the Internet is structured around the following dichotomies: Multi-agent or State-regulation vs. self-regulation[9]; deliberated decisions vs. spontaneous actions; regulation vs.

[8] See also, more recently, Post 2008.

[9] See on this point Goldsmith and Wu, 2006.

architecture; legal vs. technological normativity; materiality vs. computation; non-neutrality vs. neutrality (and so forth);
3. the governance of reality depends not only on the actors and conceptions of law but, first and foremost, on the configuration of space within which reality is shaped and can be made subject to regulation.[10] This consequence should be stressed again and again. In modernity, space is both the epistemological horizon of constitution of objective reality and the political horizon of the coexistence of its occupiers. Each change in the conception and configuration of space is likely to produce effects both from an epistemological and a political viewpoint. Objective reality, be it material or immaterial (computational or informational), is the rational basis on which we form our beliefs. Coexistence is the goal of every organizational system of politics and law. Therefore, the information revolution brought about by the evolution of digital ICTs is likely to modify both the objective basis of our beliefs and the modes of our coexistence.

The first two remarks suggest that governance of the Internet can be fruitfully analyzed according to the intertwining models of law described above. We hold that this is the case for many important issues concerning the Internet. However, the third remark says that the information revolution brought about by the evolution of digital ICTs is reshaping the concept of space in informational terms (see Chap. 2), and thus also the reality that the law is meant to govern. This means we have to take a closer look at how the informational approach examined in this book can account for traditional legal categories. In particular, we are need to understand how legal information can be construed and how it is related to the reality that law is meant to govern. To this aim, in the next section we shall examine two information taxonomies proposed by Luciano Floridi that may be relevant to the law: the first concerns the relation between information and reality, and the second concerns the relation between information and meaning.

[10] In the same sense, see Hunter's astute remark: "Thinking of cyberspace as a place has led judges, legislators, and legal scholars to apply physical assumptions about property in this new, abstract space. Owners of Internet resources think of their systems as their own little claims in cyberspace, which must be protected against the typical encroachments that we find in the physical property world" (Hunter, 2003). See also: "The Internet is a shared environment; as such, the decisions made on a sovereign basis on the geography may affect Internet users in other geographies – users in the rest of the world's Internet ecosystem. To borrow another environmental metaphor, pollution from a river that runs through one country could flow into other countries downstream. (…) Internet use should take into account the perspectives of all who have a stake, regardless whether they are part of the sovereign decision-maker's geographic territory. While the Internet is a physical artifact with components in many countries, the virtual space created by that artifact is defined by logical boundaries rather than geophysical borders" (Cerf et al. 2014).

10.4 Information Taxonomies and Legal Information

As already mentioned, Floridi's informational approach has been taken into account in the fields of law (Burk 2008), philosophy of law (Pagallo 2006), and legal informatics (Durante 2007; Durante and Pagallo 2013). Here we adopt Floridi's taxonomies of information in examining the structure of legal information in relation to reality and meaning. This allows us to circumvent a dichotomy that often arises in studies of the law (namely, the opposition between nature and culture) and to account for some of the main historical conceptions of law within a single and unified conceptual framework. To this end, we will first recall Floridi's taxonomy concerning the relation between information and reality and then apply it to the legal field as a powerful heuristic tool for interpreting the past and present history of legal conceptions. The relation between Floridi's informational taxonomy and the interpretation of the law has been already sketched out in Pagallo (2006 and 2014), against a backdrop of reflection about the relationship between law and the complexity of reality. We will make reference to these ideas and try to expand on them in the present chapter. Then we will turn our focus to the second taxonomy of information, concerned with the relation between information and meaning, and thus also with the construction of knowledge.

Each information taxonomy is premised upon a specific taxonomical criterion that serves as a LoA (see Chap. 1). As noted, Floridi's first taxonomical criterion is premised upon the relation between information and reality. On the basis of this criterion, Floridi distinguishes between: (1) information as reality; (2) information about reality; and (3) information for reality. Clearly, this taxonomy of information can be modified, by choosing a different LoA. Floridi proposes a different taxonomy (correlated, however, in many respects to the previous one), on the basis of a different taxonomical criterion, i.e., the possibility that data might be meaningful independently of an intelligent *producer/informer*. Accordingly, Floridi distinguishes between: (1) environmental information; and (2) semantic information. Let us start with the first taxonomy of information.

10.4.1 The First Taxonomy of Information

According to Floridi (2013, 30), "information can be viewed from three perspectives: information as reality (such as patterns of physical signals, which are neither true nor false), also known as *ecological* information; information about reality (semantic information, alethically qualifiable); and information for reality (instruction, like genetic information)". Now let us examine each of these perspectives.

10.4.1.1 Information *as* Reality

People often presume that the only type of information we deal with is information about reality, overlooking the existence of information *as* reality and of information *for* reality. Admittedly, information *about* reality is the most common form of information we attend to and use, but it is certainly not the only one. Quite often, reality itself is made up of information. In other words, reality is an informational resource in its own right, as in the case of patterns of physical signals mentioned by Floridi. In such cases, a distinction cannot be precisely drawn between reality and information; furthermore, as there is no hiatus – interval or distance – between reality and information, a relationship or comparison between the two terms is also impossible to define. It follows that information cannot be alethically qualifiable (it is neither true nor false), because an alethic judgment necessarily requires some form of relationship or comparison between information and reality. In such an epistemic perspective, the notion of information as reality can already be seen to displace the deep-seated dichotomy between subject and object that premises the distance and consequent relationship between reality and information upon which the entire modern philosophical tradition has been based (see Chap. 8). This has important practical and philosophical consequences (see *ibid.*), all of which concern the entrenched and risk-laden tendency of the subject to manipulate and dispose of the object, since information as reality does not support a distinction between subject and object. We can therefore see why information as reality is construed, in this wider sense, as ecological information: namely, it is a type of information that preserves the reality that it embodies.

Against this ecological backdrop, we can appreciate why information as reality has been so important historically to the legal tradition. In this perspective, Ugo Pagallo has remarked that "an example [of *ecological* or *environmental* information] is given exactly by the tradition of the philosophy of the law and, notably, by the Schools of Natural Law that, since Plato and Aristotle, were meant to infer the legal principles from the nature of human beings. More recently, we have met forms of information as reality in the studies of neuro-law and in evolutionary psychology, according to which basic legal and moral concepts may be 'hardwired' in our brains, thereby promoting the idea of a cultural evolution" (Pagallo 2014; Pagallo and Durante 2016a). There are, actually, recurring forms of law that view legal information as being embedded in reality (of things, actions, human beings and so forth). In these cases, the law may either be criticized or commended: criticized, because it is considered conservative, since legal information preserves the reality which it consists of; commended, because it is considered forward-looking and prevents people from antagonistically and destructively manipulating or disposing of the reality it comprises (see on this point Chap. 8). It is important not to overlook the fact that important political and legal institutions (such as the European Union) strongly hold that future sustainable development highly depends on our capacity to embed ICTs in our societies, since ICTs are considered to consume less energy and to foster a more efficient and intelligent use of resources. This implies that technology is embedded in our democracies and hence our democracies are technologically mediated and dependent, with the result that technological normativity (i.e., the normativity incorporated in technologies) will be increasingly perceived of and assessed as a form of legal information as reality (at least to the extent to which reality is re-ontologized and re-engineered by the current information revolution, as remarked in Floridi [2010]). This will raise concern about the possible absence of formal legitimation of the legal information embodied in technological reality. In contrast, legal information as reality is likely to acquire a significant degree of effectiveness and, potentially, of social acceptance, given that it is already embedded in the technological fabric of social reality.

10.4.1.2 Information *About* Reality

Information about reality is the most common way of construing and dealing with information. Because information tells us something about reality, it enables us to construct a meaningful representation of it. Information about reality is therefore understood in semantic terms and is alethically qualifiable. According to Floridi, "the semantic approach defines information in terms of data space (semantic information is well-formed, meaningful, and truthful data)" (Floridi 2013, 31). As remarked above, being alethically qualifiable means that information about reality may be either true or false, since it can be compared with reality. Information about reality has played a decisive role in the construction of modern politics and law (see Chap. 8) since the existing political and legal order is an artificial construction, namely, a representation of reality. In the modern age, the political and legal order is almost inextricably linked to its representation (it is *more geometrico constructo*). In fact, it is the representation of a distinct political and legal order, separate from civil society, that leads people to believe that they are members of two different data spaces i.e., the social space of community, on the one hand, and the political and legal space of citizenship, on the other (see Chap. 9). The modern constructionist dimension of politics and law mainly resides in the human capacity to construct a meaningful and differentiated representation of (both social and political-legal) reality by using information about reality. In this perspective, politics and law cease to be a built-in dimension of human experience, in that they are an intrinsic part of nature (*legal information as reality*), and become an extrinsic dimension of human experience, in that they are part of culture (*information about reality*). What is interesting to note (and we will come back to this point in our conclusions) is that this distinction (often framed in terms of an irreducible opposition between nature and culture) is theoretically reconciled (and possibly overcome) by relying on an informational approach, and this leads to the realization that these different theoretical positions and understandings of human experience are, to some extent, just different ways of considering how information might be related to reality. It is only by acknowledging all of the ways information and reality can be related (including a third way that we will examine shortly) that we can fully account for the complexity of politics and law.

Pagallo adds a further remark about information about reality that helps us understand that the reality represented by the law is necessarily framed by the legal categories that construct a specific sociological or epistemological representation of legal reality. He writes that this kind of information "is relevant for legal scholars at different levels: in doctrinal terms, it is relevant for studies in the sociology of law and for some conceptions of legal realism; in judicial terms, it is relevant for the acquisition of evidence in a trial, which is often concerned with surveys of legal experts; in practical terms, it is relevant in any case in which the reader needed to ask for legal advice, and [...] strongly hoped that what was said by the lawyer was true!" (Pagallo 2014; Pagallo and Durante 2016a). Since there is no representation of reality that is LoA-free (as seen in Chap. 1), legal information about reality is also not LoA-free. Consequently, representations of legal reality are never independent from the specific LoAs adopted (whether sociological, phenomenological, epistemological, and so forth). There may be another sense in which information about reality is decisive for politics and law today, as already touched on in the previous chapter. Information about reality forms the epistemic and cognitive basis upon which people construct their representation of reality, form their reasonable expectations and make decisions. From the political standpoint, we have noted that a sovereign State (or other current political multiagente system) today is not only concerned with the legal monopoly of the use of force, but also and above all with control of the information life-cycle (entailing the production, storage, distribution and erasure of information). This is because the capital of information coupled with the capital of attention typical of the information society[11] serves as the basis upon which political consent is produced, stored, distributed and erased. From the legal standpoint, information about reality creates the background against which we form our legal expectations (about decisions, behaviors, and so forth). However, the way this happens is different from in the past. Prior to the information revolution, these expectations were ultimately predicated and based on the bounded and tangible existence of stable and enduring structures (such as things, roles, organizations). In Robert Cooper's words, "the contemporary spread and pervasive use of information technology is challenging our conventional tendency to think about the world in terms of stable and enduring structures. The new informational world recreates reality as a transient and continuously dissolving panorama of events in space and time" (Cooper commenting on Jannis Kallinikos' book, 2006, back cover). Law – which is a way to form reasonable and stable expectations by means of information about and for reality, as we will see shortly – will be increasingly called upon to deal with the computational rendition of reality, which "does not simply transpose reality to an electronic medium" but "reorganizes the universe and reshapes the substratum

[11] Our age is characterized by the emergence of different types of capital. We can make reference to at least three forms of new capital, which are related to different aspects of information societies. The globalized and networked dimension of communication has both reinforced old forms and also created new forms of social capital (made up of an interesting and novel combination of strong and weak social ties), as noted by Taylor (2001) or Barabasi (2002). The networked economy of information coupled with the dissemination of ICTs has created a new capital of informational resources (understood as both informational inputs and outputs), that is to say, novel forms of wealth, as noted by Benkler (2006). The emergence of the Web 2.0 (user generated content as understood in Shirky 2009 and 2011) coupled with the ensuing information overload that characterizes our information societies has led to a new capital of attention (i.e., people create and share information aiming at a potential audience), on which it is now necessary to impinge in order to communicate (social capital) or to select relevant and reliable information (information capital). Needless to say, politics is indeed sensitive to the capital of attention that exists on the Net and that spreads outside the Net due to the progressive convergence of offline and online reality (Floridi 2010), since at present political consent is measured precisely by the capacity to seize this capital of attention and turn it into popularity (Durante 2013b).

upon which a substantial part of contemporary modes of action and communication are based" (Kallinikos 2006, 2). Legal information is useful because it allows us to form reasonable and stable expectations not only *about* reality but also *for* reality (that is, to realize what are our expected behaviors). Let us turn now to the notion of information *for* reality, which is the most common way of construing law in the modern and contemporary ages.

10.4.1.3 Information *for* Reality

Information for reality is a (sequence of) instructions or rules about how to behave in specific circumstances (recipes, game rules, genetic or engineered instructions or legal norms understood in positivistic terms, and so forth). Like information as reality, this type of information is neither true nor false, since it does not entail comparison with reality. However, unlike information as reality, it determines the modes of being of other entities, since it tells us how to produce, or prevent, a modification of reality. As information, it does not determine reality on its own, although it does instruct agents how to do so, thus foreseeing the possibility that agents may fail to do so.[12] This means that the accomplishment of a behavior (often framed in mental, cognitive, or intentional terms, thus becoming increasingly problematic and uncertain from a legal perspective as cognitive or neuroscience progresses) requires the agent to correctly process information for reality.[13] Perhaps many of the theoretical problems concerning the relation between the internal (either mental, cognitive or intentional stances) and the external aspects of an agent's behavior could be fruitfully dealt with in terms of the correct or incorrect, complete or incomplete, processing of information that guides the agent's behavior, particularly against the backdrop of progressive interplay between human and artificial autonomous agents (as seen in Chap. 4). What is important to note is that information *for* reality always demands collaboration from the agents to arrange or modify reality. This is very different from information *as* reality, which captures existing patterns or structures, i.e., an arrangement or organization of reality. This means, at least in principle, that information for reality is meant to reduce violence and promote coexistence, since

[12] See on this point Chap. 4, where we highlight Floridi's use of the practical counterfactual, according to which one assumes that an agent is sufficiently informed to take different and alternate courses of actions, which are parameterized not in relation to all hidden and supervening factors impeding a course of actions from occurring (this idea also confounds the lack of an ability [to close a door] with a contingent inability [to close an already closed door]), but in relation to the agent's ability to correctly process information, in order to represent and take different and alternate courses of actions. In the field of law, we repeat, since Plato, we can command someone to act only presupposing that the commanded one is free either to respect or to disrespect the injunction to act. In this sense, information for reality (for instance, positive law) is not self-executing, unlike information as reality (for instance, natural law), which is always self-executed.

[13] We do not wish to enter here into the intricate debate about whether or not the accomplishment of a complex behavior based on instructions necessarily requires from the agent a form of intelligence or other computational processing of information or may be the mere execution of a task requiring the automated processing of data. According to Floridi, these qualifications are not LoAs-free; hence, "a good way of posing the problem is not: 'Is '*x* is *y*' adequate?' but rather 'If '*x* is *y*' at LoA *z*, is *z* adequate?" (Floridi 2004a, b, 566).

it necessarily requires agents to work together to arrange or modify reality. This is the secular project of modernity: the notion that reality is constructed and arranged by means of norms of coexistence that requires the agents' co-operation. It is thus within the theoretical and practical framework of constructivism (see Chap. 3) that we can understand the role of legal norms (information for reality) in the more comprehensive design of society and of democracy. It is true, of course, that collaboration between agents may also at times be used against other agents, thus producing forms of exclusion and violence (see in this sense Chap. 9).

At this point, let us turn to how information for reality has been historically treated in the tradition of legal thought. As has been noted, this type of information has had a decisive role in the understanding and construction of law in the modern and contemporary ages. Pagallo remarks that: "in the legal field, we should focus the attention on the various conceptions of the law in positivistic terms, which find their harbinger in the father of modern law and politics, Thomas Hobbes (1588–1679). Hobbes himself argues in Chapter 26 of the Leviathan that 'the law of nature and the civil law are reciprocally included and are coextensive", in essence seeming to endorse the idea of information as reality. However, as the chapter proceeds, the laws referred to are merely those which the constituted power has sanctioned as such: 'since the law is a command, and a command consists of a declaration or manifestation of the will of the one who is in command – by means of voice, writing or other certain indication of his will –, one can understand that the command of the State is the law only for those that can have cognition of it" (Hobbes, ed. 2008, 223–224) (Pagallo 2014). Once again, Hobbes is seminal in giving rise to the modern conception of legal information understood both as information *about* and *for* reality. In this perspective, the law of nature is superseded by civil law, and law itself is somehow dislodged from nature and conceived of as part of culture, by means of an opposition (between nature and culture) that will later be exacerbated in the contemporary age and, notably, through the resurgence of the new Schools of Natural Law following World War II.

Understood as information for reality, legal norms can be conceived of as instructions or rules that set our expectations, granting them a certain degree of stability. In other words, legal norms coordinate our behaviors by giving stability to our expectations. In this sense, information for reality is essential for us, since it enables us to behave correctly and modify reality consistently with our expectations. It also furnishes us with reasonable and stable expectations about others' behaviors, since legal norms tell us what the expected collective behaviors are on the basis of shared information for reality. This information thus establishes a twofold relation with freedom. On the one hand, instructions can only be directed at those who are free to act, meaning they can choose whether or not to follow the instructions. Information for reality is thus not self-executing, and requires collaboration from the agents, thereby presupposing some form of freedom. On the other hand, shared information for reality informs us of legal expectations concerning possible limits on our behavior, letting us know the extent of the sphere of freedom people have agreed upon to delimit through pre-established expectations. Here, the informative dimension of information for reality is crucial, since the (*ex post*) limitation of our behaviors (sanctioned by means of the judicial process) should be coextensive to the (*ex ante*) delimitation of our sphere of freedom, and should never exceed it. In this sense, information for reality entails some form of (*ex ante*) delimitation of freedom that should never be superseded by a wider (*ex post*) limitation of freedom (information about reality). The required respect for freedom calls for consistency and coordination between information for reality and about reality and, as observed in the previous chapter in reference to the relationship between ethics and infraethics, it requires us to coordinate the syntactical dimension of information for reality (which is never purely syntactical[14]) with the semantic dimension of information about reality. This leads us to the second taxonomy, concerning information that is specifically related to the possibility that data might be meaningful independently of an intelligent *producer/informer*. The next section examines this information taxonomy.

10.4.2 The Second Taxonomy of Information

10.4.2.1 Environmental Information

In many respects, environmental information correlates (but is not identical) with information as reality. As already mentioned, we speak of "environmental information when we wish to stress the possibility that data might be meaningful independently of an intelligent *producer/informer*. One of the most well-known examples of environmental information is the series of concentric rings in the wood of a cut tree trunk, which may be used to estimate its age" (Floridi 2010, 32). This means either that data may be provided with meaning regardless of the interpretative activity of a producer/informer, who in this case is only an observer, or that an entity may be "capable of making practical use of environmental information even in the absence of any semantic processing of *meaningful* data" (Floridi 2010, 34). In the latter case, for instance, an entity may be capable of processing data (i.e., it produces an output from an input) in merely syntactical terms. Besides, according to Floridi, environmental information does not need to be *natural* (Floridi 2010, 32). In fact, an "*engineered* signal too can be interpreted as an instance of environmental information" (Floridi 2010, 32). In this case, a signal "is normally defined relative to an observer (an informational organism or informee), who relies on it instead of having direct access to the original data in themselves. It follows that environmental information requires two systems, let us call them *a* and *b*, which are linked in such a way that the fact that *a* has a particular feature *F* is correlated to the fact that *b* has a particular feature *G*, so that this connection between the two features tells the

[14] Let us recall what Floridi observes with regard to computer (as possibly endowed with some form of artificial intelligence): "computers are often and rightly described as purely syntactic machines, yet 'purely syntactic' is a comparative abstraction, like 'virtually fat free'. It means that the level of semantic stance is negligible, not that is completely nonexistent. Computers are capable of (responding to) elementary discrimination (the detection of an identity as an identity and of a difference not in terms of perception of the peculiar and rich features of the entities involved but a simple registration of an invariant lack of identity constituting the relata as relata) and this is after all a protosemantic act" (Floridi 2004a, b, 569–570).

observers that *b* is *G*" (Floridi 2010, 32–33). This is true, for example, in the case of legal evidence in crime scenes, as Floridi quite properly remarks: "Viewers of *CSI*: *Crime Scene Investigation*, the crime television series, will also be acquainted with bullet trajectories, blood spray patterns, organ damage, fingerprints, and other similar evidence" (Floridi 2010, 32). In such cases, the correlation between two systems (which may require or involve no semantics at all, since they "may consist of networks or patterns of correlated data understood as mere physical differences" (Floridi 2010, 33)) follows some law or rule guiding the observer (an informational organism or informee) in the processing of data. The very fact that the correlation between two systems follows some law or rule allows the observer to reproduce and examine, by means of simulation, the correlation between the systems under exam. Furthermore, it also allows the observer to infer new data (in terms of predictions) from large quantities of networks or patterns of correlated data. Hence, environmental information supports both the third and the fourth paradigm of contemporary science, as reconstructed and accounted for by John Gray, which are respectively the paradigm of computational science based on simulation and the paradigm of data-intensive science based on big data.[15]

10.4.2.2 Semantic Information

Information as semantic content, although not identical, correlates with information for and about reality. As Floridi remarks: "when data are well formed and meaningful, the result is also known as *semantic content*. Information, understood as semantic content, comes in two main varieties: *instructional* and *factual*" (Floridi 2010, 34). Information is understood as semantic content when data might not be meaningful independently of an intelligent *producer/informer*. Information is instructional when it conveys the need for a specific action: in this sense, "instructional information is not *about* a situation, a fact, or a state of affairs *w* and does not model, or describe, or represent *w*. Rather, it is meant to (contribute to) bring about *w*"

[15] See T. Hey, S. Tansley, K. in Tolle (eds.) (2007), "Jim Gray on eScience: A Transformed Scientific Method", based on the transcript of a talk given by Jim Gray to the NRC-CSTB1 in Mountain View, CA, on January 11, 2007, xvii–xxxi, online at: http://research.microsoft.com/en-us/um/people/gray/talks/NRC-CSTB_eScience.ppt.: "Then, for many problems, the theoretical models grew too complicated to solve analytically, and people had to start simulating. These simulations have carried us through much of the last half of the last millennium. At this point, these simulations are generating a whole lot of data, along with a huge increase in data from the experimental sciences. People now do not actually look through telescopes. Instead, they are "looking" through large-scale, complex instruments which relay data to datacenters, and only then do they look at the information on their computers. The world of science has changed, and there is no question about this. The new model is for the data to be captured by instruments or generated by simulations before being processed by software and for the resulting information or knowledge to be stored in computers. Scientists only get to look at their data fairly late in this pipeline. The techniques and technologies for such data-intensive science are so different that it is worth distinguishing data-intensive science from computational science as a new, *fourth paradigm* for scientific exploration" (xvii-xviii). And also as to ecological information (xviii): "If you look at ecology, there is now both computational ecology, which is to do with simulating ecologies, and eco-informatics, which is to do with collecting and analyzing ecological information".

(Floridi 2010, 35). Therefore, information is factual when, in contrast, it is *about* a situation, a fact, or a state of affairs *w* and hence models, or describes, or represents *w* (Floridi 2010, 34–35). This also means that instructional information may be either environmental or semantic, "depending on whether meaning is a required feature" (Floridi 2010, 35).[16] Semantic instructional information is essential to law in many ways, as one can understand by considering the different contexts in which a piece of information can count as semantic instructional information or in which factual information may acquire an instructional value:

> There are many plausible contexts in which a stipulation ('let the value of x be 3' or 'suppose we genetically engineer a unicorn'), an invitation ('you are cordially invited to the college party'), an order ('close the window'), an instruction ('to open the box turn the key'), a game move ('1.e2–e4 c7–c5' at the beginning of a chess game) may be correctly qualified as kinds of semantic instructional information. (…) Such semantic instances of instructional information have to be at least potentially meaningful (interpretable) to count as information. Finally, there are performative contexts in which we do things with words, such as christening (e.g. 'this ship is now called *HMS The informer*') or programming (e.g. as when deciding the type of variable). In these cases, factual (descriptive) information acquires an instructional value (Floridi 2010, 35–36).

Legal information may thus be the content of different forms of semantic instructional information in potentially all of the above-mentioned contexts, ranging from stipulations, invitations and orders to instructions, game-moves and so on (thus also including performative contexts in which factual, descriptive legal information may acquire instructional value). In this perspective, legal norms could be considered as instances of semantic instructional information. We may wonder whether or not environmental instructional information may at times qualify as legal information: namely, whether we can speak of legal information or norms, independently of an intelligent *producer/informer*. As mentioned with reference to information as reality, this can happen whenever networks or patterns of correlated data (understood as mere physical differences) follow some law or rule and, therefore, guide the observer (an informational organism or informee) in the processing of data. In these cases, the fact that networks or patterns of correlated data following some law or rule may also guide the observer in the ensuing enunciation of an item of legal information or norm (acquiring a secondary and derived semantic value) is merely a side-effect of the environmental instructional information.

Factual semantic information is also essential to law, or more precisely, to legal science. Factual semantic information is, in fact, "the most common way in which information is understood and also one of the most important, since information as

[16] Floridi gives the following examples: "… the logic gates in the motherboard of a computer merely channel the electric voltage, which we may interpret in terms of instructional information (logic instructions), such as 'if…then'. In this case, there is no semantics involved at the level of the gates. The car's operation manual, on the contrary, provides *semantic* instructional information, either imperatively – in the form of a recipe: first do this, then do that – or conditionally – in the form of inferential procedure: if such and such is the case do this, otherwise do that" (Floridi, 2010, 35).

true semantic content is a necessary condition for knowledge" (Floridi 2010, 36). We do not propose to describe in full detail here Floridi's view of how information may upgrade to knowledge (see Floridi 2011a), but suffice it to recall what we have said in this regard with reference to a specific feature of legal adjudication, i.e., the process of legal balancing (see Durante 2013c). This is important, since legal knowledge (and hence legal science) is mainly based on legal factual semantic information. For this reason, we have to resort to two related concepts, elaborated by Floridi as part of his PI, which are both relevant to legal knowledge: the epistemological *Maker's Knowledge* approach (2011b) and the theory of knowledge as a *network account* (2011a).

10.4.2.3 The *Maker's Knowledge* Approach and the Theory of Knowledge as a *Network Account*

The *Maker's Knowledge* approach is an *engineer-friendly* approach to epistemology, according to which "knowing" is knowing how something is construed, and is thus characteristic of Floridi's epistemology in terms of a new form of *constructionism* (Floridi 2011b. For a detailed analysis of this concept, see Durante 2011). Let us see in more detail how this approach is conceived from an informational standpoint:

> If genuine knowledge is knowledge of the intrinsic nature of the object known (knowledge of the ontology of the known), and if there is no innate acquisition of such blueprint, then knowing a phenomenon, an artifact, or, in our case, gaining information and being able to account for it, means being able to produce it and reproduce it, to assemble and disassemble it, to build and dismantle it, to improve it and answer questions about it, and all this for the right reasons (Floridi 2011b, 290).

Furthermore, the *Maker's Knowledge* approach is not a-temporal and single-agent. On the contrary, it qualifies knowledge as a dynamic and collaborative epistemological enterprise which is rooted in our practical and creative interactions with reality and culminates in the informational representation of the object known. In Floridi's words:

> The maker's knowledge approach, on the contrary, requires trial and error and time-consuming processes of accumulation, exactly like other engineering tasks, so knowledge becomes a collaborative enterprise of growth and refinements in a multi-agent system (humanity), across generations (Floridi 2011b, 291).

> We do things with information, to paraphrase Austin. So it is because we *know how* to do something creatively, interactively, and collectively that we can rightly report to *know that* such and such is the case passively and individually. Propositional knowledge is the glorious conclusion of the informational process, not its humble beginning (Floridi 2011b, 284).

These epistemological aspects are indeed consistent with the understanding of legal reasoning in the process of legal adjudication as a creative, interactive, time-consuming, and collaborative informational enterprise of growth and refinements in a multi-agent system, a description that is perfectly suited to the legal tradition as a whole. Another aspect of Floridi's *Maker's Knowledge* approach is of great interest from the standpoint of legal theory: Floridi interprets constructionism as middle grounds between the Scylla and Charybdis of discovery, or invention, in which the study of the process of legal adjudication still seems to be entangled:

> We need to identify and follow the middle course, represented by the *design* of the world. This hardly thrills young minds, smacks of compromise to older ones, and, worst of all, cannot escape the constant risk of being confused with Scylla or Charybdis, *discovery* or *invention*. During an arm wrestling event, you neither expect nor look forward to a balanced draw between the two wrestlers. That is not the exciting outcome of the competition. Likewise, in philosophy we seek clear-cut alternatives and resolutions. In epistemology, we wish either knowledge or reality to pin the other's arm onto the surface of a conclusive answer over primacy once and for all. Equilibrium requires more energy than resolution, so we can hardly hold firm the view that *constructionism* is neither *realism* nor *constructivism*, because knowledge neither *describes* nor *prescribes* how the world is but inscribes it with semantic artifacts. The powerful and intuitive polarization between realism and idealism, discovery and invention, naturalism and anti-naturalism represents the intellectual temptation that makes our difficult task so delicate. For we need to ensure that what we appreciate as the highest and most cherished form of knowledge—our increasingly successful capacity to capture the world in a network of propositional contents and relevant accounts—maintains its deserved high status, keeps flourishing, and remains open to further progress, while replacing the foundations that make it so reliable (Floridi 2011b, 285).

The latter part of this noteworthy quotation explicitly relates the concept of constructionism, characteristic of the *Maker's Knowledge* approach, to another concept mentioned above: the theory of knowledge as a *network account* (Floridi 2011a). This theory further explains how to distinguish between information and knowledge and what knowledge is for, i.e., what knowledge enables us to do with it. Let us recall what qualifies as semantic information within the context of the theory of knowledge:

> Each piece of semantic information is an *answer to a question*, which, as a whole, poses further questions about itself that require the right sort of information flow in order to be answered correctly, through an appropriate network of relations with some informational source (Floridi 2011a, 274; emphasis is mine).

This definition is important for two reasons. First, it helps us understand why a legal dispute may have a basic heuristic function. In a sense, a legal dispute is nothing more than a 'question' within whose framework an answer arises to provide us with a new piece of semantic information. However, this new piece of information cannot yet be considered proper knowledge (a single item of information cannot be upgraded to legal knowledge), although it can once it is part of an appropriate network of relations with another information source. The second reason why this definition is important, in fact, relates to the difference between the key concepts of information and knowledge:

> The difference is that relevant semantic information lacks the necessary structure of relations that allow different packets of information to account for each other. It follows that, for relevant semantic information to be upgraded to knowledge, it is necessary to embed it

> in a network of equally relevant questions and correspondingly correct answers (Floridi 2011a, 278–279).

As stated above, knowing something presupposes understanding *how* a semantic artifact (a phenomenon, an object, a legal case, etc.) is constructed by means of a creative, interactive, time-consuming and collaborative enterprise. This epistemological enterprise requires us to construct "a network of equally relevant questions and correspondingly corrects answers" (Floridi 2011a, 279), that is to say that:

> We need to construct a network through which the right sort of information flows from a source *s* to a sink target *t*. In this network, *t* poses the relevant questions and *s* accounts *fort* if and only if *s* provides the correct answers. If the bi-conditional holds, we shall say that the whole network yields an account *of t* (Floridi 2011a, 274).

In other words, this means (Floridi 2011a, 277) that the relevant semantic information to be accounted for is the sink *t*, which on the one hand provides an answer to a question and, on the other, gives rise to further questions in relation to itself. Each question is, therefore, transformed into a Boolean interrogative. So *t* has an informational deficit, quantifiable by the number of Boolean answers required to satisfy the deficit. Hence, accounting for *t* means providing correct answers to all the questions that arise from *t* itself, so as to provide "the necessary flow of information that can satisfy *t*'s Boolean deficit satisfactorily" (Floridi 2011a, 277). The idea that emerges from these technicalities is that knowledge is not a sum of different elements of information relating to a given reality, but "a web of mutual relations that allow one part of it to account for another" (Floridi 2010, 51). The production of knowledge depends primarily on the relevant questions that we are able to ask and account for. Intelligence resides first and foremost in the questions asked, and only afterwards in the answers that are prompted:

> The information analysis of knowledge is more *engineer-friendly*. According to it, the production of knowledge that *t* relies, ultimately, on the *intelligent* mastery of the practical expertise (including modeling or, more mundanely, story-telling) required to produce not only *t* but also its correct account *A*. 'Knowing that' is grounded on 'knowing how', hardly surprising from an evolutionary perspective (Floridi 2011a, 287; emphasis is mine).

The *network theory of account* thus leads us back to the *maker's knowledge* approach, introducing a radical change of perspective in our understanding of knowledge: "we no longer try to define knowledge doxastically and by relying on a logic of subjective justification, but informationally, and by using a logic of objective accounting" (Floridi 2011a, 285).

10.5 Informational Notions and Legal Categories

Floridi's approach offers us some consistent criteria and theoretical tools for updating three basic legal notions in informational terms: (1) agents: legal subjects are understood as legal informational systems; (2) norms: legal provisions and expectations are understood as legal information; (3) reality: legal objects are understood as a new informational environment. Let us recall some issues already touched on and discussed in other parts of the book (see Chaps. 5 and 8), including the previous section, which is entirely concerned with the notion of legal information.

10.5.1 Legal Subjects

In the information society, legal subjects can no longer be conceived in merely anthropocentric terms. First, the notion of agents has been expanded to include autonomous artificial agents, to whom we delegate a growing number of tasks. Secondly, the activity of collecting and processing information is no longer only achieved by a single (human or artificial) agent, but by multi-agent systems or by distributed and pervasive systems (such as an autonomic computing system: Kephart and Chess 2003). Legal agency is thus increasingly made up of automated operations: "The nature of coding and computationally produced information are such that they make indispensable the relentless and meticulous parsing of reality and its reconstruction as large, often huge, series of automated operations" (Kallinikos 2006, 6). In this perspective, legal subjects cannot be understood merely as single and human centers of legal imputation, but also as systems of interaction between human or artificial, single or distributed, agents that share information. This requires us to devise new legal forms of personhood, accountability and responsibility (Solum 1992; Karnow 1996; Teubner 2007; Sartor 2009; Hildebrandt et al. 2010; Pagallo 2010 and Pagallo 2013a, b, c). The informational approach does not just show how agents communicate and interact with each other by sharing information in terms of positive or negative messages (Floridi 2013). Thanks to its ontocentric perspective, it offers a unified framework for the varying status and regime involving the nature of agents, their relations and the content of shared information (see Chaps. 2 and 8). All agents, relations and data may be understood as informational entities, which are to be treated as part of the informational environment, the infosphere, to which they belong *qua* informational systems. This applies not only to the moral domain but, potentially, also to the legal realm, and it may call for expansion of both the class of agents that are held responsible and of the class of actions for which they are held responsible. Furthermore, as seen in Chap. 8, the informational approach suggests that, in the long run, the distinction itself between legal subjects and objects may be blurred and conflated in favor of a unified notion of the information system (understood as any entity capable of producing, storing, communicating and sharing information).

10.5.2 Legal Provisions and Expectations

In the information society, the capability of legal norms to predict future behaviors and establish expectations needs to be rethought. A legal norm implies a rather static representation of reality, in contrast with the ability of the technological world to change itself.[17] The amount of information contained in a legal norm (set by a deliberative institutional body) may often be insufficient to account for the complexity of technological reality and its rapid self-modification. On this basis, we can redefine the notion of a legal norm by starting from a deeper and more systematic analysis of the informational content of a norm. In fact, the idea of treating the legal norm as information produced not only by a single center but, first and foremost, by a decentered multi-agent system, is not new in the field of philosophy of law (Robilant 1973; Pagallo 2006; Pagallo and Durante 2016b; Durante 2013a). What is novel at present is the need to treat a legal norm as legal information that is part of an ontological reinterpretation of reality, which we have sketched out in the previous section. As already noted, this requires us to make reference to a specific philosophy of information that considers not only the syntactical features of information (as in many studies of AI and the law) but also its semantic dimension (Floridi 2011a). An informational approach to the idea of a legal norm understood as a provision and an expectation containing a certain amount of information should be able to deal with the two essential features of the (a) quality and the (b) quantity of information. Floridi's concept of information accounts for both a qualitative (concerned with meaning) and a quantitative concept of information (concerned with the quantity of semantic content). We have already considered the qualitative aspect of meaning. Let us now focus on the quantity of information that a legal norm should contain. According to Floridi, "the quantity of semantic information in *p* can then be calculated in terms of distance of *p* from the situation *w* that *p* is supposed to address" (Floridi 2010, 59). Floridi provides us with an example: "Imagine there will be exactly three guests for dinner tonight. This is our situation *w*. Imagine John is cooking the meal and he is told that: A. there will or will not be some guests for dinner tonight; or B. there will be some guests tonight; or C. there will be three guests tonight; or D. there will and will not be some guests tonight. The *degree of informativeness* of A is zero because, as a tautology, A applies both to *w* and to its negation. B performs better, while C has the maximum degree of informativeness because, as a fully accurate, precise, and contingent truth, it 'zeros in' on its target *w*. And since D is false (it is a contradiction), it does not qualify as semantic information at all, just mere content" (Floridi 2010, 59; for a more analytical account of the quantitative aspect of semantic information, Floridi 2011a, 117–133). Hence, we adopt Floridi's semantic concept of information because it allows us to account for both the qualitative and the quantitative aspects of information. Both aspects of information are relevant and involved in the fields of law. Most of the time, people make decisions and act on the basis of the information that they have. In this sense, information is crucial for many legally relevant decisions and actions. In such cases, people need information from both a quantitative and a qualitative standpoint: namely, they need to have a certain amount of information, the semantic content of which is relevant for and aimed at the situation in which the agent has to decide and act. People can decide and

[17] However, this is not always the case. Sometimes, law may rapidly intervene to determine or to affect the development of a technology. In effect, the relation between law and technology is more circular than one normally tends to acknowledge (see on this point, Durante and Pagallo 2013).

act efficiently and efficaciously only when they have the right combination of quantitative and qualitative information. To put it simply, one can decide and act correctly when in possession of all (quantitative) the relevant information.[18]

10.5.3 Legal Objects

In the information society, the evolution of ICTs is no longer viewed, according to the informational approach, as merely a question of applied ethics or empirical examination, but as something that constitutes a new environment that brings about a re-ontologization of reality made up of informational entities. This may require the law to protect both the informational entities recognized as valuable in the information society as well as the agent's capacity to be a source of information and produce informational entities, according to the four laws of the infosphere (see Chap. 2), understood as the *fundamental law* of a new social contract or ontic trust of the information society (see Chap. 8). The four laws, along with ontological friction (seen in Chap. 7), tend to establish a basic principle that underlies the informational approach to law, according to which the informational environment should be ruled and governed on the basis of a presumption in favor of the most liberal creation, circulation and distribution of information (*rectius*: informational entities). This means that the burden of proving that restrictions in the creation, circulation and distribution of information are justified should be placed, first, on those who invoke them (Pagallo and Durante 2010). Furthermore, it is important to note that Floridi's ecological approach to information (for his notion of e-environmentalism see Floridi 2010; see also Chap. 8) is deeply consistent with EU sensitivity towards the idea that the sustainable development of globalized societies mainly relies, nowadays, on the evolution of digital ICTs, which are not only less energy-consuming but can also provide us with new ways to use energy in a smarter and more efficient way. Any fragmented and merely instrumental approach to law and technology fails to notice that we are part of a whole (see Chaps. 3 and 9) that requires a systemic approach to moral and legal issues. Objects (including legal objects) are related to the whole, since they are bundles of variable relations rather than solidified entities (according to an ontology based on interaction: see Chap. 2). Therefore, legal objects are to be protected not only because they are encroached in either material or immaterial forms of property, but also because they entail bundles of relations between interacting agents or information systems (see Chaps. 6 and 8). In this sense, objects today play an increasingly important normative function in that they enable us to establish relations and share information with each other and with the environment.

[18]Things are, of course, much more complicated in real life than in abstract representations. For instance, in some legal contexts (e.g. some contracts), the amount of information (numerous contractual terms) can obscure our perception of what the most relevant information actually is. As a result, we often end up signing contracts without thoroughly reading and understanding them first. Our assumption is that, in most cases, we will be provided with the relevant information (information not too distant from the targeted situation) to allow us decide and act properly in the situation under exam.

10.6 Conclusions

The information revolution brought about by the technological evolution of digital ICTs may have a far more profound and complex impact on the law than ever imagined before. The current literature has examined some of the main consequences of this impact, such as the production and dissemination of information across international borders (including informational agents and objects). The resulting problems of legal jurisdiction and the exponential growth in the number of sources of legally relevant information tend to undermine the modern territorial State's claim to absolute sovereignty within its borders and, with it, the hierarchy of norms or powers established by national law. As a consequence, networked models of law based on unbounded, decentralized and horizontal forms of legal organization are emerging alongside more traditional models of law based on bounded, central and vertical forms of legal organization. Moreover, as a normative system, contemporary law is being confronted with new challenges arising from other increasingly important normative systems, such as economics, architecture, design, social norms, and - above all - technology. Legal scholars have begun to investigate the role of technological normativity in information societies and, more generally, to examine how technology is embedded in our democracies and information societies (Lessig 2006; Hildebrandt 2008; Pagallo 2014; Durante 2015; Floridi 2015).

Although these issues are clearly important and relevant, the literature has fallen short in capturing the most profound implication of the information revolution stemming from the technological evolution of digital ICTs: the re-ontologization of the reality that the law is intended to govern. What is at stake is nothing less than a paradigm shift in our normative mind-set towards the representation of the world. Our normative beliefs are no longer regulated and based solely on a traditional and deep-seated representation of reality (i.e., the material objects of the world), but also on its informational representation (i.e. virtual reality, informational entities, and streams of information).

If we are to deal effectively with this nascent ontology of reality, it is useful to apply an informational approach to the philosophy of law. In this chapter, we have availed ourselves of the informational approach provided by Luciano Floridi's philosophy and ethics of information. First, we provided an outline of the evolution of models of law from modernity to industrial and post-industrial societies up to information societies. We then adopted Floridi's information taxonomies, based on the relation between (1) information and reality, and (2) information and meaning, the two keystones of legal normativity, to re-examine the content and structure of normativity in terms of legal information. Finally, we tried to envisage how the traditional legal categories of legal subjects, norms and objects are likely to change in light of the ontological and ecological informational approach required by the technological evolution of digital ICTs.

Floridi's ontological and ecological approach as applied to the philosophy of law shows us that: (1) information societies need to be founded on a novel social contract or ontic trust that is consistent with the four laws of the infosphere (Chap. 8); (2) politics in information societies is no longer merely concerned with the art of making collective decisions (from a normative standpoint) or with control over a territory (from a descriptive standpoint), but, also and above all, with control and management of the life-cycle of information (Chapter 9); (3) law in information societies can no longer be understood according to the traditional opposition between culture and nature, on the one hand, and between subject and object, on the other.

An informational approach to law also allows us to abandon the traditional dichotomy between culture and nature (by adopting - according to Floridi's information taxonomies - a LoA of legal information), and that between subject and object (by adopting a LoA of information systems) (Chaps. 8 and 10). The information revolution thus makes us realize that we live in a smart and animated world, or e-life, in which our decisions and behaviors constantly generate new information and modify the distribution of existing information, thus renewing the context in which we continue to make decisions and to act. This communicative and recursive interaction with the world and with the (human or artificial) agents that populate it is, and will remain, at the center of the most decisive future debates, particularly in the moral, political and legal fields. The theoretical and practical task we now face is that of understanding that this communicative interaction will always be less than one-way: on the contrary, it must be conceived as an exchange and a potential form of enrichment, on the assumption that as simple as inevitable what is relevant to information is likewise relevant to our existence (Chaps. 1 and 2).

As observed by di Robilant, law may thus be conceived as an open normative system, located "in the environment and exposed to the influence of the environment, i.e., is in a situation of mutual interference: it introduces information in the environment and receives information from it, it modifies it and is modified by it" (di Robilant 1973, 253). Thus, "in an open system normativity, as a result of multiple interferences between normative inputs and outputs, that is, between information flows, is understood as an attempt to achieve a reduction of complexity that is consistent with as much as possible of information" (di Robilant 1973, 256). To rephrase di Robilant's commentary on the industrial society, the existence of the information society is tied in with a plurality of inputs and outputs, that is, with the multiplicity of information and choices (di Robilant 1973, 256). Choices are also important, in fact, since they concern the way in which we select relevant legal information. This selection posits an axiological problem, which is concerned with the values that are encroached in an open normative system. According to di Robilant, the openness of the normative system concerns not only norms, understood as legal information, but also values, which, like information, also circulate and transmit new information and are understood as suggestions for the selection of relevant legal information (di Robilant 1973, 257).

In this perspective, "a closed system tends to defend itself from the flow of new information, different from that introduced in the system by the centers of emission, and thus tends to refute new values, which are perceived as forms of disturb or of violation of existing values; whereas an open system tends to introduce new values, which stem from the interference and the mutual interaction between information flows, and hence from the adjustments required by the need to reduce complexity.

In an open system, the [information] *feedback* (…) is not a function of a merely *negative self-regulation* of the system, that is aimed to eliminate forms of disturb and to keep the system in equilibrium; on the contrary, it is aimed to let new information flows, as well as new values, to be selected, assimilated and incorporated in the system. In this case, the [information] *feedback* is a function of a *positive self-regulation* of the system that is directed to create a new situation, different from the starting one" (di Robilant 1973, 258).

The operative closure of the normative system, as noted by di Robilant (1973, 253–255), is not only brought about by particular legal conceptions (which are more concerned with the structure than with the function of the normative system), but also by specific ethical conceptions (mainly based on the ideas of fault, expiation and regeneration, which point out the need to always restore a broken equilibrium, by bringing the system back to its presumed starting point [see in this perspective what we have said in the previous chapter about the start-end principle]). This means that the openness of the normative system (as well as of the information society) requires not only an informational approach to the law but also and above all it requires a new perspective for the ethical conception. Floridi's information ethics, examined in the first part of this book, provides a powerful framework for pursuing detailed investigations of this ontological shift, whose meaning and scope are still in the making.

References

Barabasi, A.-L. 2002. *Linked: The New Science of Networks*. New York: Basic Books.

Benkler, Y. 2006. *The Wealth of Networks: How Social Production Transforms Markets and Freedom*. New Haven CT: Yale University Press.

Burk, D.-L. 2008. Information Ethics and the Law of Data Representations. *Ethics and Information Technology* 10: 135–147.

Castells, M. 2009. *Communication Power*. Oxford: Oxford University Press.

Cerf, V., P. Ryan, and M. Senges 2014. Internet Governance is our shared responsibility. *Journal of Law and Policy for the Information Society*. Online at: http://ssrn.com/abstract=2309772

Ceruti, M. 2009. *Il vincolo e la possibilità*. Milano: Raffaello Cortina Editore.

Cohen, J. 2007. Cyberspace as/and Space. *Columbia Law Review* 107: 210–256.

Di Robilant, E. 1973. Il diritto nella società industriale. *Rivista internazionale di filosofia del diritto* 50 (2): 225–262.

Durante, M. 2007. Il futuro del web: etica, diritto, decentramento. Dalla sussidiarietà digitale all'economia dell'informazione in rete, Giappichelli, Torino.

———. 2010. The Value of Information as Ontological Pluralism. *Knowledge, Technology & Policy* 23 (1): 149–161.

———. 2011. Rethinking Human Identity in the Age of Autonomic Computing: The Philosophical Idea of the Trace. In *Law, Human Agency and Autonomic Computing. The Philosophy of Law Meets the Philosophy of Technology*, ed. M. Hildebrandt and A. Rouvroy, 85–103. London: Routledge.

———. 2013a. How to Cross Boundaries in the Information Society: Vulnerability, Responsiveness, and Accountability. *Acm Sigcas Computers and Society* 43 (1): 9–21.

———. 2013b. Informazione e regolazione. Internet come problema democratico. *Teoria politica* 3: 39–65.

———. 2013c. Dealing with Legal Conflicts in the Information Society. An Informational Understanding of Balancing Competing Interests. *Philosophy & Technology* 26 (4): 437–457.
———. 2015. The Democratic Governance of Information Societies. A Critique to the Theory of Stakeholders. *Philosophy & Technology* 28 (1): 11–32.
Durante, M., and U. Pagallo (eds.). 2013. *Manuale di informatica giuridica e diritto delle nuove tecnologie*. Torino: UTET.
Floridi, L. 2004a. On the Morality of Artificial Agents. *Minds and Machines* 14 (3): 349–379.
———. 2004b. Outline of a Theory of Strongly Semantic Information. *Minds and Machines* 14 (2): 197–222.
———. 2007. Global Information Ethics: The Importance of Being Environmentally Earnest. *International Journal of Technology and Human Interaction* 3 (3): 1–11.
———. 2010. *Information. A Very Short Introduction*. Oxford: Oxford University Press.
———. 2011a. *The Philosophy of Information*. Oxford: Oxford University Press.
———. 2011b. A Defence of Constructionism: Philosophy as Conceptual Engineering. *Metaphilosophy* 42 (3): 282–304.
———. 2013. *Information Ethics*. Oxford: Oxford University Press.
———. 2015. Toleration and the Design of Norms. *Science and Engineering Ethics* 21 (5): 1095–1123.
Galloway, A. 2004. *Protocol. How Control Exists After Decentralization*. Cambridge, MA: MIT Press.
Galloway, A., and E. Thacker. 2007. *The Exploit. A Theory of Networks*, Electronic Mediations Series. Minneapolis/London: Minnesota University Press.
Goldsmith, J., and T. Wu. 2006. *Who Controls the Internet? Illusions of a Borderless World*. Oxford: Oxford University Press.
Gould, C. 2004. *Globalizing Democracy and Human Rights*. Cambridge, MA: Cambridge University Press.
Hey, T., S. Tansley, and K. Tolle. 2007. *Jim Gray on eScience: A Transformed Scientific Model*, accessible online at: http://research.microsoft.com/en-us/collaboration/fourthparadigm.
Hildebrandt, M. 2008. Legal and Technological Normativity: More (and Less) Than Twin Sisters. *Techné: Research in Philosophy and Technology* 12 (3): 169–183.
Hildebrandt, M., B.-J. Koops, and D.-O. Jaquet-Chifelle. 2010. Bridging the Accountability Gap: Rights for New Entities in the Information Society? *Minnesota Journal of Law, Science & Technology* 11 (2): 497–561.
Hobbes, T. 2008. *Leviathan [1651]*. Oxford: Oxford University Press.
Hunter, D. 2003. Cyberspace as Place and the Tragedy of the Digital Anticommons. *California Law Review* 91 (2): 439–519.
Johnson, D.-R., and D.-G. Post. 1996. Law and Borders. The Rise of Law in Cyberspace. *Stanford Law Review* 48: 1367–1404.
Kallinikos, J. 2006. *The Consequences of Information*. In *Institutional Implications of Technological Change*. Cheltenham/Northampton, MA: Edward Elgar.
Karnow, C.E.A. 1996. Liability for Distributed Artificial Intelligence. *Berkeley Technology and Law Journal* 11: 147–183.
Kephart, J.O., and D.M. Chess. 2003. The Vision of Autonomic Computing, IEEE Society. Online at: www.research.ibm.com/autonomic/manifesto.
Lessig, L. 2006. *Code: And Other Laws of Cyberspace, Version 2.0*. New York: Basic Books.
Murray, A. 2007. *The Regulation of Cyberspace: Control in the Online Environment*. Abingdon: Routledge Cavendish.
Ost, F., and M. van de Kerchove. 2002. *De la pyramide au réseau ? Pour une théorie dialectique du droit*. Bruxelles: Publications Faculté St. Louis.
Pagallo, U. 2003. *Prolegomeni d'informatica giuridica*. Padova: Cedam.
———. 2006. *Teoria giuridica della complessità*. Torino: Giappichelli.
———. 2010. Robotrust and Legal Responsibility. *Knowledge, Technology and Policy* 23: 367–379.
———. 2013a. *The Laws of Robot: Crimes, Contracts, and Torts*. Dordrecht/Berlin: Springer.

———. 2013b. What Robots Want: Autonomous Machines, Codes and New Frontiers of Legal Responsibility. In *Human Law and Computer Law: Comparative Perspectives*, ed. M. Hildebrandt and J. Gaakeer. Dordrecht: Springer.

———. 2013c. Online Security and the Protection of Civil Rights: A Legal Overview. *Philosophy and Technology* 26 (4): 381–395.

———. 2014. Il diritto nell'età dell'informazione. Il riposizionamento tecnologico degli ordinamenti giuridici tra complessità sociale, lotta per il potere e tutela dei diritti, Giappichelli, Torino.

Pagallo, U., and M. Durante. 2010. Three Roads to P2P Systems and Their Impact on Business Practices and Ethics. *Journal of Business Ethics* 94 (4): 551–564.

———. 2016a. The Philosophy of Law in an Information Society. In *The Routledge Handbook of Philosophy of Information*, ed. L. Floridi, 396–407. London/New York: Routledge.

———. 2016b. The Pros and Cons of Legal Automation and its Governance. *European Journal of Risk Regulation* 7 (2): 323–334.

Post, D. 2008. *In Search of Jefferson's Moose. Notes on the State of Cyberspace*. Oxford/New York: Oxford University Press.

Sartor, G. 2009. Cognitive Automata and the Law: Electronic Contracting and the Intentionality of Software Agents. *Artificial Intelligence and Law* 17 (4): 253–290.

———. 2015. Reasoning with Normative Systems. In *The Cognitive Foundations of Group Attitudes and Social Interaction*, ed. A. Herzig and E. Lorini, 177–190. Dordrecht: Springer.

Shirky, C. 2009. *Here Comes Everybody: How Change Happens when People Come Together*. London: Penguin.

———. 2011. *Cognitive Surplus: Creativity and Generosity in a Connected Age*. London: Penguin.

Solum, L. 1992. Legal Personhood for Artificial Intelligence. *North Carolina Law Review* 70: 1231–1287.

Taylor, M. 2001. *The Moment of Complexity: Emerging Network Culture*. Chicago: Chicago University Press.

Teubner, G. 2007. *Rights of Non-humans? Electronic Agents and Animals as New Actors in Politics and Law*. Max Weber Lecture at the European University Institute of Fiesole, Italy, January 17.

Bibliography

Abensour, M. 2006. L'extravagante hypothèse, in Levinas, collectif aux éditions Bayard, Paris, 73–105.

Allo, P. (ed.). 2011. *Putting Information First: Luciano Floridi and the Philosophy of Information*, Hoboken: Wiley-Blackwell.

Alpaydin, E. 2010. *Introduction to Machine Learning*. II ed. Cambridge, MA: MIT Press.

Amichai-Hamburger, Y., K. McKenna, and S.A. Tal. 2008, September. E-empowerment: Empowerment by the Internet, Special Issue: *Internet Empowerment. Computers in Human Behaviour* 24 (5): 1776–1789.

Antonelli, C. 2005. "Prefazione" a M. Antonelli, C. 2005. "Introduzione" to M. Taylor, Il momento della complessità.Taylor, Il momento della complessità. L'emergenza di una cultura a rete. transl. by it.di Benedetta Antonelli D'Oulx, Codice Editore, Torino, pp.B. Antonelli D'Oulx, Codice Editore, Torinoix-xx.

Arendt, H. 2011. *Quaderni e diari 1950–1973*. Trans. C. Marazia. Milano: Neri Pozza.

Barabasi, A.-L. 2002. *Linked: The New Science of Networks*. New York: Basic Books.

Barberis, M. 2013. La fine dello Stato e altri racconti. *Filosofia Politica* 2: 317–329.

Bateson, G. 1973. *Steps to an Ecology of Mind*. Frogmore, St. Albans: Paladin.

Beavers, A.-F., and D. Jones, eds. 2014. Philosophy in the Age of Information: A Symposium on Luciano Floridi's The Philosophy of Information. *Mind and Machines* 24 (1): 1–141.

Benasayag, M., and A. del Rey. 2007. *Eloge du conflit*. Paris: Editions La Découverte.

Benkler, Y. 2006. *The Wealth of Networks: How Social Production Transforms Markets and Freedom*. New Haven CT: Yale University Press.

———. 2011. *The Penguin and the Leviathan: The Triumph of Cooperation Over Self-Interest*. New York: Crown Business.

Blumenberg, H. 1985. *The Legitimacy of the Modern Age* [1976]. Trans. R.-M. Wallace from the 2ed ed. Cambridge, MA: MIT Press.

Brandt, R. 1991. *D'Artagnan und die Urteilstafel. Über ein Ordnungsprinzip der europäischen Kulturgeschichte*. Stuttgart: Franz Steiner.

Brey, P. 2008. Do We Have Moral Duties Towards Information Objects? *Ethics and Information Technology* 10 (2–3): 109–114.

Burk, D.-L. 2008. Information Ethics and the Law of Data Representations. *Ethics and Information Technology* 10: 135–147.

Butler, J. 2005. *Giving an Account of Oneself*. New York: Fordham University Press.

Capurro, R. 2008. On Floridi's Metaphysical Foundation of Information Ecology. *Ethics and Information Technology* 10 (2–3): 167–173.

Castells, M. 1996. *The Rise of the Network Society, The Information Age: Economy, Society and Culture*. Vol. I. Cambridge, MA/Oxford: Blackwell.

———. 1997. *The Power of Identity, The Information Age: Economy, Society and Culture*. Vol. II. Cambridge, MA/Oxford: Blackwell.

M. Durante, *Ethics, Law and the Politics of Information*, The International Library of Ethics, Law and Technology 18, DOI 10.1007/978-94-024-1150-8

———. 1998. *End of Millennium, The Information Age: Economy, Society and Culture*. Vol. III. Cambridge, MA/Oxford: Blackwell.

———. 1999. *The Information Age: Economy, Society, and Culture*. Vol. 1–3. Malden, MA: Wiley-Blackwell.

———. 2009. *Communication Power*. Oxford: Oxford University Press.

———. 2012. *Networks of Outrage and Hope: Social Movements in the Internet Age*. New York: Polity Press.

Cavarero, A. 2010. *Horrorism: Naming Contemporary Violence*. Trans. W. Mc Cuaig. New York: Columbia University Press.

Cavell, S. 1991. *Conditions Handsome and Unhandsome: The Constitution of Emersonian Perfectionism*. Chicago: University Of Chicago Press.

———. 2005. *Cities of Words: Pedagogical Letters on a Register of the Moral Life*. Cambridge, MA: Belknap Press of Harvard University Press.

Cerf, V., P. Ryan, and M. Senges 2014. Internet Governance is our shared responsibility. *Journal of Law and Policy for the Information Society*. Online at: http://ssrn.com/abstract=2309772

Ceruti, M. 2009. *Il vincolo e la possibilità*. Milano: Raffaello Cortina Editore.

Cohen, J. 2007. Cyberspace as/and Space. *Columbia Law Review* 107: 210–256.

Comensoli Antonini, L. 2013. Gauchet lettore di Kantorowicz. *Apporti alla teoria del disincanto, Filosofia Politica* 2: 271–294.

Davidson, D. 1984. *Inquiries into Truth and Interpretation [1974]*. Oxford: Clarendon Press.

Deleuze, G., and F. Guattari. 1994. *What Is Philosophy?* New York: Columbia University Press.

Demir, H. (ed.). 2010. Luciano Floridi's Philosophy of Technology: Critical Reflections. *Knowledge, Technology & Policy*, 23.

———. (ed.). 2012. *Luciano Floridi's Philosophy of Technology: Critical Reflections*. Dordrecht: Springer.

Dey, A.-K. 2001. Understanding and Using Context. *Personal and Ubiquitous Computing Journal*, 5(1): 4–7. Available at: http://www.cc.gatech.edu/fce/pubs/PeTe5-1.pdf.

Di Robilant, E. 1973. Il diritto nella società industriale. *Rivista internazionale di filosofia del diritto* 50 (2): 225–262.

Dicker, G. 2004. *Kant's Theory of Knowledge. An Analytical Introduction*. Oxford: Oxford University Press.

Doyle, T. 2010. A Critique of Information Ethics. *Knowledge, Technology and Policy* 23 (1–2): 163–175.

Durante, M. 2002. *Comunità e alterità nell'opera di Emmanuel Levinas: il terzo, la legge, la giustizia*. Torino: Thélème.

———. 2007. Il futuro del web: etica, diritto, decentramento. Dalla sussidiarietà digitale all'economia dell'informazione in rete, Giappichelli, Torino.

———. 2008. "What Model of Trust for Networked Cooperation? Online Social Trust in the Production of Common Goods (Knowledge Sharing)", in T.W. Bynum, M. Calzarossa, I. De Lotto, S. Rogerson, "Living, Working and Learning Beyond Technology", Proceedings of the Tenth International Conference Ethicomp2008, Tipografia commerciale, Mantova, 211–223.

———. 2009. Re-designing the Role of Law in the Information Society: Mediating between the Real and the Virtual. In *Law and Technology: Looking into the Future*, ed. M. Fernandez-Barrera, N. Gomes de Andrade, P. de Filippi, M. Viola de Azevedo Cunha, G. Sartor, and P. Casanovas, 31–50. Florence: European Press Academic Publishing.

———. 2010. The Value of Information as Ontological Pluralism. *Knowledge, Technology & Policy* 23 (1): 149–161.

———. 2011a. Normativity, Constructionism, and Constraining Affordances. *Etica & Politica/ Ethics & Politics*, Symposium on Luciano Floridi's Philosophy of Information, XIII(2): 180–200.

———. 2011b. Rethinking Human Identity in the Age of Autonomic Computing: The Philosophical Idea of the Trace. In *Law, Human Agency and Autonomic Computing. The Philosophy of Law Meets the Philosophy of Technology*, ed. M. Hildebrandt and A. Rouvroy, 85–103. London: Routledge.

———. 2012. E-democracy as the Frame of Networked Public Discourse. Information, Consensus and Complexity, In ed. P. Mindus, A. Greppi, and M. Cuono. Legitimacy 2.0. E-Democracy and Public Opinion in the Digital Age, Paper Series – 25th IVR World Congress: Law, Science and Technology, Frankfurt am Main, Goethe University Press, 1–28.

———. 2013a. How to Cross Boundaries in the Information Society: Vulnerability, Responsiveness, and Accountability. *Acm Sigcas Computers and Society* 43 (1): 9–21.

———. 2013b. Informazione e regolazione. Internet come problema democratico. *Teoria politica* 3: 39–65.

———. 2013c. Dealing with Legal Conflicts in the Information Society. An Informational Understanding of Balancing Competing Interests. *Philosophy & Technology* 26 (4): 437–457.

———. 2015. The Democratic Governance of Information Societies. A Critique to the Theory of Stakeholders. *Philosophy & Technology* 28 (1): 11–32.

Durante, M., and U. Pagallo (eds.). 2013. *Manuale di informatica giuridica e diritto delle nuove tecnologie*. Torino: UTET.

Esposito. 2013. Politica e metafisica. *Filosofia Politica* 3: 465–478.

Ess, C. 2009. Floridi's Philosophy of Information and Information Ethics: Current Perspectives, Future Directions, Introduction to a Special issue on "Floridi's information and Computer Ethics". *The Information Society – The Philosophy of Information, its Nature, and Future Developments* 25 (3): 159–168.

Ethics and Information Technology. 2008. Special issue edited by C. Ess on "Luciano Floridi's Philosophy of Information and Information Ethics: Critical Reflections and the State of the Art", 10(2–3).

Etica & Politica/Ethics & Politics. 2011. Symposium on "Luciano Floridi's Philosophy of Information", XIII, 2.

Fernandez-Barrera, M., N. Gomes de Andrade, P. de Filippi, M. Viola de Azevedo Cunha, G. Sartor, and P. Casanovas (eds.). 2009. *Law and Technology: Looking into the Future*, Florence: European Press Academic Publishing.

Floridi, L. 1999. Information Ethics: On the Philosophical Foundation of Computer Ethics. *Ethics and Information Technology* 1: 37–56.

———. 2003. On the Intrinsic Value of Information Objects and the Infosphere. *Ethics and Information Technology* 4 (4): 287–304.

———. 2004a. On the Morality of Artificial Agents. *Minds and Machines* 14 (3): 349–379.

———. 2004b. Outline of a Theory of Strongly Semantic Information. *Minds and Machines* 14 (2): 197–222.

———. 2006. Information Technology and the Tragedy of the Good Will. *Ethics and Information Technology* 8 (4): 253–262.

———. 2007a. A Look into the Future Impact of ICT on Our Lives. *The Information Society* 23 (1): 59–64.

———. 2007b. Global Information Ethics: The Importance of Being Environmentally Earnest. *International Journal of Technology and Human Interaction* 3 (3): 1–11.

———. 2008a. Information Ethics, Its Nature and Scope. In *Moral Philosophy and Information Technology*, ed. J. van den Hoven and J. Weckert, 40–65. Cambridge: Cambridge University Press.

———. 2008b. Information Ethics: A Reappraisal. In Ess, C. (ed.). Luciano Floridi's Philosophy of Information and Information Ethics: Critical Reflections and the State of the Art. *Ethics and Information Technology*, 10(2–3): 189–204.

———. 2008c. The Method of Levels of Abstraction. *Minds and Machines* 18 (3): 303–329.

———. 2010a. *Information. A Very Short Introduction*. Oxford: Oxford University Press.

———. 2010b. The Philosophy of Information as a Conceptual Framework. In Demir, H. (ed.). Luciano Floridi's Philosophy of Technology: Critical Reflections. *Knowledge, Technology & Policy*, 23.

———. 2010c. Information Ethics. In *The Cambridge Handbook of Information and Computer Ethics*, ed. L. Floridi, 77–99. Cambridge: Cambridge University Press.

———. 2011a. *The Philosophy of Information*. Oxford: Oxford University Press.

———. 2011b. A Defence of Constructionism: Philosophy as Conceptual Engineering. *Metaphilosophy* 42 (3): 282–304.

———. 2011c. The Informational Nature of Personal Identity. *Minds & Machines* 21: 549–566.

———. 2012. Hyperhistory and the Philosophy of Information Policies. *Philosophy and Technology* 25: 129–131.

———. 2013. *Information Ethics*. Oxford: Oxford University Press.

———. 2014a. *The Fourth Revolution. On the Impact of Information and Communication Technologies on Our Lives*. Oxford: Oxford University Press.

———. (ed.). 2014b. *The Onlife Manifesto. Being Human in a Hyperconnected Era*, Dordrecht: Springer.

———. 2015. Toleration and the Design of Norms. *Science and Engineering Ethics* 21 (5): 1095–1123.

Foessel, M., J.-F. Kervégan, and M. Revault d'Allonnes. 2007. *Modernité et sécularisation: Hans Blumenberg, Karl Löwith, Carl Schmitt, Leo Strauss*. Paris: CNRS Editions.

Foucault, M. 1988. In *Power/Knowledge: Selected Interviews and Other Writings 1972–1977*, ed. C. Gordon. New York: Pantheon Books.

———. 2010. *The Birth of Biopolitics: Lectures at the Collège de France, 1978–1979*. New York: Picador.

Frankfurt, H. 1969. Alternate Possibilities and Moral Responsibility. *Journal of Philosophy* LXVI: 829–839.

Galli, C. 2010. Genealogia della politica. Carl Schmitt e la crisi del pensiero politico moderno, il Mulino, Bologna.

Galloway, A. 2004. *Protocol. How Control Exists After Decentralization*. Cambridge, MA: MIT Press.

Galloway, A., and E. Thacker. 2007. *The Exploit. A Theory of Networks*, Electronic Mediations Series. Minneapolis/London: Minnesota University Press.

Gardner, J. 2013. Putting Legal Philosophy at Its Place. *Rivista di filosofia del diritto* 2: 253–266.

Gauchet, M. 1999. *The Disenchantment of the World: A Political History of Religion* [1985], foreword by C. Taylor, Trans. O. Burge. Princeton: Princeton University Press.

Gilman, S. 1991. *The Jew's Body*. New York: Routledge.

Glorioso, A. 2012. Un nuovo concetto di 'autodeterminazione informazionale' come bussola concettuale per navigare il nuovo mondo digitale. In Durante, M., and U. Pagallo (ed.). 2013. Manuale di informatica giuridica e diritto delle nuove tecnologie, 383–394. Torino: UTET.

Goldsmith, J., and T. Wu. 2006. *Who Controls the Internet? Illusions of a Borderless World*. Oxford: Oxford University Press.

Gould, C. 2004. *Globalizing Democracy and Human Rights*. Cambridge, MA: Cambridge University Press.

Heidegger, M. 1996. *Being and Time* [1927]. Trans. J. Stambaugh. New York: SUNY.

———. 1997. *Kant and the Problem of Metaphysics*, 5th ed. enlarged, Trans. R. Taft. Bloomington: Indiana University Press.

———. 2004. *What is called thinking?* [1954]. Trans. J. Glenn Gray. New York: Harper Perennial.

Hey, T., S. Tansley, and K. Tolle. 2007. *Jim Gray on eScience: A Transformed Scientific Model*, accessible online at: http://research.microsoft.com/en-us/collaboration/fourthparadigm.

Hildebrandt, M. 2008. Legal and Technological Normativity: More (and Less) Than Twin Sisters. *Techné: Research in Philosophy and Technology* 12 (3): 169–183.

———. 2011. Autonomic and Autonomous 'Thinking': Preconditions for Criminal Accountability. In *Law, Human Agency and Autonomic Computing. The Philosophy of Law Meets the Philosophy of Technology*, ed. M. Hildebrandt and A. Rouvroy, 141–160. London: Routledge.

———. 2013. Balance or Trade-Off? Online Security Technologies and Fundamental Rights. *Philosophy and Technology* 26 (4): 357–379.

Hildebrandt, M., and B.-J. Koops. 2010. The Challenges of Ambient Law and Legal Protection in the Profiling Era. *The Modern Law Review* 73 (3): 428–460.

Hildebrandt, M., B.-J. Koops, and D.-O. Jaquet-Chifelle. 2010. Bridging the Accountability Gap: Rights for New Entities in the Information Society? *Minnesota Journal of Law, Science & Technology* 11 (2): 497–561.

Himma, K.-E. 2004. There's Something About Mary: The Moral Value of Things Qua Information Objects. *Ethics and Information Technology* 6 (3): 145–159.

———. 2009. Artificial Agency, Consciousness, and the Criteria for Moral Agency: What Properties Must an Artificial Agent Have to Be a Moral Agent? *Ethics and Information Technology* 11 (1): 19–29.

Hobbes, T. 2008. *Leviathan* [1651]. Oxford: Oxford University Press.

Hongladarom, S. 2008. Floridi and Spinoza on Global Information Ethics. In Ess, C. (ed.). Luciano Floridi's Philosophy of Information and Information Ethics: Critical Reflections and the State of the Art. *Ethics and Information Technology*, 10(2–3), 175–187.

Hunter, D. 2003. Cyberspace as Place and the Tragedy of the Digital Anticommons. *California Law Review* 91 (2): 439–519.

Huxley, A. 1932. *Texts & Pretexts: An Anthology with Commentaries*. London: Chatto & Windus.

Ihde, D. 2002. *Bodies in Technology. Electronic Mediations*. Minneapolis: University of Minnesota Press.

———. 2003. Postphenomenology – Again?, Working Paper n. 3, The Centre for STS Studies, Aarhus.

Jacobs, B. 2003. Kantian Character and the Problem of a Science of Humanity. In *Essays on Kant's Anthropology*, ed. B. Jacob. Cambridge: Cambridge University Press.

Johnson, D.-R., and D.-G. Post. 1996. Law and Borders. The Rise of Law in Cyberspace. *Stanford Law Review* 48: 1367–1404.

Journal of Experimental and Theoretical Artificial Intelligence. 2015. Special issue edited by Jones, D. and A. Beavers on Inforgs and the Infosphere: Themes from Luciano Floridi's Information Ethics and Philosophy of Artificial Intelligence, 27(1).

Kallinikos, J. 2006. *The Consequences of Information*. In *Institutional Implications of Technological Change*. Cheltenham/Northampton, MA: Edward Elgar.

———. 2011. *Governing Through Technology. Information Artefacts and Social Practice*. Houndmills, Basingstoke: Palgrave Macmillan.

Kallinikos, Y., and N. Tempini. 2012. Post-material Meditations: On Data Tokens, Knowledge and Behavior. Accessible online at: www.tigair.info/docs/kalltemp_egos11.pdf.

Kant, I. 1992. In *Theoretical Philosophy, 1775–1770*, ed. D. Walford and R. Meerbote. Cambridge: Cambridge University Press.

———. 2003. *Critique of Pure Reason* [1781]. Trans. N. Kemp Smith. Hampshire: Palgrave Macmillan.

Karnow, C.E.A. 1996. Liability for Distributed Artificial Intelligence. *Berkeley Technology and Law Journal* 11: 147–183.

Kephart, J.O., and D.M. Chess. 2003. The Vision of Autonomic Computing, IEEE Society. Online at: www.research.ibm.com/autonomic/manifesto.

Knowledge, Technology and Policy. 2010. Special double issue edited by Demir, H., and M. Taddeo on Luciano Floridi's Philosophy of Technology: Critical Reflections. 23(1–2) and 24(3–4).

Lessig, L. 2006. *Code: And Other Laws of Cyberspace, Version 2.0*. New York: Basic Books.

Levi, P. 1989. *The Drowned and the Saved* [1986]. Trans. R. Rosenthal. New York: Vintage Books.

Levinas, E. 1969. *Totality and Infinity: An Essay on Exteriority* [1961]. Trans. A. Lingis. Pittsburgh: Dusquene University Press.

———. 1990. Reflections on the Philosophy of Hitlerism [1934]. Trans. S. Hand. *Critical Inquiry*, 17: 63–71.

———. 1998. *Otherwise Than Being or Beyond the Essence* [1974]. Trans. A. Lingis. Pittsburgh: Dusquene University Press.

———. 2006. *Entre Nous: Thinking of the Other*. Trans. M. Smith and B. Harshaw. London/New York: The Athlone Press.

Loraux, N. 1997. *La cité divisée. Oubli The dans la mémoire d'Athenes*. Paris: Payot & Rivages.

Lowith, K. 1957. *Meaning in History: The Theological Implications of the Philosophy of History [1949]*. Chicago: Chicago University Press.

Lyon, D. 2007. *Surveillance Studies: An Overview*. New York: Polity.

Lyon, D., and Z. Bauman. 2013. *Liquid Surveillance: A Conversation*. New York: Polity.

Lyotard, J.-F. 1984. *The Postmodern Condition: A Report on Knowledge* (1979). Trans. G. Bennington and B. Massumi. Manchester: Manchester University Press.

MacKay, D.M. 1969. *Information, Mechanism and Meaning*. Cambridge, MA: MIT Press.

Margulis, S.-T. 2003. Privacy as a Social Issue and Behavioral Concept. *Journal of Social Issues* 59 (2): 243–261.

Martin, K. 2012. Information Technology and Privacy: Conceptual Muddles or Privacy Vacuums? *Ethics and Information Technology* 14 (4): 267–284.

Matheson, D. 2007. Unknowableness and Informational Privacy. *Journal of Philosophical Research* 32: 251–267.

Mathieu, V. 2004. *Privacy e dignità dell'uomo. Una teoria della persona*. Torino: Giappichelli Editore.

Mayer-Schonberger, V. 2009. *Delete: The Virtue of Forgetting in the Digital Age*. Princeton: Princeton University Press.

McDowell, J.H. 1996. *Mind and World*. Cambridge MA/London: Harvard University Press.

McKenna, M. 2009. *Compatibilism, Stanford Encyclopedia of Philosophy*, (first published 2004; substantively revised 2009), online at: http://plato.stanford.edu/entries/compatibilism/.

Metaphilosophy. 2010. Special issue edited by P. Allo on Luciano Floridi and the Philosophy of Information 41(3): 247–459.

Metzinger, T. 2004. *Being No One: The Self-Model Theory of Subjectivity*. Cambridge, MA: MIT Press.

Minsky, M. 1988. *The Society of Mind*. New York: Simon & Schuster.

Mitchell, M. 1998. *An Introduction to Genetic Algorithms*. Cambridge, MA/London: MIT Press.

Moor, J.H. 1985. What Is Computer Ethics? *Metaphilosophy* 16 (4): 266–275.

Moore, G.E. 2004. *Principia Ethica [1903]*. Cambridge: Cambridge University Press.

Morozov, E. 2011. *The Net Delusion: How Not to Liberate The World*. New York: Penguin.

———. 2013. *To Save Everything, Click Here: Technology, Solutionism, and the Urge to Fix Problems that Don't Exist*. London: Allen Lane.

Motwani, R., and P. Raghavan. 1995. *Randomized Algorithms*. Cambridge: Cambridge University Press.

Murray, A. 2007. *The Regulation of Cyberspace: Control in the Online Environment*. Abingdon: Routledge Cavendish.

Nielsen, M. 2011. *Reinventing Discovery: The New Era of Networked Science*. Princeton: Princeton University Press.

Nissenbaum, H. 1998. Protecting Privacy in an Information Age: The Problem of Privacy in Public. *Law and Philosophy* 17 (5–6): 559–596.

———. 2010. *Privacy in Context: Technology, Policy, and the Integrity of the Social Life*. Stanford: Stanford Law Books.

Nye, J. 2008. *The Powers to Lead: Soft, Hard, and Smart*. Oxford: Oxford University Press.

Ost, F., and M. van de Kerchove. 2002. *De la pyramide au réseau ? Pour une théorie dialectique du droit*. Bruxelles: Publications Faculté St. Louis.

Pagallo, U. 2003. *Prolegomeni d'informatica giuridica*. Padova: Cedam.

———. 2006. *Teoria giuridica della complessità*. Torino: Giappichelli.

———. 2008. *La tutela della privacy negli Stati Uniti d'America e in Europa. Modelli giuridici a confronto*. Milano: Giuffré.

———. 2010. Robotrust and Legal Responsibility. *Knowledge, Technology and Policy* 23: 367–379.

———. 2013a. *The Laws of Robot: Crimes, Contracts, and Torts*. Dordrecht/Berlin: Springer.

———. 2013b. What Robots Want: Autonomous Machines, Codes and New Frontiers of Legal Responsibility. In *Human Law and Computer Law: Comparative Perspectives*, ed. M. Hildebrandt and J. Gaakeer. Dordrecht: Springer.

———. 2013c. Online Security and the Protection of Civil Rights: A Legal Overview. *Philosophy and Technology* 26 (4): 381–395.
———. 2014. Il diritto nell'età dell'informazione. Il riposizionamento tecnologico degli ordinamenti giuridici tra complessità sociale, lotta per il potere e tutela dei diritti, Giappichelli, Torino.
Pagallo, U., and M. Durante. 2010. Three Roads to P2P Systems and Their Impact on Business Practices and Ethics. *Journal of Business Ethics* 94 (4): 551–564.
———. 2014. Legal Memories and the Right to be Forgotten. In *Protection of Information and the Right to Privacy – A New Equilibrium?* Law, Governance and Technology Series, ed. L. Floridi, vol. 17, 17–30. Dordrecht: Springer.
———. 2016a. The Philosophy of Law in an Information Society. In *The Routledge Handbook of Philosophy of Information*, ed. L. Floridi, 396–407. London/New York: Routledge.
———. 2016b. The Pros and Cons of Legal Automation and its Governance. *European Journal of Risk Regulation* 7 (2): 323–334.
Post, D. 2008. *In Search of Jefferson's Moose. Notes on the State of Cyberspace*. Oxford/New York: Oxford University Press.
Prigogine, I., and I. Stengers 1981. Vincolo, Enciclopedia Einaudi, Einaudi, Torino, vol. 14, 1064–1080.
Ralws, J. 1971. *A Theory of Justice*. Cambridge, MA: Belknap Press of Harvard University Press.
Rorty, R. 1989. *Contingency, Irony, and Solidarity*. Cambridge: Cambridge University Press.
Russell, S., and P. Norvig. 2010. *Artificial Intelligence: A Modern Approach*. III ed. London: Pearson.
Salinger, J.-D. 1963. *Raise High the Roof Beam, Carpenters and Seymour: An Introduction*. New York: Little, Brown and Company.
Santoni De Sio, F. 2013. *Per colpa di chi. Mente, responsabilità e diritto*. Milano: Raffaello Cortina Editore.
Sartor, G. 2009. Cognitive Automata and the Law: Electronic Contracting and the Intentionality of Software Agents. *Artificial Intelligence and Law* 17 (4): 253–290.
———. 2015. Reasoning with Normative Systems. In *The Cognitive Foundations of Group Attitudes and Social Interaction*, ed. A. Herzig and E. Lorini, 177–190. Dordrecht: Springer.
Schmitt, C. Der Gegensatz von Parlamentarismus und moderner Massendemokratie (1926), in Positionen und Begriffe im Kampf mit Weimar-Genf-Versailles , 1923–1939, Hamburg, Dunker & Humblot, 1940; trad.Schmitt C. (1940), *Der Gegensatz von Parlamentarismus und moderner Massen demokratie* (1926), in *Positionen und Begriffe im Kampf mit Weimar-Genf-Versailles,* 1923–1939. Hamburg: Dunker & Humblot.
———. 2006. *Political Theology: Four Chapters on the Concept of Sovereignty.* Trans. G. Schwab. Chicago: Chicago University Press.
———. 2007a. *The Concept of the Political* [1932], (expanded edition). Trans. G. Schwab. Chicago: Chicago University Press.
———. 2007b. *Theory of the Partisan.* Trans. G.-L. Ulmen. New York: Telos Press.
Sen, A. 1985. Well-Being, Agency and Freedom: The Dewey Lectures 1984. *Journal of Philosophy* LXXXII: 169–221.
Serres, M. 1995. *The Natural Contract*, Trans. E. MacArthur and W. Paulson. Ann Arbor: University of Michigan Press.
———. 2009. *Temps des crises*. Paris: Editions Le Pommier.
Shirky, C. 2009. *Here Comes Everybody: How Change Happens when People Come Together*. London: Penguin.
———. 2011. *Cognitive Surplus: Creativity and Generosity in a Connected Age*. London: Penguin.
Simmel, G. 1964. *Conflict & The Web of Group Affiliations*. New York: Free Press.
Solum, L. 1992. Legal Personhood for Artificial Intelligence. *North Carolina Law Review* 70: 1231–1287.
Tavani, H.-T. 2007. Philosophical Theories of Privacy: Implications for an Adequate Online Privacy Policy. *Metaphilosophy* 38 (1): 1–22.
———. 2008. Floridi's Ontological Theory of Informational Privacy: Some Implications and Challenges. *Ethics and Information Technology* 10 (2–3): 155–166.

Taylor, M. 2001. *The Moment of Complexity: Emerging Network Culture*. Chicago: Chicago University Press.

Teubner, G. 2007. *Rights of Non-humans? Electronic Agents and Animals as New Actors in Politics and Law*. Max Weber Lecture at the European University Institute of Fiesole, Italy, January 17.

Valery, P. (1998). La crise de l'esprit. In *Varieté I et II*, Folio essais. Paris: Gallimard.

Wellman, B., et al. 2003. The Social Affordance of the Internet for Networked Individualism. *Journal of Computer-Mediated Communication* 8 (3.), available online.

Williams, B. 1981. *Moral Luck: Philosophical Papers 1973–1980*. Cambridge: Cambridge University Press.

Yakovits, J. 2011. The Tragedy of the Data Commons. *Harvard Journal of Law and Technology* 25 (1 Fall): 1–67.

Ziccardi, G. 2012. *Resistance, Liberation Technology and Human Rights in the Digital Age*. Dordrecht/Berlin: Springer.

Index

M. Durante, *Ethics, Law and the Politics of Information*, The International Library of Ethics, Law and Technology 18, DOI 10.1007/978-94-024-1150-8